Continuing to Disrupt the Status Quo?

Young and New Women Professors of Educational Leadership

A volume in
*New Directions in Educational Leadership:
Innovations in Research, Teaching, and Learning*
Noelle Witherspoon-Arnold, *Series Editor*

Continuing to Disrupt the Status Quo?

Young and New Women Professors of Educational Leadership

edited by

Whitney Sherman Newcomb
Virginia Commonwealth University

INFORMATION AGE PUBLISHING, INC.
Charlotte, NC • www.infoagepub.com

Library of Congress Cataloging-in-Publication Data

A CIP record for this book is available from the Library of Congress
http://www.loc.gov

ISBN: 978-1-62396-640-9 (Paperback)
        978-1-62396-641-6 (Hardcover)
        978-1-62396-642-3 (ebook)

Copyright © 2014 Information Age Publishing Inc.

All rights reserved. No part of this publication may be reproduced, stored in a retrieval system, or transmitted, in any form or by any means, electronic, mechanical, photocopying, microfilming, recording or otherwise, without written permission from the publisher.

Printed in the United States of America

CONTENTS

Acknowledgments vii

Preface ix
Whitney Sherman Newcomb

1 Breaking into the All-Male Club and Continuing to Disrupt the Status Quo 1
Whitney Sherman Newcomb

2 Cage Fighting in Higher Education: Same Old Fight in a 21st Century Ring 7
Whitney Sherman Newcomb

3 Navigating Unchartered Territories in Academe Through Mentoring Networks 25
Gaëtane Jean-Marie

4 Young, Gifted, Female, and Black: The Journey to Becoming Who I Am 41
April L. Peters

5 The Invisible Other: Ruminations on Transcending "La Cerca" in Academia 55
Azadeh F. Osanloo

6 My Transition to the Academy: Lessons and Community 65
Karen Sanzo

7   Having It All: Wait, What Does "All" Mean? 77
    Jennifer K. Clayton

8   Still I Rise: An Early-Career African-American Female
    Scholar's Told Truths on Surviving Academia 87
    Cosette M. Grant

9   Navigating My Career as a Trailing Spouse 117
    Melanie C. Brooks

10 Reflections on Perpetual Liminality 129
    Katherine Cumings Mansfield

11 My Relationship with Academia as a Latina Scholar 145
    Melissa A. Martinez

12 Earning a Doctorate in Educational Leadership:
    The Perspectives and Experiences of a Deaf Female Scholar 157
    Catherine O'Brien

13 Since She is Gone, Who Will Get Me Through? 177
    Anjalé Welton

14 Sense Making: The Fight to Claim and Continuously Reclaim
    a Space in Higher Education 193
    Whitney Sherman Newcomb and Catherine Ruziak Gorman

15 Then... and Now: Reflections on Women Faculty
    in Educational Administration 213
    Norma T. Mertz

    Chronology of Young and New Women Professors' Entry
    Into Departments of Educational Leadership and Their Ages
    Upon Entrance 219

    About the Contributors 221

ACKNOWLEDGMENTS

As with any endeavor of this kind, contributions to the fruition of this book extend both to the individuals directly involved with the writing and to those who have provided tremendous support to the writers and to the project itself. First, I would like to extend my heartfelt gratitude to the courageous women who contributed their stories to this book. Each of these women are friends and colleagues who inspire me and serve as sources of strength for many. Second, I want to extend my sincere appreciation to Norma Mertz, who created the space to begin the conversation with her book on veteran women professors, and who graciously contributed to this book as well. Third, I want recognize and thank all of the veteran woman who shared their stories in Norma's book, many of whom have been mentors and advocates for the women authors in this book. Fourth, I would like to thank Noelle Witherspoon Arnold, the editor of the *New Directions in Educational Leadership* series and the Information Age team for their belief in and support of this project. Finally, I would like to thank my family for their enduring support and unconditional love.

PREFACE

Whitney Sherman Newcomb

Continuing to Disrupt the Status Quo? Young and New Women Professors of Educational Leadership was conceptualized as a follow-up to *Breaking Into the All-Male Club: Female Professors of Educational Administration* (Mertz, 2009), a book about and by many women who were the first women faculty admitted into departments of educational administration primarily in the 1970s and 1980s. As pioneers to the field, it was important for them to tell their stories; how they experienced graduate school, how they came to be the first women faculty in their departments, and what they faced once they secured positions. The idea behind the later book was that giving veteran women a public space to share stories about their experiences could help women continuing to enter the field of educational administration negotiate their own acceptance and navigate any barriers that still exist.

Themes that emerged from *Breaking Into the All-Male Club* included: Experiences fitting in (or not fitting in) once having entered all male departments; Experiences gaining entrance, primarily by gatekeepers who had been their sponsors in graduate school; Experiences becoming firsts (i.e., many never aspired to become professors and planned to return to the K–12 environment, many were brokered into their positions due to Title IX pressures); Experiences making their way (some were welcomed, some ignored; most tended never to ask for help when problems arose; feeling silenced and actually self-silencing; feeling invisible; surprise at overt sexism after being admitted to departments as full members); and Lessons learned (becoming masters of managing their own situations, choosing battles, finding mentors, the importance of developing a strong sense of self). When I first read this book, I was intrigued by the stories of many of the veteran women, as they resonated with experiences that I had or am still having as a young woman professor years later. For instance, Ellen Bueschel wrote about Nelda Cambron-McCabe's story on being described by a colleague as a young girl who "came bopping down the steps of the plane in her ponytail and jeans" (Mertz, p. 56) to an interview with a university (when, she, in fact, had dressed up as people did back then to fly and had certainly not worn her hair in a ponytail) and as someone who broke the traditional path to the professoriate in educational leadership as she had no previous administrative experience in public schools when she entered the academy. She wrote about students seeming surprised that they actually learned something from her classes (p. 56) and the feeling that while she seemed to be acknowledged by her colleagues for her overall scholarship, she was still somehow invisible in her day-to-day interactions with them. Norma Mertz shared stories of colleagues who, while addressing themselves with the title of "Doctor," insisted upon calling her by her first name rather than granting her the respect of referring to her as "Dr. Mertz," a title she had earned, as her colleagues had, with the achievement of a doctorate. She talked about refusing to "get along just to get along" (p. 72) and how this was seen as intimidating to some colleagues. And, Nona Prestine recounted the difficulties of being a single woman in the academy as colleagues told her, "You're single, so you have time to write and do research... you're not like us who have family and obligations" (p. 118). I experienced each one of these instances in my own life as a young and relatively new professor in the field of educational leadership. Furthermore, I knew from informal conversations with the few other young women in the field at the time that they too experienced similar instances.

In *Breaking Into the All-Male Club*, while reflecting on the past and looking ahead to the present in her narrative, Edie Rusch posed the question, "How many department faculty have mastered the art of healthy gender dynamics?" (Mertz, p. 184). I took pause at this question because, at the time I read the book, I was painfully aware of how unhealthy many of the departments I had been a member of were along the lines of gender. Edie went on to describe the stories in the veteran women's book as sense-making starters (p. 185) for retrospective learning and used Dorothy Smith's (1987) notion of fault lines—the point of rupture between socially organized practice and lived experience—to situate the veteran women's narratives. As I reflected on the stories of the veteran women, I was inspired to share my own story and to encourage my young women colleagues to share their stories as well. I invited Danna Beaty, Karen Sanzo, and April Peters to join me on an autoethnographic project to record our stories and share them with one another as a process of healing and continuing to move forward in a field that was not always accepting of us. We shared our stories for the first time in 2009 at the American Educational Research Association's (AERA) annual conference in San Diego, California (see Sherman, Beaty, Crum, & Peters, 2010; Newcomb, Beaty, Crum, & Peters, 2013). Edie Rusch contacted me after this conference and invited us to join a session with the veteran women authors of *Breaking Into the All-Male Club* that was planned for the University Council of Educational Administration's (UCEA) annual meeting the following fall in Anaheim, California. It was during this session, as veteran women and young/new women in the field joined together to share and understand one another's stories, that the idea for the present book was inspired.

It seemed clear to me at the time that the underlying mission of Norma's book in regard to how the stories and women could inspire change rather than just a handling of the current situation might best be considered if a current accounting of women's experiences in the field of educational leadership was gathered and then compared to the veteran women's stories years earlier. I had heard rumblings of veteran women's frustration with women new to the field continuing to report "the same old thing" along gender lines in their research agendas thirty and forty years later that veteran women had initially reported and, in turn, rumblings from women new to the field justifying their work by maintaining that reporting the same findings along gender lines for thirty years and counting indicates that little has changed and is, in and of itself, an important finding and message to faculty in educational leadership. Thus, the idea for *Continuing to Disrupt the Status Quo?* was born. It seemed reasonable to try to gather narratives of those women new to the field of educational leadership and make comparisons to those stories shared by the veteran women in the field to highlight both similarities and differences. *Continuing to Disrupt the Status Quo? Young and New Women Professors of Educational Leadership* is a literary way to preserve and continue the tradition of the sharing/addition of voices to the field of educational leadership that was begun with *Breaking Into the All-Male Club*. It begs the question, "If the women from *Breaking Into the All-Male Club* are "firsts," "pioneers," and "groundbreakers," then who are we, the young and new women of the field? If the entrance of women into the field of educational leadership was threatening enough for the veteran women (and still is for many of the young and new women), then the addition of age and ethnicity as confounding factors has likely created a cacophony of dissonance forty years later!

Continuing to Disrupt the Status Quo? represents a decade of stories (2002–2012) from young and new women to the field of educational leadership. I contacted twelve young women who I knew to be reasonably new to their careers in the academy in March 2012 and invited them to participate in this book project with me. Each of the women responded enthusiastically and agreed to join me by committing to write her narrative and share it publicly in the form of a chapter in this book (one woman pulled out of the project later due to an overabundance of writing deadlines). They were asked to free write their narratives and stories any way they chose, but were asked to include information on their experiences with general themes including: background; preparation for the academy/graduate school; job searches; positions; getting tenure; socialization; mentoring; healthy/unhealthy networks; etc. The result is twelve narratives (including my own) rich in context that, together, represent the experiences of many young and new women to the field of educational leadership. While the stories of these women in no way represent all young and new women's experiences in the field, they encompass a variety of institutions and geographic locations and, in contrast to *Breaking Into the All-Male Club*, include the voices of women from multiple ethnic backgrounds. As more women of color have entered the field, stories of multiple marginality have made their way to the surface.

I am honored to be the editor of *Continuing to Disrupt the Status Quo?* and humbled by the women's stories of survival and triumph. My relationship with this project has been one of both love and hate as writing my own narrative and reading those of others has brought forth mixed emotions of love and laughter, but also of anger and sadness at the realization that young and new women professors have, in some ways, experienced the same sexist and racist practices that the veteran women experienced thirty years ago. I am thankful for the bravery these women displayed by sharing their stories in such an open, public venue (particularly risky to those women who had not achieved tenure at the time of this writing) and wish to express my gratitude to all of the women authors, to Information Age Publishing, and to Noelle Witherspoon Arnold, editor of the IAP series *New Directions in Educational Leadership*. I am also grateful to the veteran women for sharing their stories several years ago and, particularly, to Norma Mertz as she has been a vital part of this book as well.

REFERENCES

Mertz, N. T. (2009). *Breaking into the all-male club: Female professors of educational administration*. Albany: State University of New York (SUNY) Press.

Newcomb, W. S., Beaty, D., Crum, K. S., & Peters, A. (2013). Finding our stride: Young women professors of educational leadership. *Journal of School Leadership, 23*(4).

Sherman, W. H., Beaty, D., Crum, K. S., & Peters, A. (2010). Unwritten: Young women faculty in educational leadership. *Journal of Educational Administration, 48*(6), 741–754.

Smith, D. (1987). *The everyday world as problematic: A feminist sociology*. Boston: Northeastern University Press.

CHAPTER 1

BREAKING INTO THE ALL-MALE CLUB AND CONTINUING TO DISRUPT THE STATUS QUO

Whitney Sherman Newcomb

While teaching in schools has long been associated with females, from the very beginning, males were preferred for the job and dominated its ranks. Females entered the profession in the 1800s because the unprecedented growth of common schools across the United States required more teachers. The demand outstripped the number of males available and willing to work for the low wages being paid to teachers. By 1900, men had largely deserted teaching for other occupations, and women made up 70% of the teachers. The trend continued, and by 1920, women constituted 86% of the teachers.

—(Mertz, 2009, p. 2)

According to Blount (1998), while men accounted for nearly all teachers at the beginning of the nineteenth century, women were in the majority one hundred years later. This gender transformation birthed the creation of a domain for men—school administration. The feminization of the profession of teaching, in concert with societal beliefs about women and their place in society, spearheaded a domain that would allow men to monitor female teachers and "keep them from getting out of line"

(Blount, p. 26). The "reestablishment of male hegemony in school administration" (Mertz, 2009, p. 3), along with the growing need for administrators, coincided with the establishment of university-based programs for preparing school leaders in the early 1900s. These programs began to flourish in the 1950s and the departments were almost exclusively male; "professors of administration could and did control not only who studied school administration (was admitted to programs) but, in many cases, who was recommended and subsequently hired to be administrators in schools" (Mertz, p. 3). Women were not only excluded from school administration practice, but from participation as students and as faculty in school leadership preparation programs as well.

From the 1970s to the 1990s, "A confluence of factors led to unlocking the door and setting the stage for women to move into the club, in schools and into the ranks of faculty of administrator preparation programs" (Mertz, 2009, p. 4). The civil rights movement and legislation such as the Equal Pay Act of 1963 and Title IX of the Education Amendments of 1972 resulted from mounting concern for equity in education and inspired change, albeit slow. Recent data indicate that women are 83% elementary teachers, 52% elementary principals, 57% central office administrators, and 33% assistant superintendents (Grogan, 2005). Women fill more than half of elementary principalships and have made inroads in school leadership. However, the most recent American Association of School Administrators (AASA) study reports that women represent only 18% of the superintendents in the nation (Brunner & Grogan, 2005). The percentage of women earning doctorates increased from 11% in 1972 to 40% in 1982 (Blount, 1998) and the number of women faculty in educational administration increased from 2% in 1972 to 20% in 1994 (McCarthy, 1999).

More current statistics (2003–2004) indicate that women account for 38% of faculty in the United States and are most well-represented at community colleges and least represented at doctoral institutions (Faculty Salary and Faculty Distribution Sheet, AAUP). Women are 58% of instructors, 54% of lecturers, and hold 51% of unranked positions. They are 46% of assistant professors, 38% of associate professors, and 23% of full professors. While the number of women in faculty positions has increased, women report difficulties with the expectation that they adopt the same working patterns as men (Loder, 2005), while also being responsible for maintaining their households (Hochschild, 1989). This division of labor is problematic (Newton et al., 2003), and women report difficulty with finding a balance between their academic work and family responsibilities (Ward & Wolf-Wendel, 2004). In fact, Ward and Wolf-Wendel (2004) found that women faculty have learned to practice the art of satisficing (Simon as cited in Ward & Wolf-Wendel), the act of doing things that are "good enough" but not "the best" to manage increasing expectations and responsibilities (i.e., "good enough is the new perfect"). Wolfinger, Mason, and Goulden (2008) found that having children accounts for the lower rate at which women obtain tenure-track jobs and achieve tenure. Though the number of women in university faculty positions steadily increased, it was not without hardships and setbacks; the percentage of women with tenure fell from 52% in 1998 to 43% in 2007 (Marcus, 2007).

Sandler and Hall (1986) report a "chilly" climate for women at many higher education institutions. Women identify overwhelming workload as a problem more frequently than men (Kochan, Spencer, & Matthews, 1999) and receive support for child care and domestic responsibilities (Myers & Ginsberg, 1994). Acker and Feuerverger (1996) report women's feelings of disappointment in regard to faculty life and related them to the inequitable reward system in academic life, feelings of an unequal division of labor, and an expectation that women will take greater responsibility for the housekeeping side of academic life. Furthermore, the salary advantage held by male faculty over female faculty persists across all ranks and all institutional types (AAUW, 2007; Porter, Toutkoushian, & Moore, 2008), as, on average, women earn only 80% of what men earn.

Though experienced at varying degrees, the aforementioned conditions were experienced by both veteran *and* young/new women to the field of educational leadership upon entrance. The narratives of veteran women faculty who broke into the field of educational leadership as "pioneering firsts" in *Breaking Into the All-Male Club* (Mertz, 2009) helped to lay the foundation for the study of university women on their own terms; by women, of women, and for women. "Because higher education organizations are essentially people and because these individuals bring their own personal and professional backgrounds to their interpretation of organizational life, narrative approaches are particularly useful" (Safarik, 2003, p. 419). The current book was conceived from a feminist perspective that allows gender as the category of attention, data to be collected on the lived experiences of women, results that answer questions about women's lives, and research that is change oriented (Bensimon & Marshall, 1997). *Continuing to Disrupt the Status Quo?* is an effort to continue the storytelling tradition of veteran women in the field and to fan the flame of dialogue and conversation around issues of gender, race, and age in departments of educational leadership. It is a unique opportunity to learn about how departments have either changed or remained the same for women faculty over the years.

Sharing the stories of women faculty's lives is powerful because these narratives allow us to know what young and new women to the field value, believe, and experience (Benham, 1997). These stories, particularly when combined with the stories from veteran women, may help to create an understanding that redefines traditions and generates space for new department dynamics and entirely different stories. The autobiographical narrative format of the chapters (Sanders-Lawson, Smith-Campbell, & Benham, 2006; Sheilds & Edwards, 2005) is based on reflective practice and aims to inspire continued dialogue due to the understanding that these aspects of leadership are "synergistic components of holistic leadership practice" (Brooks & Tooms, 2008, p. 134). The examination of our experiences as young and new women faculty with issues related to equity creates a dialogue for learning that is supported by a growing body of literature (Andrews & Grogan, 2001; Brooks & Tooms, 2008; Brown, 2004; Osterman & Kottkamp, 1993; Shields & Edwards, 2005; Shields, LaRocque & Oberg, 2002; Short & Rinehard, 1993).

Following this first contextual chapter, twelve autobiographical narrative chapters are presented in chronological order according to when the authors attained their first full-time, tenure-track positions in educational leadership. The narratives represent a decade of stories (2002–2012) about personal experiences in the academy as young and new women professors. When combined with the stories of veteran women (Mertz, 2009), the storytelling spans over forty years. The next to the last chapter shares themes across the individual narratives of the young and new women to the field in an attempt at sense-making across the stories. The final chapter offers insight into themes that are similar and different between the veteran women's stories from *Breaking Into the All-Male Club* and the young/new women's experiences as faculty members in *Continuing to Disrupt the Status Quo?*

This book allows us a window into women's lives; an opportunity to experience how women have experienced and are experiencing their faculty positions in departments of educational leadership across the United States. It allows us to consider whether change has occurred in university settings and, if change has occurred, how and to what extent. Though women have increased in number in departments of educational leadership, are young and new women to the field still experiencing the same obstacles and sexist behaviors as their veteran counterparts? How do age and race complicate these experiences? Have legislative shifts and workplace policies helped women? Are women balancing work and home expectations more effectively as time has passed? The stories are complex and rich; full of honest reflections about personal struggles and triumphs. As a whole, this book is a type of makeshift handiwork akin to the knitting of a quilt (Denzin & Lincoln, 2000) that offers readers an assemblage of individual stories that create a new whole; the weaving of stories together facilitates a connection between the readers and writers (Newcomb, 2013). Multiple perspectives are pieced together to form a body of perspectives that, together, help readers understand a complex phenomenon (young and new women's experiences in higher education) that cannot be explained by one of the perspectives alone (Denzin & Lincoln, 1994, p. 4).

REFERENCES

Acker, S., & Feuerverger, G. (1996). Doing good and feeling bad: The work of women university teachers. *Cambridge Journal of Education, 26*(3), 401–422.

AAUP. American Association of University Professors (2001). *Statement of principles on family responsibilities and academic work.* Retrieved March 13, 2009 from http://www.aaup.org/AAUP/pubsres/policydocs/contents/workfam-stmt.htm.

AAUW. American Association of University Women (2007). *Behind the pay gap.* Retrieved March 13, 2009 from http://www.aauw.org/research/upload/behindPayGap.pdf.

Andrews, R., & Grogan, M. (2001, September). *Defining preparation and professional development for the future.* Paper commissioned for the first meeting of the National Commission for the Advancement of Educational Leadership Preparation, Racine, WI.

Bensimon, E. M., & Marshall, C. (1997). Policy analysis for postsecondary education: Feminist and critical perspectives. In C. Marshall (Ed.), *Feminist critical policy analysis: A perspective from post-secondary education* (pp. 1–21). London: Falmer Press.

Benham, M. K. (1997). Silences and serenades: The journeys of three ethnic minority women school leaders. *Anthropology and Education Quarterly, 28*(2), 280–307.

Blount, J. M. (1998). *Destined to rule the schools: Women and the superintendency, 1873–1995.* Albany: SUNY.

Brooks, J., & Tooms, A. (2008). A dialectic of social justice: Findings synergy between life and work through reflection and dialogue. *Journal of School Leadership, 18*(2), 134–163.

Brown, K. (2004). Leadership for social justice and equity: Weaving a transformative framework and pedagogy. *Educational Administration Quarterly, 40*(1), 79–110.

Brunner, C. C., & Grogan, M. (2005). Women leading systems: Latest facts and figures on women and the superintendency. *The School Administrator, 2*(62), 46–50.

Denzin, N. K., & Lincoln, Y. S. (1994). (Eds.) *Handbook of qualitative research.* Thousand Oaks: Sage Publications.

Denzin, N. K., & Lincoln, Y. S. (2000). (Eds.) *Handbook of qualitative research,* (2nd ed.), London: Sage Publications.

Faculty Salary and Faculty Distribution Fact Sheet 2003–04. Prepared by John W. Curtis, American Association of University Professors (AAUP) Director of Research, for the Committee on Women in the Academic Profession. Retrieved at http://www.aaup.org/AAUP/pubsres/research/2003-04factsheet.htm.

Grogan, M. (2005). Echoing their ancestors, women lead districts in the United States. *International Studies in Educational Administration, 33,* 21–30.

Hochschild, A. R. (1989). *The second shift: Working parents and the revolution at home.* New York: Viking Press.

Kochan, F. K., Spencer, W. A., & Matthews, J. (1999, April). *The changing face of the principalship in Alabama: Role, perceptions, and gender.* Paper presented at the annual meeting of the American Educational Research Association, Montreal, Canada.

Loder, T. L. (2005). Women administrators negotiate work-family conflicts in changing times: An intergenerational perspective. *Educational Administration Quarterly, 41*(5), 741–776.

Marcus, J. (2007). Helping academic families have families and tenure too: Universities discover their self-interest. *Changes, 39*(2), 27–32.

McCarthy, M. M. (1999). The evolution of educational leadership preparation programs. In J. Murphy & K. Seashore-Louis (Eds.), *Handbook of research on educational administration* (2nd ed.). San Francisco: Jossey-Bass.

Mertz, N. (2009). *Breaking into the all-male club: Female professors of educational administration.* Albany: State University of New York.

Myers, S., & Ginsberg, R. (1994). Gender, marital status, and support systems of public school principals. *Urban Review, 26,* 209–223.

Newcomb, W. S. (2013). A bricolage of voices: Lessons learned from feminist analyses in educational leadership. In I. Bogotch & C. Shields (Eds.), *The international handbook on social [in]justice and educational leadership* (pp. 199–216). New York, NY: Springer Publishing Co.

Newton, R., Giesen, J., Freeman, J., Bishop, H., & Zeitoun, P. (2003). Assessing the reactions of males and females to attributes of the principalship. *Educational Administration Quarterly, 39*(4), 504–532.

Osterman, K. F., & Kottkamp, R. B. (1993). *Reflective practice for educators: Improving schooling through professional development.* Newbury Park, CA: Corwin Press.

Porter, S. R., Toutkoushian, R. K, & Moore, J. V. (2008). Pay inequities for recently hired faculty, 1988–2004. *The Review of Higher Education, 31*(4), 465–487.

Safarik, L. (2003). Feminist transformation in higher education: Discipline, structure, and institution. *The Review of Higher Education, 26*(4), 419–445.

Sanders-Lawson, E. R., Smith-Campbell, S., & Benham, M. K. P. (2006). Wholistic visionioning for social justice: Black women theorizing practice. In C. Marshall & M. Oliva, (Eds.), *Leadership for social justice: Making revolutions in education.* New York: Allyn & Bacon.

Sandler, B., & Hall, R. M. (1986), *The campus climate revisited: Chilly for women faculty, administrators, and graduate students.* Washington, DC: Association of American Colleges.

Shields, C. M., & Edwards, M. M. (2005). *Dialogue is not just talk: A new ground for educational leadership.* New York, NY: Peter Lang.

Shields, C. M., LaRocque, L. J., & Oberg, S. L. (2002). A conversation about race and ethnicity: Struggling to understand issues in cross-cultural leadership. *Journal of School Leadership 12*(2), 116–137.

Ward, K., & Wolf-Wendel, L. (2004). Academic motherhood: Managing complex roles in research universities. *The Review of Higher Education, 27*(2), 233–257.

Wolfinger, N. H., Mason, M. A., & Goulden, M. (2008). Problems in the pipeline: Gender, marriage, and fertility in the ivory tower. *The Journal of Higher Education, 79*(4), 388–405.

CHAPTER 2

CAGE FIGHTING IN HIGHER EDUCATION

Same Old Fight in a 21st Century Ring

Whitney Sherman Newcomb

Writing this narrative was a struggle. I put it off for months. The longer I remain in the university setting, the more often I put off writing until the last possible minute. I'm not a procrastinator; rather, a thinker...one who walks around shaping my writing projects as I multitask doing other things throughout the day (one of my colleagues likes to make fun of me and says I practice what she calls "walk-abouts"); and, then, weeks after walking around thinking (while doing other things of course), the writing spills out in a matter of 24 to 48 hours. Luckily, I'm a quick writer and, once I'm ready, the process flows. As I sat in my office struggling to find "readiness" to write in the early hours of many mornings, however, I was frustrated and, honestly, more angry than I wanted to admit. I waited...and waited...and waited to craft my story in a more positive and peaceful frame of mind. This frame of mind never came. Perhaps writing from a positive frame of mind would not have allowed me to tell my truth anyway.

I was recently in Vienna, Virginia for a Ben Harper concert and was intrigued by lyrics that included the phrase "break the silence even if you're letting go" as, even at that concert, I considered how to tell my story. I had become increasingly tired of carrying the burden of being angry for so long about experiences I had weathered in the academy. I felt that I might be at a place in my career where I needed to make a choice between continuing to hold the anger and letting it go. I was at a crossroads of sorts because toxicity from the anger was close to taking over in regard to how I was feeling about my career and I knew I needed to find a way to move on to create space for more positive and peaceful reflections and forthcoming experiences. I doubted, however, whether I could truly let go without breaking the silence I had kept for so many years; thus, my intrigue with the notion of breaking the silence and letting go simultaneously.

After watching several Ultimate Fighting Championship (UFC) fights with my husband while considering how to craft my story to, eventually, feel able to "let go," I was compelled to use Mixed Martial Arts (MMA) metaphors for some of my experiences in higher education. For me, nothing explains the micro politics and hallway ethnographies of higher education as viscerally as MMA moves such as "the rear naked choke, heel hook, the slam, hammer fist, and foot sweeps." And, to my surprise, I found myself identifying with several lyrics by the artist Eminem (who has been criticized by some for his negative lyrics about women) while I ran in the mornings ("25 to Life," "Lose Yourself"). It is fairly clear that reflections on my career in higher education had aggressive undertones.

I'll begin here with the difficult problem of telling the truth and protecting the names of institutions and individuals that have impacted and interacted with me in my academic journey. What follows is a summary of my career trajectory (see also Sherman, Beaty, Crum, & Peters, 2010) to give readers a holistic sense of my journey under themes which protect the identity of both institutions and people.

THE BLOW-BY-BLOW

I grew up in a family that provided, and still does, a nurturing and supportive environment. My parents encouraged me to be whoever I wanted and to do whatever I wanted (Hence, I was the only girl on my childhood soccer team while also the "girly" type who was on homecoming court and participated in a pageant... I love my heels, running shoes, bare feet, and Ugg boots equally). I never aspired to be a professor in the academy. I taught kindergarten and first grade for several years, and this seemed fairly natural to me. After a short while, I attended school at night after long days of teaching to attain a master's degree in leadership because becoming a principal seemed like the logical next step. Unfortunately, I didn't find the K–12 environment accepting of someone who didn't fit the traditional administrator "mold" (i.e., I was told I'd never make it because I didn't have serious enough hair) and decided to pursue a doctorate at the University of Virginia while I decided what to do. In the back of my mind, I thought that gaining a doctorate would give me the credibility that some in K–12 were so reluctant to give me.

My pursuit of a doctorate opened up a new way of thinking and approaching the world. I was encouraged by my mentor and dissertation chair, Dr. Margaret Grogan, to pursue a career in higher education, something I had never really considered before. She played a prominent role in my readiness for a role in the academy and an even more significant role in the development of my self-confidence. Margaret buffered me when I wanted to conduct research on women in leadership when this was not acceptable to some at my doctoral institution. Imagine my surprise when, in 2000, decades after Dr. Catherine Marshall had been told by an advisor that a thesis on women was not a significant topic (Marshall, 2010), I received the same response. Margaret helped me design a program of study that would prepare me to conduct a dissertation on women in leadership that included taking coursework outside of the School of Education and completing a comprehensive exam that consisted of an extensive literature review on feminist theory rather than sitting for the traditional question-and-answer exam typical at the time. I immersed myself in the writings of feminist theorists and philosophers of education such as Belenky et al. (1997), Davies (1994), Fraser and Nicholson (1990), Frye (1993), Gilligan (1982), Harding (1989), Lather (1992), Noddings (1984), Weedon (1997) as well as the writings of feminist scholars who had emerged specific to the field of educational leadership such as Alston (1999), Benham (1997), Brunner (2000), Gardiner, Enomoto, and Grogan (2000), Grogan (1996), Marshall (1981), and Shakeshaft (1989). However, I, like many veteran women in the field, found the study of women sometimes a lonely and, often, unsupported task (Marshall, 2010).

Margaret also buffered me when, after being selected to teach a doctoral level class as a doctoral student myself, several students in my class complained about my age and the assignments I had chosen (interestingly, these students were the very individuals who acted as barriers to me in the school district I worked in before leaving K–12 to pursue a doctorate). More importantly, Margaret supported me when my mom was diagnosed with breast cancer. My mother had a mastectomy and went through chemotherapy for a year. That first year of my doctoral program was a whirlwind as I taught half-day kindergarten, went to graduate school as a full-time student with a Graduate Assistantship, and watched my mom bravely struggle through the worst time of her life as she spent days vomiting from chemotherapy, and, eventually chose to shave her head bald so that she did not have to watch herself lose her hair slowly, day-by-day due to the chemotherapy. The last year of my program, I was selected to attend the David L. Clark Leadership Seminar[1] in spring 2001 at the American Educational Research Association (AERA) in Seattle, WA; and this proved to be a turning point in my decision to pursue an academic career as I had the chance to network with both veteran and aspiring scholars in the field of educational leadership.

With some trepidation, I secured my first university faculty position in Georgia immediately after receiving my doctorate in May 2002. Most of the educational policy department members at this university embraced me. I had mixed feelings about moving so far away from home (I told myself that I would only move to another state if I could drive back to Virginia in less than a day—this city fit the bill since I could make the trip in ten hours), but took the plunge and dove into the academic environment. Even though my doctoral program had prepared me for a university career, the world I entered still required a change in mindset. For example, I assumed that I needed to be at work at 8:00 in the morning on the first day of my contract. I laugh hysterically when I look back and think about myself sitting in the lobby of my office building as the sole human being in the building for over an hour (I didn't have a key to my office). I also shake my head with slight disgust when I remember wearing ridiculously ugly suits that first year and tying my long hair in a bun to make myself look "academic" and to hide my youth. I gave up the strategy of "dressing for the part" quickly and returned to wearing clothes that fit my personality (which seem to vacillate between my weakness for designer, but youthful-looking suits, and my passion for "hippy" and "bohemian" clothing). A significant point for readers, however, is that women entering the academy decades after Catherine Marshall broke through the glass ceiling as the first and only woman in her department, still felt it necessary to wear things akin to "suits with little bow ties" (Marshall, 2010).

Furthermore, after teaching in an elementary school environment, I was shocked at what could be the cold reality of the higher education setting when I was pulled aside at my first university and warned not to ask people personal questions like, "How was your weekend?" because, for some, this was invasive, and would be answered with something akin to, "None of your f-ing business!" I owe much of the survival of my first year in academia to Dr. Mary Beth Gasman and Dr. Darlene Opfer. I was extremely thankful for their guidance and friendship after moving to a city where I knew no one to begin a new career. They reminded me daily to have fun and not take my job too seriously. In fact, I looked forward to our lunch meetings many days (because our topics of conversation were outrageous and random and had nothing to do with work or academia) and still laugh today when I think about the practical jokes Darlene and I played on Mary Beth.

In February 2003, about six months into my new career, my brother was in a car accident in Virginia and sustained a traumatic brain injury. There are no words to express what I felt when my dad called to tell me what had happened (I was in a hotel in New Orleans preparing to give a presentation at the American Association of School Administrators Conference). To this day, if the phone rings in my hotel room, I panic and freeze. In fact, if anyone calls me at any time and for any reason and seems to be struggling to tell me something, I practically scream into the phone and demand to be told exactly what is going on because I, literally, feel like I am going to have a heart attack. For the rest of the academic year, I flew back and forth between Virginia and Georgia to fulfill both academic and family duties. Those days were, without a doubt, the worst, most dark times of my life. While I was grateful for those doctors, nurses and staff that were competent, I was horrified by those who were not and almost cost my brother his life multiple times. The things I watched some people do to helpless patients like my brother because they hated their lives and jobs were unspeakable acts of terror and evil. After 100 days, many spent around the clock at the hospital with my brother, I made the decision not to return to the university. While several people told me leaving the academy after only a year would ruin my career, it struck me as odd that anyone would think I was really concerned about my career at that point. I found myself asking people, "If *you* had *one opportunity* to bring a person back to life, would *you* walk away?" I had one goal and one goal only: To bring my brother as far back to life as possible.

For the next two years my family and I took on the major responsibilities for my brother's rehabilitation (this meant around-the-clock responsibilities that left no room for the academy). In 2005, my brother's recovery progressed to the point that I could return to the academy. After dropping everything for two years and doing nothing but focusing on my brother's recovery, my self-confidence in regard to my work had plummeted. I wasn't sure I fit in any more (actually, I wasn't sure I ever had in the first place). Despite my lack of self-confidence, I secured a position at a university in Virginia (but lived in a city an hour and a half away to share caregiving duties for my brother) and held this position from 2005–2007.

I made a third career move in fall 2007 and joined the faculty at another institution in Virginia in an attempt to bring my work and home lives back into balance (or at least into the same city). I joined the faculty of a department that was in transition from a focus on primarily teaching to one that included a focus on both teaching and scholarship. The transition for the department has been labor-intensive (we redesigned our PhD, MEd, and PMC programs and birthed an EdD program), but worth it, as the department has been able to increase its national and international reputation in the field of leadership education. The transition for my career, personally, has been difficult and has required sacrifices (i.e., my own scholarship has been completed during second and third shift night work so that I have been able to focus on program development and coursework/teaching during the day). However, I received tenure in 2009. I am extremely proud of the academic work that I have accomplished despite living in a constant state of family crisis (ten years at the time I wrote this narrative). And, in 2011, I took on a new role as wife and partner to my husband, who is a musician, and was deemed the "professor who married the rock star" by the local newspaper (my "title" just isn't quite as catchy as his). I currently remain at this university and will soon go under consideration for promotion to full professor.

WEATHERING SUBMISSION AND KNOCKOUT MOVES IN EDUCATIONAL LEADERSHIP

I mentioned previously that I feel like a good amount of my academic journey has been rather colorful and not unlike a series of Mixed Martial Arts matches. Thus, in the sections that follow, I utilized several MMA submission and knockout moves as metaphors for prominent events and obstacles that I experienced in the decade prior to writing this. I struggled as I put these events to paper because, while I prefer not to give negative events any significant portion of my memory, they are part of my truth. And, telling these stories might help someone else who is struggling with/has struggled with similar circumstances. At the very least, they are yet another accounting of how sexism and ageism are still alive and kicking in the academy.

Foot Sweeping Early Years

According to CagePotato.com (yes, you read that correctly), one of the top ten signature moves in MMA is the Foot Sweep. According to this website,

> Double-leg takedowns are for the commoners—when a true martial artist wants to get you to the mat, he simply hooks his foot out and delicately pushes you over it. Yes, it's a little strange to see a technique from the karate classes of our youth being used to punk some of the world's top fighters. But Lyoto Machida [a fighter known for his foot sweeps] isn't concerned with inflicting more damage than anybody else, or finishing fights as quickly as possible. His only goal is to showcase the superiority of his style. He'd rather break an opponent down mentally than physically. Hence, the foot-sweep, which comes out of nowhere, turns your momentum against you, and frustrates you out of your game plan.

The early years of the professoriate were rough and sometimes lonely. In 2002, there were few young faces in departments of educational leadership and even fewer young female faces (I was 27 at the time). There were few departments of educational leadership that would even consider hiring a young woman with little K–12 experience touting a social justice agenda (that seemed scary to some at the time). In fact, I was interviewed by only one university and was made an offer by that same university. Actually, that university seemed to seek out and embrace all that I was and stood for. I accepted the offer with trepidation because I didn't really want to move by myself 10 hours away from my family and friends. Nevertheless, I began my career in higher education in Georgia and have moved forward ever since.

While the majority of the events that I describe in this section occurred during the earliest years of my time in the university setting, they span across several campuses. I categorize the experiences below as Foot Sweeps because: (a) many involve efforts to break me down mentally by people who had low self-esteem and self-soothed by putting others, particularly young faculty, down; and (b) while foot sweeps knock you off of your feet, there is always the chance that you will recover quickly and manage to land on your feet. Though these events were hurtful and stressful, I became more agile as time went on and more apt to land on my feet as if I had merely stumbled along my career trajectory rather than had my feet swept completely out from under me.

Foot Sweep #1—Being told, as a doctoral student, that "There are enough studies on women these days. Pick a dissertation topic that is more current and really matters." While my doctoral and dissertation experiences were positive, for the most part, due to my chair's direction and protection of my desire to study gender, my choice of topic presented several hurdles to jump as well as a loss of funding and recognition for my work.

Foot Sweep #2—Being told as a doctoral teaching assistant by one of the doctoral students in my class, "Just who do you think you are anyway? You look like you're 18!"

Foot Sweep #3—Being asked during an interview for an academic position why my study entitled "Women's Experiences with a District-Based Aspiring Leadership Program" didn't include men to make it more equitable.

Foot Sweep #4—Being referred to as "Whitney Spears" (in reference to Britney Spears) behind my back by other faculty in a job interview.

Foot Sweep #5—Repeatedly (and continuing into the present) being asked by students if they can call me by my first name rather than Dr. Sherman or Dr. Newcomb. Or even worse, simply being called Miss Sherman or Miss Newcomb by students as a sign of disrespect. This doesn't happen to male faculty of any age and, to my knowledge, it does not happen to the veteran women faculty with whom I have worked.

Foot Sweep #6—Often being scorned by the very women I interview for studies in an effort to give them greater voice because of resentment that I have a doctoral degree. ("Well, if I had decided not to get married and if I didn't have children, I could be where you are today too.") Many of these same women (as well as women faculty colleagues) have been nasty to me because I am childless as well. They assume that since I do not have children, I can't empathize with mothers and parents of students or with working mothers. There is an assumption made by many women with children that women without children have no responsibilities. There is a belief by some that women faculty with no children should have to shoulder the burden of travel to conferences or more service work and that they don't need salary raises because they have no families to support. The work that I do as the caregiver of a person with a disability is often greater than that of the care of the average child or children. But, it is discounted nonetheless.

Foot Sweep #7—Being confronted by senior male faculty at conferences because of a disbelief that any university would actually want to hire me. ("I can't believe University X hired you! They must have been desperate?!")

Foot Sweep # 8—Being told by a department chair after I made a presentation to the Dean of the College of Education that he was so impressed that I was able to speak coherently in front of him... "Good job sweetie! I'm proud of you!"

Foot Sweep #9—Writing papers with an older male colleague, doing the bulk of the work, and then being told our names as authors should be presented in alphabetical order because everyone knows when names are listed alphabetically, it means the contributions from authors were equal.

Foot Sweep #10—Making countless suggestions in department faculty meetings only to be ignored and then have the male colleague sitting next to me repeat my suggestion and be told it is an amazing idea.

Foot Sweep #11—Being told by an older male student that when I wear pants, I don't look very professional.

Foot Sweep #12—Having to hide in a colleague's office from a hypersexual male colleague who made countless visits to my office and refused to leave me alone or to cease calling me for dates on my home telephone.

Foot Sweep #13—Having a male colleague go from office to office in the department to campaign against my "worthiness" in the academy because we disagreed on an interview candidate.

Foot Sweep #14—Being told by a veteran female colleague that my shoes make me look like a hooker. Being told by another veteran female faculty member that my tattoo makes me look like a biker.

Foot Sweep #15—Being screamed at by a male student who said that because I'm a woman, I can't take his brand of intellect.

Foot Sweep #16—Being told by the editor of a journal that the article I had submitted for publication was great, but needed to be toned down and my feminist lens of analysis changed to a human resource lens for the comfort of the editorial board before publication.

Foot Sweep #17—Being told by a journal reviewer that my use of feminist poststructuralism as a lens for the meaning-making of data was akin to a "jelly and ketchup sandwich."

Needless to say, the early years were interesting and full of foot sweeps, some that knocked me off of my feet and some that didn't, but despite scores of instances such as the above, I never really considered quitting and, for the most part, enjoyed my work and tried to focus on the positive aspects of being a professor and relied on my mentors for venting and advice.

Continuous Ground-and-Pound Hammer Fists

Although I learned to escape, overcome, and, eventually, ignore the mental and emotional obstacles/foot sweeps lodged at me in the higher education environment, efforts toward my submission/knockout weren't over. They became increasingly aggressive and physical, not in the literal sense, but in the way I felt the blows coming at me. These attempts at knockouts were almost impossible to ignore, more continuous than those described above (although some above were and still are continuous as well), and more difficult to overcome. According to CagePotato.com, Brock Lesnar's (an enormous MMA fighter known for a neck that resembles a tree trunk) "trademark ground-and-pound hammer fist attacks are: . . . short, rapid, furious, and performed by a panting, red-faced man . . . a 280-pound behemoth with XXXL fists." The website goes on to say that, "When he's [Lesnar] on top and there's blood in the water, the frenzy takes over. *It's less about the one-punch knockout and more about creating an onslaught that his opponent can't breathe under.*"

Hammer Fist #1—Repeatedly being expected to carry more than my fair share of the service load in some departments to help male faculty carve out time for their families. While male faculty are worshipped for being family centered, women are not. In fact, several faculty colleagues have resented the priority I place on my family as a woman. And, in my experience, family is defined by most as a wife and children in the academic setting. The fact that women are often caregivers of aging parents or that I share responsibility for the care of a sibling with a disability doesn't count for many as family. Being asked to carry more than your fair share of the load in a department can be devastating to a faculty member on a tenure line. It is exhausting and often carries with it health implications.

Hammer Fist #2—Being the constant target of an unhappy colleague that was akin to being married to an abusive spouse who makes efforts to bruise only in places that are unseen by most others. The circumstances and events that are encompassed by Hammer Fist #2 are those that I am unable to tell without compromising anonymity. They are numerous. They are nasty. And, they are unknown by all but a small number of people.

Hammer Fist #3—Having a faculty member tell other department faculty that I was responsible for said member's woes. This statement, while completely false (and verified to be false by administrators), caused huge rifts and irreparable damage.

Hammer Fist #4—Being told in an e-mail by an administrator who completed an evaluation on me at one point in time that all of the senior administrators wanted to change my evaluation from a positive one to a negative one (the e-mail was a "just so you know" sort of communication). Feeling like I'd been punched in the stomach (or hammer fisted) after reading this news, I scheduled face-to-face meetings with each of these individuals to gain helpful feedback as to why they felt this way. After discussions with each of them, it became apparent that none of them had any idea what I was talking about. Each of them said the e-mail was completely false. However, they chose not to confront the administrator who had lied about them. It was easier not to address the issue because it would have been uncomfortable for them.

Hammer Fist #5—Being lied to repeatedly by an administrator so as to always keep me unsure of the actual truth (i.e., Hammer Fist #4).

Hammer Fist #6—Being repeatedly left out of key e-mail communications by a faculty member (for some reason, all other faculty members consistently received these communications) with the intent of making me look incompetent. Lack of access to information is one of the most difficult punches to overcome because you have no idea what you've missed out on until it's too late.

Hammer Fist #7—Spending time in a department as the only tenured faculty member among many tenure-line faculty, but making the least amount of money. I repeatedly tried to negotiate an equity adjustment and was always told "I'm sorry. I know you need an equity adjustment, but we just don't have the money for it." Meanwhile, I was asked to take on increasing responsibilities "to protect junior faculty" (who were men) and "to allow untenured faculty time to focus on their writing" (although this was never afforded to me when I was struggling to work toward tenure). When I finally got what was deemed as an equity adjustment, it was an increase of three percent (and I still made the least amount of money). Meanwhile, I watched other faculty members get raises/adjustments (enormous increases . . . upwards of $10,000).

As stated previously, I experienced these hammer fist events in a different way than the foot sweeps that, while problematic, were more frustrating than anything else. These events were emotionally and physically draining and, in some cases, wasted precious time that could have been devoted to my work or personal life. They were less about the "one-punch knockout" and more about the overall "onslaught" that took the breath out of me. Still, none of these circumstances or events made me question my decision to become a professor or whether to remain in the academic field of educational leadership. As time went by, I had not only my mentors to rely upon, but a growing group of men and women colleagues from across the globe that were amazing support systems.

Fending Off Rear Naked Chokes

According to Extremeprosports.com, "The major thing that separates MMA from boxing is the ground game. And the most exciting parts of the ground game are the moves that end fights, the ones we call submissions." Submission moves were made famous when Royce Gracie started causing his opponents to tap (the signal fighters give to referees indicating that they will concede the fight due to excruciating pain being inflicted on them from their opponents). When inflicting a rear naked submission choke,

> The performer must have access to their opponent's back to pull this off. From there they curl one arm around the their neck, bicep against one side of the neck, forearm against the other. Then the performer tugs it close and places the hand of the choking arm on the bicep of their other arm as that arm comes up behind the opponent's head and touches their hair. Last, the applier tucks their head, expands their chest, and squeezes.

Why, readers might ask, would I dare to turn my back to anyone in higher education after experiencing so many attempts at submission and knockout? It didn't take many years to learn to love and like multitudes of colleagues, but to trust a precious few. But, however naive it might be, and no matter how many storms I weathered, I always thought some sense of safety and/or relief could eventually be found with those in high leadership positions at universities (i.e., Associate Deans, Deans, Provosts, etc.). Thus, I allowed myself to be placed in vulnerable positions with my back open to attack in several circumstances. The events I describe here are fewer, but more profound or larger in scope in regard to the impact they had on me in comparison to those described in previous sections. They are, for lack of a better way of putting it, the events that came the closest to causing my total submission or knockout. They are the events that made me wonder whether I should "tap out" and leave the field.

Rear Naked Choke #1—One year, I was initially astounded at and then furious with my faculty evaluation. After meeting with my evaluator and another administrator, I made the decision to contest the evaluation by writing a letter of rebuttal. I spent a week writing my rebuttal and included many appendices and supporting documents that proved the negative statements in my evaluation to be not only biased, but entirely untruthful. I followed university policy and gave both my evaluator and the other administrator a copy of the rebuttal and supporting documents. After getting no response from either person after a month passed, I scheduled a meeting with the administrator to discuss the contents of the rebuttal. As I sat in front of the administrator, it became glaringly obvious that this person had not read the rebuttal. When I pushed and asked why I had received no response, the administrator said, "I'm not required to read the rebuttal or do anything with it other than file it. Policy only requires me to file it." When I proceeded to push the administrator along ethical lines suggesting that the allowance of lying about a faculty member (defamation of character) when proof was available that disputed and disproved the lies was a dereliction of duty, the administrator, with a nasty look, replied, "Why can't you just leave things alone? Things will change with the evaluation process next year and this won't happen again." When I let the administrator know that not only would I not leave things alone when my character was at stake, but I would continue to meet with the university omsbudperson for further guidance about the lack of response I was receiving from administration, this person's response was, "Well, I guess I'll just have to contact Dr. XX because I have no idea what to do!"

I characterize this story as a rear naked choke because it was one of the few times in my higher education career that I considered "tapping" or giving up the fight. I can't express how profoundly sad it made me to have gone to a leader for help only to be dismissed as an "emotional female faculty member" who simply "can't get along with another faculty member" or who "has a strong ego." And, how telling it was that the administrator had hoped I would look the other way so that he did not have to figure out what to do! I had always believed that those individuals in the highest positions of power at a university would have my back if ever called upon. So, I entered this experience with my back open to attack. These days, my back is never fully open to attack. This experience left me a changed faculty member.

Rear Naked Choke #2—I was once asked to join a meeting with several faculty for the purposes of working out a conflict that had occurred with other faculty. Thinking nothing of this and, once again, believing in a system of general equality and fairness, I went into this meeting with my gloves off and back open to attack (I had no other reason to act otherwise) because I assumed that whatever the purpose of the meeting, it was for the good of the faculty as a whole and would result in a positive outcome. Instead, I spent an hour and a half being verbally and emotionally assaulted by two of the faculty (I was not the only one to be assaulted in this meeting, but share only the comments directed toward me) and was told things that included:

- "You are the youngest female we have ever known who has had conflict with so many university administrators... they are probably sick of seeing your face!"
- "Your personality is too strong." (Most of my colleagues and family describe me as quiet and thoughtful. I wonder if the problem is that my personality is too strong or whether it just isn't acceptable for a young female faculty member to speak her mind and defend herself when attacked?)
- "Are you always going to insist on taking a social justice stance on everything? Why can't you just take a chill pill and tone it down a notch?" When I didn't understand this question/comment and asked for clarification, I was told, "You're being combative."[2]
- "We've reviewed your CV and have determined there are several gaps and much room for improvement."

Needless to say, I left this meeting furious, yet wondering if I had somehow been punked[3] by other faculty because it was just that kind of experience that leaves you so unsteady of your feet that you think what you have just experienced can't possibly have just happened. I paced back and forth talking on the phone with a colleague for an hour and then spent another hour meeting face to face with yet another colleague trying to convince myself to remain in higher education and at the institution I was working for at the time. It took the better part of a month to overcome the urge to tap out of this rear naked choke experience and throw in the higher education towel.

LOSING ROUNDS, BUT WINNING THE FIGHT

While writing this narrative, I struggled to find a way to represent the most unspeakable events that I weathered as a young woman faculty member. But, no matter what I did to mask them or to, grudgingly, protect individuals who don't deserve to be protected, I was not able to bring myself to the task of "outing" them and, in essence, publicly destroying them. My ethic of care for even those individuals who have repeatedly tried to push me down, step on me, and strangle me will not allow me. Thus, I tried to find a way to represent these events and individuals without words or without describing the events and people themselves. At first, I thought providing a blank space in this narrative would represent all that is left unspoken (similar to a moment of silence). However, after running and listening to my ipod one morning, I determined that the lyrics, while aggressive, to

Eminem's song "25 to Life" represent what I feel about these events, individuals, and experiences in higher education over the past decade. Clearly, when Eminem performs these lyrics, he is speaking of entirely different circumstances than I have experienced and wish to represent here. So, instead, I ask readers to consider the lyrics as if I'm telling a story about my experiences (both in general and with specific individuals) in the university environment and describing the loss of round after round, but emerging victorious in the overall fight to claim a space in educational leadership that isn't chilly (Sandler & Hall, 1986), but open, warm and inviting to me.

25 to Life

Took me for granted took my heart and ran it straight into the planet
Into the dirt I can no longer stand it
Now my respect I demand it
Imma take control of this relationship
Command it, and imma be the boss of you now damnit
And what I mean is that I will no longer let you control me
So you better hear me out this much you owe me
I gave up my life for you, totally devoted to you while I've stayed…

I feel like when I bend over backwards for you all you do is laugh
Cause that ain't good enough you expect me to fold myself in half
Til I snap
Don't think I'm loyal
All I do is rap
How can I moonlight on the side
I have no life outside of that
Don't I give you enough of my time
You don't think so do you
Jealous when I spend time with the girls
Why I'm married to you still man I don't know
But tonight I'm serving you with papers
I'm divorcing you
Go marry someone else and make em famous
And take away their freedom like you did to me
Treat em like you don't need them and they ain't worthy of you
Feed em the same shit you made me eat
I'm moving on forget you

Ain't changing my mind
I'm climbing out this abyss

—Eminem

Honestly, I'm unable to say anything more to describe why these lyrics best represent some of what I've gone through, so I'm left having to say to readers, "Enough said." Those who find metaphors and forms of art as outlets for expression and descriptions of feelings and experiences will most likely understand the gist of what I'm using these words to represent (or, if they don't, they will, at the very least, understand the use of metaphors to describe feelings or to represent events). Others will find the lyrics strange and incomprehensible. And, I just have to accept as the writer that this is okay. Using these lyrics as a metaphor has allowed me to, in a sense, divorce all of the ugliness that I've experienced in the past and embrace the good aspects and people that surround me in the academic world.

Breaking the Silence and Letting Go?

I know it's over, but is it ever really done?
Please break the silence. Even if you're letting go.
My eyes are heavy and so is my heart.
Please break the silence. Even if you're letting go.
Even if you're letting go.
Break the Silence

—Ben Harper

I had numerous inclinations on how to end my narrative. I think the most important thing, for me, is to leave readers with an honest, true accounting of some of the obstacles I faced in the past decade as a young woman professor of educational leadership; not simply to provide a negative accounting of my time as a professor, but to help new professors see that they are not alone in some of the experiences they have had and to help veteran professors understand that much of the sexism (and/or ageism) that they experienced decades ago continues to be omnipresent in the lives of women professors new to the field. Writing this narrative, in essence, allowed me the opportunity to break my own silence. Breaking silence is important because without doing so, nothing changes; nothing can move forward.

I began this narrative with a heavy heart, but conclude it with the freedom of knowing I can now take bigger steps toward letting go. I can move toward the light. I can change the world with my own two hands (or, parts of it at least, particularly my own reality); I can make it better (if not for myself, for others); I can, unequivocally, make it kinder (Ben Harper, *With my own Two Hands*). This does not mean that I naively think that circumstances, in some instances, will change for myself or for others anytime soon. After all, I and many of the women scholars represented in this book have continued to experience similar sexist and stereotypical behaviors that veteran women experienced years ago.

Returning to mixed martial arts as a metaphor for some of the things I have experienced as I conclude this narrative provides interesting fodder for discussion. Interestingly, the first recorded prize fight was in the *Illiad* as it is widely known that men dueled/fought to the death in Ancient Greece and Rome. In fact, fighting has often been used as a metaphor for good vs. evil and intellect vs. brawn as, traditionally, two men face one another and brutally assault one another for pride and victory. Furthermore, according to McKay and McKay (2009) in their historical accounting of boxing, a precursor to MMA,

> The 1780's ushered in the first golden age of modern boxing. The aristocracy's interest in the sport, which had waned..., experienced a resurgence. And England's war with France spurred a sense of nationalism and a desire for men to take up this "truly British art." The popularity of a series of fights between Richard Humphries and Daniel Mendoza also created widespread interest in the sweet science... Mendoza's fighting style also changed the nature of the sport. Pugilists had formerly stood toe to toe and simply slugged each other back and forth. Fighters would block shots but there was very little weaving, bobbing, and fancy footwork. No floating like a butterfly; just stinging like a bee. Mendoza brought in the dancing and the defense, making him highly successful, although also the object of scorn. Some spectators found this agile style to be "ungentlemanly." (http://artofmanliness.com/2009/05/30/boxing-a-manly-history-of-the-sweet-science-of-bruising/)

I wonder if Humphries' style of fighting is what exhausted veteran women in the field as they spent countless hours in the ring in defense positions blocking shots, but having little space to weave and move. And, conversely, I wonder if Mendoza's style of fighting is how women have learned to return punches and make counter moves as they remain in the field and increase in number. Are we floating like butterflies or stinging like bees? Are we dancing and, if so, have we been successful while also becoming the object of scorn for some? Are veteran and young/new women to the field experiencing the same old fight in a new ring? Perhaps we should take lessons from Ronda Rousey, the first UFC Women's Bantamweight Champion.

Completing this narrative has rejuvenated my commitment to doing what I can to advocate for myself and for others; despite the knowledge that doing so will stereotype me as a "loud mouth," "bitch," "problem-child" and earn me a good deal of "eye-rolling" (and much worse) from those who love to bully (see Westhues', 2009 work on academic mobbing). It has reminded me to make more of an effort to move toward the light, remain in the light, and bring others to the light. Most important, it will push me to, legitimately, claim (and continuously reclaim) the space that I have created for myself in the academy. I may have to continue to weave, bob, and duck in defense of punches (stings), but this doesn't prevent me from dancing around and looking for spaces to float into in the most ungentlemanly way possible. And, once I claim the space, I can lift others up to join me.

NOTES

1. The David L. Clark National Graduate Student Research Seminar is sponsored by the University Council for Educational Administration (UCEA), Divisions A and L of the American Educational Research Association (AERA), and SAGE Publications, and brings emerging and veteran scholars in educational leadership together for two days of professional growth.
2. As someone who often uses humor to navigate frustrating experiences, I hope readers can imagine me responding to this comment with a resounding REALLY?! In the voice of either Seth or Amy from Saturday Night Live's Really!?! Skits.
3. Punk'd is an American hidden camera (practical joke) reality television series that first aired from 2003–2007 and was created by Ashton Kutcher and Jason Goldberg.

REFERENCES

Alston, J. A. (1999). Climbing hills and mountains: Black females making it to the superintendency. In C. C. Brunner (Ed.), *Sacred dreams. Women and the superintendency* (pp. 79–90). Albany, NY: SUNY.

Belenky, M. F., Clinchy, B. M., Goldberger, N. R., & Tarule, J. M. (1997). *Women's ways of knowing. The development of self, voice, and mind.* New York: Basic Books.

Benham, (1997). Silences and serenades: The journeys of three ethnic minority women school leaders. *Anthropology and Education Quarterly, 28*(2), 280–307.

Brunner, C. C. (2000). Unsettled moments in settled discourse: Women superintendents' experiences of inequality. *Educational Administration Quarterly, 36*, 76–116.

Davies, B. (1994). Poststructuralist theory, gender and teaching. In B. Davies (Ed.), *Poststructuralist theory and classroom practice* (pp. 1–43). Victoria, Australia: Deakin University Press.

Fraser, N., & Nicholson, L. J. (1990). Social criticism without philosophy: An encounter between feminism and postmodernism. In L. J. Nicholson (Ed.), *Feminism/postmodernism* (pp. 19–38). New York: Routledge.

Frye, M. (1993). The possibility of feminist theory. In A. Jaggar & P. S. Rothenburg (Eds.), *Feminist frameworks* (pp. 103–112). New York: McGraw-Hill.

Gardiner, M. E., Enomoto, E., & Grogan, M. (2000). *Coloring outside the lines. Mentoring women into school leadership.* Albany: State University of New York Press.

Gilligan, C. (1982). *In a different voice. Psychological theory and women's development.* Cambridge, MA: Harvard University Press.

Grogan, M. (1996). *Voices of women aspiring to the superintendency.* Albany: State University of New York Press.

Harding, S. (1989). Women as creators of knowledge. *American Behavioral Scientist, 32*(6), 700–707.

Lather, P. (1992). Critical frames in educational research: Feminist and post-structural perspectives. *Theory Into Practice, 31*(2), 87–99.

Marshall, C. (1981). Organizational policy and women's socialization in administration. *Urban Education, 16*(2), 205–231.

Marshall, C. (2010). Surviving while dismantling one's professional culture: The honor/struggle for the Feminist Academic. In A. K. Tooms & C. Boske (Eds.), *Bridge leadership: Connecting educational leadership and social justice to improve schools* (pp. 3–25). Greenwich, CT: Information Age Publishing.

McKay, B., & McKay, K. (2009). Boxing: A manly history of the sweet science of bruising. http://artofmanliness.com/2009/05/30/boxing-a-manly-history-of-the-sweet-science-of-bruising/.

Mertz, N. T. (1991). Females in school administration: Making sense of the numbers. *Planning and Change, 22,* 34–45.

Noddings, N. (1992). *The challenge to care in schools: An alternative approach to education.* New York: Teachers College Press.

Sandler, B., & Hall, R. M. (1986). *The campus climate revisited: Chilly for women faculty, administrators, and graduate students.* Washington, DC: Association of American Colleges.

Shakeshaft, C. (1989).*Women in educational administration.* NewburyPark, CA: Corwin Press.

Sherman, W. H., Beaty, D., Crum, K. S., & Peters, A. (2010). Unwritten: Young women faculty in educational leadership. *Journal of Educational Administration, 48*(6), 741–754.

Weedon, C. (1997). *Feminist practice and poststructuralist theory* (2nd ed.). Cambridge, MA: Blackwell.

CHAPTER 3

NAVIGATING UNCHARTERED TERRITORIES IN ACADEME THROUGH MENTORING NETWORKS

Gaëtane Jean-Marie

INTRODUCTION AND PURPOSE

Mentoring relationships over the years have been instrumental in my career development in academe. These relationships are a combination of same race and gender, cross-race and gender with colleagues locally and nationally. As such, I have engaged in numerous collaborative initiatives to include research and scholarly endeavors. As a Haitian-American scholar, my collaboration with others of different backgrounds provided opportunities to engage in dialogue about race, class, and gender issues which created opportunities to learn about our diverse cultural backgrounds. Over the years, these networks have been instrumental in my professional career and I attribute my successes to the supportive relationships I have established.

In this chapter, I chronicle my journey of navigating uncharted territories as a Haitian-American scholar in the academy. As the first in my family of Haitian descent to pursue a PhD and go on to be a professor, the

Continuing to Disrupt the Status Quo?, pages 25–39
Copyright © 2014 by Information Age Publishing
All rights of reproduction in any form reserved.

successes I've achieved are based on trials and errors, and what I've learned from mentors and colleagues who provided guidance and helpful insights along the way.

WOMEN OF COLOR AND MENTORING IN HIGHER EDUCATION LITERATURE

Scholarly interest in mentoring for women in general has been developing as a distinct body of literature and research over the last two decades (Holmes &Terrell, 2004; Johnston & McCormack, 1997). This is part of a response to a range of widespread changes affecting higher education including the increasing presence of women in college, faculty, and administrative roles. Additionally, Tuitt, Sagaria and Turner (2007) report that colleges and universities have undertaken a mission to increase the representation of people of color on their faculties. While men and women of color are underrepresented of the total full-time faculty, even more so, women faculty of color remain a small part of the professoriate (Jean-Marie, 2011; Ryu, 2010; Turner, Gonzalez & Wood, 2008).

Women of color who gain entry to academe may experience isolation and exclusion, and reports of the culture of academia have been described as less hospitable to navigate the various aspects of academic life (Gibson, 2006; Glazer-Raymo, 1999; Holmes, Land, & Hinton-Hudson, 2007). In the existing structure of academia, women faculty of color often view themselves as "outsiders" because of professional and personal demands, and are less likely to gain access to networks and organizational systems for their success (Gibson, 2006; Rios & Longnion, 2000; Tillman, 2001). Though women faculty of color in the academy differ in experiences, they are connected in their struggle to be accepted and respected, and on how issues of marginalization, racism, and sexism can be manifested as unintended barriers to navigating the tenure process successfully (Diggs, Garrison-Wade, Estrada & Galindo, 2009).

As research supports, informal and formal mentoring and supportive networks can enhance the socialization (Gibson, 2006), impact scholarly productivity (Jean-Marie & Brooks, 2011), and the persistence of women faculty of color (Holmes et al, 2007; Jean-Marie & Lloyd-Jones, 2011). As more women faculty of color enter the professoriate, they are reevaluating, clashing with, and challenging old practices, while simultaneously articulating new ones (James & Farmer, 1993). Yet, to do so effectively, they are better served by a portfolio of mentors (Baugh & Scandura, 1999; Higgins & Kram, 2001) who can facilitate their development of career competencies, help them understand "the rules of the game" for scholarly activity, and transform the normalized construction of academic environments that is sometimes exclusionary of women faculty of color (Jean-Marie & Brooks,

2011; Jean-Marie & Lloyd-Jones, 2011; Tillman, 2001). Mentoring networks are vital contributions to a successful academic career in an increasingly complex and changing academic environment, particularly for women faculty of color (Sorcinelli & Yun, 2007). Given that the training for faculty roles all too often is happenstance (Johnson, 2007; Sorcinelli & Yun, 2007), drawing from a variety of mentoring relationships assists women faculty of color in building collegial networks in research and teaching. New models of mentoring (deJanasz, 2004; Girves, Zepeda, & Gwathmey, 2005; Johnson, 2007) offer frameworks for helping women faculty of color faculty build robust networks that are nonhierarchical, collaborative, and cross-cultural partnerships to address specific areas of faculty activity.

Women faculty of color benefit more in seeking out "multiple mentors" (de Janasz & Sullivan, 2004), "constellations of mentors" (van Emmerik, 2004), "networks of mentors" (Girves, Lepeda, & Gwathmeny, 2005), or a "portfolio of mentors" who can address a variety of career competencies (Bauch & Scandura, 1999; Higgins & Kram, 2001). Mentoring networks are ideal for women faculty of color because they expand the constellation of developmental relationships (Higgins & Kram, 2001) to make connections with a broad array of faculty and colleagues in and outside of the profession.

METHODS

As part of a larger study capturing my life experiences as an immigrant adolescent into my professional career, for this chapter, I draw upon an autoethnographic approach (Anderson, 2006; Ellis & Bochner, 2000) to chronicle significant experiences in the academy. Consistent with qualitative inquiry rooted in traditional symbolic interactionism (Anderson, 2006), auto-ethnography is a term that has been in use for at least two decades and includes a wide range of research and writing approaches, which connect the personal to the cultural (Ellis & Bochner 2000, p. 739). According to Richardson (2000), "auto-ethnographies are highly personalized, revealing texts in which authors tell stories about their own lived experiences, relating the personal to the cultural (p. 931)." The five key features of analytic auto-ethnography that I propose include (a) complete member researcher (CMR) status; (b) analytic reflexivity; (c) narrative visibility of the researcher's self; (d) dialogue with informants beyond the self; and (e) commitment to theoretical analysis (Anderson, 2006).

This research enabled me to think through influential moments in my life, which included some of my experiences in which I began to embrace teaching as a possible career choice. Through my reflections, I wrote about difficult moments as well as the successes and key turning points. Through the process of writing, the past became more meaningful. As van Manen

(1990) explained, "writing became more meaningful" (p. 124). Through my writings, I relived pieces of my life, and reignited memories and events that influence the work in which I am deeply entrenched in.

Poststructuralist theories offer support to auto/ethnography research approaches, firstly, by directing us to "understand ourselves reflexively as persons writing from particular positions as specific times; and second, it frees us from trying to write a single text in which we say everything at once to everyone" (Richardson, 2000, p. 929). Writing from a particular position (i.e., childhood experiences on marginalization and its influence) provided me an opportunity to reflect on a particular period in my life that played a significant role in my adult life (i.e., professional career).

Data Collection and Analysis

Data collected for this self-study included my journals focusing on writings about my experiences, and email correspondence I have kept over the years. The data collected from these sources provided contextual information to help [me] investigate and examine my subjectivity (Reissman, 1993). In addition to old journals I have kept for keepsake, in particular my faded blue notebook, for four months, I wrote about my experiences as an immigrant in the United States.

To analyze the multiple data sources collected for the study, I read and reread my journals to bring into light the structure and content of the narratives (Reissman, 1993). I examined specific events that had profound effect on my professional career. What ensues in the following section is how I threaded my analysis and interpretation of my behaviors, thoughts, and experiences to provide a portraiture of my journey in academe.

FINDINGS

Four major findings emerged from the auto-ethnographic study which are addressed in the ensuing discussion: (a) surrendering to the call of teaching; (b) cementing my call to teach: learning the craft of teaching through mentoring; (c) rocky entry to the professoriate: surviving "bumps" through mentoring relationships; and (d) paying it forward by mentoring women of color.

Surrendering to the Call of Teaching

As early as 8th grade, I considered teaching as a profession but rejected it because I learned very early on education privileged some people and marginalized others based on cultural markers such as race, gender, class and sexual orientation (Jean-Marie & Mansfield, 2013). Therefore, my evolution as an educator took a circuitous route, even to arriving at this juncture in my professional career as a tenured faculty member in educational leadership. I best characterize my entry to the field of education as one who stumbled into teaching. The more I tried to distance myself from the teaching profession, the more I felt a tug to go in that direction.

I started teaching during my sophomore year of undergraduate study in a precollege program at a local university in a metropolitan city. I was hired as a teaching assistant to work with disenfranchised students from the three largest urban schools which the program recruits students. Working at precollege was an opportunity to generate an income stream during the remainder of my undergraduate study. As a political science major and English minor, I had my sights set on law school and did not intend to go into teaching. Although I had my sights on a different career trajectory, the experience at precollege revealed the effects of inequitable educational opportunities in urban school districts. I am reminded of Walker and Dimmock (2005) who argue that the challenges accompanying the education of diverse groups and ways to provide worthwhile, socially responsible, and equitable education are both exhilarating and alarming. When I first started as a teacher's assistant, I struggled working with my students' behavioral issues. Despite my struggle, I was beginning to embrace the challenge of finding ways to connect with my students by building relationships. It took time but I achieved success developing positive relationships with my students, a valuable lesson that would remain with me over the years.

After undergraduate school while still working at precollege, I decided to pursue a masters' degree in criminal justice as I contemplated law school. However, toward the end of my masters' degree, I had the opportunity to go to law school to get a joint degree but that was short-lived. After I graduated with my masters, I realized that I did not want to work with adolescents after they became entrenched in the criminal justice system. I felt a tug toward the teaching profession but for a long time I did not heed to the voice inside me. I would continue to struggle with my resistance during graduate school in North Carolina in pursuit of my doctorate.

Cementing My Call to Teach: Learning the Craft of Teaching Through Mentoring

When I relocated to Greensboro, North Carolina, I was charting a new path, one with uncertainties. The year before I moved, my dad died at 59 years old after a short battle with cancer, and three months prior, my eight-year-old cousin died of leukemia. Culturally, a female leaving her parents' home to live independently is frowned upon. Nevertheless, I was in search of a new path, one that would lead to a fulfilling career. After the first semester living in a 250 square foot room, I pursued full-time work so I could have a steady income and more spacious living arrangements. I was hired in the dean's office in the College of Education and was promoted in less than a year to a higher-level position. Now that I was working full time and attending graduate school three nights a week, my goal was to finish my doctorate in four years.

As a doctoral student, I had the opportunity to teach an upper level foundation course for preservice teachers. It was while teaching the course the culmination of what I learned and was learning in graduate school influenced my interest in and love of teaching. In my doctoral program, my professors encouraged me to develop my intellectual acumen as I grappled with my "outsider-within" status (McDemmond, 1999) as an emerging Black female scholar (Jean-Marie, 2009). Modeling my professors, I sought to create an open, inclusive classroom environment that was invigorating but at times difficult because many students expected this course to be value-neutral. However, the assigned readings sought to stimulate and challenge students to expand their experiential base. As Bickford (2008) asserts, "new knowledge has the potential to create outrage" (p. 142).

Realizing my students needed an outlet to express their thoughts, I used journals so that students could reflect on their experiences and pose questions to themselves and me. They also engaged in action-research projects (i.e., an assignment on poverty included eating on a $1 daily budget for a few days) to help them link theory to practice. Further, these activities were for the purpose of encouraging students to take an active rather than a passive role in their self-development, and advance critical analyses of racism, sexism and classism, and other markers of difference. However, for many students this was their first time exploring multifaceted critical social issues (i.e., equity and access, social justice, affirmative action, etc.) and their implications for educational practice. Similarly, I was learning from my students on how we can explore a democratic process about teaching and learning as they encountered texts that pushed them beyond their comfort zone.

Many of my White students resisted, became defensive, or simply disengaged from the process of critical inquiry. As a woman of color in a predominantly White university, my students' resistance did not surprise me. As hooks (1994) posits, "the choice to work against the grain, to challenge the status quo, often has negative consequences" (p. 201). Initially, I struggled to find a space where engagement and criticality were welcomed features of the classroom discourse. There was a dissonance between the students who I taught and the course content. No matter how I structured my course syllabus in an honest effort to disclose through course objectives and student learning outcomes, the evaluations usually criticized the amount of time spent discussing race or more precisely "bashing Whites." At times, I developed a hypersensitivity to these tensions and consistently had to adjust my "mask" to fit the classroom environment, as Paul Dunbar avers in *We Wear the Mask* (1993): We wear the mask that grins and lies. It hides our cheeks and shades our eyes..." However, there were momentary lapses in the adjustment process of my mask where a rage flooded my being.

In that moment when the rage was present, I managed to readjust the mask and transcend this emotional storm. The transcendence enabled me to see through the fog, haze and rage to students" potential and possibility for developing a critical consciousness and struggling for social justice. For that, I am thankful because it allowed the more empowering feelings of care and nurture to emerge and dominate my classroom in order that the potential and the possibility for change might evolve (Noddings, 2002). Truly believing in the possibility of change, I persisted in my efforts to help my preservice teachers take an active role in self-development, and give voice to new ways of thinking about education, teaching and learning. In the course of one semester, it was difficult to observe the transformation in students' thinking about the various issues examined in class. However, students' reflections provided a snapshot of their growth.

While teaching another undergraduate course that same year for freshmen Teaching Fellows, Brandy (pseudonym for a student) shared her thoughts about the effect the course had on her. She wrote:

> One night a week, I return to my dorm room with my thoughts racing with confusion, happiness, sadness, anger and complacency. Sometimes I feel like crying; other times, I feel as if I am well on my way to understanding. And yet, with all these contradicting emotions and thoughts, I find myself eager to return to the same class the very next week. As this spring semester has flown by, I feel that the seminar in Teaching Fellows has been one of the most beneficial of all my classes. I accredit these most complex thoughts and feelings to the assigned readings and to the sincere discussions that are evoked by the text. If I had to characterize this semester with one word, it would have to be "awareness." I feel that the issues raised and discussed in class have made me more aware and which made me truly think about the teaching profession in a more critical manner.

For Brandy, the classroom was a safe place for her to further explore her thoughts about schooling and education, which challenged her to interrogate the teaching profession more closely. Similar to hooks (1994), I conscientiously work to make my classroom a "democratic setting where everyone feels a responsibility to contribute, a central goal of transformative pedagogy" (p. 39). Sharing was not relegated only to my students by also to me as the instructor of the class. My willingness to share my thoughts and feelings about the topic under discussion was to create a climate of openness and intellectual rigor. It was also important that no student would be invisible; so I called on different students all the time although some resented having to make a verbal contribution. If a student did not want to participate, I moved on to the next student and always reminded the class that I will call on all students. Participation was an important aspect of the course. Over time, students felt they were part of a classroom community where they felt free to talk and "talk back" (hooks, 1994). Engaged in mutual participation, I was learning from my students, listened, and observed in class and in their reflective journals their struggles of giving up old ways of thinking, knowing and learning new approaches. Together, we "surrendered to the wonder of relearning and learning ways of knowing that went against the grain" (hooks, 1994, p. 44).

For Brandy, as her comfort level increased over the course of the semester, she participated more in class and her reflection revealed the growth she experienced by the end of the semester:

> The articles have brought to my attention many problems and issues that need to be addressed and need solutions. And every class I sit and almost laugh at the notion that 30 or so educators-to-be, sit and try to come up with solutions that have been plaguing education as we know it. Then, I think, this is how problems are solved and solutions are reached...As I have been given much, almost too much to think about this semester, I feel extremely lucky to have the opportunity to discuss and bring to attention issues and problems I would've not have otherwise thought of prior to this class. I leave this class with such mixed emotions; but for once, I am thankful for being so indecisive. I have learned that we may never know the right answers but that does not mean we quit searching.

This student's reflection depicts how she grappled with encountering multiple perspectives in an effort to become mindful of her actions on the world in order to gain new knowledge, cross-cultural barriers and encounter multiple perspectives that generate new possibilities (Greene, 1988). Years later, I still read students' reflections from my very first two courses because they represent the development of my pedagogical skills.

In addition to the opportunity to teach, my professors in graduate school provided frameworks for me to examine hard questions regarding the intersection of social class, race, and gender; they challenged me to think seriously about pedagogy (Freire, 2000; hooks, 1994). They encouraged me to learn (unlearn/relearn) and critique without fear and helped push the boundaries of what I knew as I grappled with my "outsider-within" (McDemmond, 1999) status as a Black emerging scholar in academe. In addition, they approached the classroom environments as open spaces where students from diverse cultural experiences could engage in discourse, understand the fluidity of a complex society and bridge gaps through cultural understandings. I learned through them what hooks (1994) explicates about her insights, strategies, and critical reflections on pedagogical practice. She asserts, "teaching is a performative act. And it is that aspect of our work that offers the space for change, invention, spontaneous shifts, that can serve as a catalyst drawing out the unique elements in each classroom" (p. 11). Through this perfomative act, my professors helped me become more engaged and an active participant in learning, an activist process that I was being oriented to and one I wanted to reciprocate.

Not only did I yearn to practice this kind of activism in pedagogy (James, 1993), I was also beginning to embrace the teaching profession as part of my calling. Seeing how my professors approached teaching from a standpoint that sought to educate for critical consciousness (hooks, 1994) and ignite activism in pedagogy (James, 1993), I knew I could help my students uncover the underlying political, social, cultural and economic foundations of the larger society (McLaren, 1998). With this recognition, the period of my graduate school provided me rich opportunities to learn and enrich my understanding about critical pedagogy, to gain greater personal awareness through reflection, and to develop a passion to engage in praxis as an agent of social change.

Beyond my classes, I sought my professors and, in particular, their mentorship. Specifically, my doctoral advisor, a White female tenured faculty was very supportive of the women of color in the program. Therefore, my colleagues and I gravitated toward her for mentorship; we wanted to broaden our knowledge and understanding so we would be well prepared for the next journey in our career trajectory. Another professor, a White female untenured faculty, who continued to be a mentor after she left the institution was also instrumental in providing support to my peer networks and me. As working professionals, my colleagues (i.e., seven Black women) and I were challenged to develop strong mentoring relationships with our professors in which we could study under and work with them. Most of us worked full time and attended classes in the evening; therefore, there were limited opportunities to interact with our professors beyond class. However, to compensate for the lack of mentoring, we would meet bi-weekly on Sundays to work on scholarly endeavors to enhance our doctoral experience given our aspirations to become professors in the university setting. We recognized that our White counterparts' colleagues would often meet to work collaboratively on conference proposals and publications, but no invitations were extended to us. As a group, we organized and developed the Scholars of Color Network (SCN), which served as not only a professional network, but also a sisterhood. As I reflect on my doctoral program, the bonds I developed with the women in SCN have evolved into lasting friendships because of the shared experiences and rapport we developed with each other. As one of the first three to graduate and transition to the professoriate, I would often reach out to this group for support over the years and other women of color I have developed relationships with from other institutions.

Rocky Entry to the Professoriate: Surviving "Bumps" Through Mentoring Relationships

My circuitous journey to the teaching profession in academe began in undergraduate where I had the opportunity to teach in precollege but the university classroom was truly my training ground for what was to become my passion and calling. Towards the completion of my doctoral studies, I reflected deeply on whether I wanted to pursue academe as a faculty member or stay on the current path as a full-time administrator in higher education. After much contemplation, I accepted a tenure-track faculty position in a graduate program in educational leadership.

Several incidents during *my* first semester gave me insights on the challenges I would confront due to my race, gender, and age (Jarmon, 2001; Jean-Marie, 2012). These are what I call academic stressors. I recall an incident in my first semester in an instructional leadership class of thirty-one master level students. On the first night of class, one middle-aged, White male student, who, on several occasions in class referred to my colleagues as "Dr. so and so," stayed to talk to me after class ended. On our way to the parking lot, he turned and asked me, "Can I call you by your first name?" I did not respond to his question but instead said, "Have a good evening and I'll see you next week." On my ten minute drive home, I reflected on his question and was curious as to why he felt it was appropriate to want to call me by first name but referred to my White male colleagues by "Dr. so and so" in class. Was this about race, gender or age? Why did I have a heightened sensitivity to this incident? My research on Black women administrators in historically Black institutions (Jean-Marie, 2005; 2006; 2009) revealed the subtle and explicit prejudice that generation of 1960s women encountered. I began to ponder if this incident was an introduction to what I would encounter in the professoriate.

In search of an answer about what I was feeling regarding my student's question, after arriving home, I sent an email to my White female mentor, a former professor in my graduate program. She was a person I trusted and would be candid with me. In the subject line of my email, I titled it, "What's in a name?" In short, I interrogated why this student might felt it appropriate to ask to call me by my first name. Under a different circumstance, I would be receptive to being called by my first name, but this was different. The undertone of his question led to me ponder that perhaps, I am perceived as undeserving of the title "Doctor" or "Professor." My disposition is to always address an issue directly so it doesn't escalate because it was unaddressed. The following week, I returned to class and stated that since the common practice in our department is that students refer to my colleagues by their professional title (i.e., Professor X or Dr. X), the same applies to me.

In another incident that semester, the department secretary was having a conversation with me and another colleague about a particular matter. When she mentioned my colleague's and another person's name, she referred to them as "Dr." but when it came to me, it was Gaëtane. It was so noticeable that my colleague responded and said, "Well, Dr. Jean-Marie should have..." Over the years I have encountered subtle practices that intended to undermine my credibility or challenge my authority in the classroom as a woman of color in academe. However, those moments were opportunities to engage in meaningful dialogue about issues of social justice. While I will have my momentary relapse of anger and frustration (hooks, 1994; Jean-Marie, 2009), my supportive networks within and outside academe were outlets to talk about my experiences.

Another colleague who was instrumental in resolving a conflict prior to my arrival to my new institution and later would become a mentor was a senior White female full professor. When I butted heads with my department chair about my teaching load for the fall semester, she intervened. I had negotiated a one course fall/two courses spring teaching load for my first year. Prior to moving, I was contacted by the program coordinator who informed me about the two classes I was scheduled to teach. In learning about this error, I contacted the department chair who told me I misunderstood the terms of my contract and it was a 2/2 load. His statement clearly contradicted what my legally binding contract indicated about my teaching load. In addition, I had copies of my email correspondence with the dean about my teaching load during negotiation.

For a while, the department chair and I went back and forth because he insisted that I misunderstood my contract. He was dismissive. I was angry and stressed about the situation. This was not the way I wanted to begin my career at the institution. Therefore, I reached out to my department chair who served on my doctoral committee. He was a close friend to my new colleague; however, I did not know that at the time. He contacted my colleague raising concerns about how the department chair was in violation of my contract. By then several individuals became aware of the situation and shortly after arriving to the university, my colleague informed me that the matter had been resolved and my teaching load was one course fall /two courses spring.

Over the years, in addition to being a colleague and mentor, the aforementioned person was also a close friend. A highly respected and productive scholar, I learned a lot from her and she became a role model on how to balance work and family life. In addition to this colleague, I also have had opportunities to benefit from the mentoring of senior women of color during the course of my professional career. Many of them are the first women of color to receive promotion and tenure at their universities and I have benefitted from their experiences. My encounters with some of these scholars were through their research; they were studying and living the intersection of race, gender and leadership. I also engaged in peer mentoring with others of cross-race and cross-gender during my professional career. The culmination of my mentoring experiences has influenced the success I have achieved in my professional career. Through great mentoring and my commitment to maintain an active research agenda, I was successfully promoted and received tenure at a research-intensive institution.

Paying it Forward by Mentoring Women of Color

In reciprocity, as a way to pay forward (Holmes & Terrell, 2004) the mentoring support I have benefitted from, in 2011, I cofounded a mentoring network, Advancing Women of Color in the Academy (AWOCA). AWOCA is a scholarly network of eight women of color, connected through research in the field of education and their affiliation in higher education. We are an interethnic, transdisciplinary, and cross-institutional collaborative group dedicated to advancing women of color in the academy. The vision of AWOCA is to emerge as a distinguished network for supporting and promoting the retention and achievement of women of color scholars in the academy. Its mission is to provide mentoring support to advance of women of color scholars in the academy, including collaboration through research, publishing, and grant-writing opportunities, and seminar workshops to foster and enhance knowledge and research. To date, AWOCA members have collaborated on nine scholarly endeavors (i.e., edited book, grant, national conferences, special issue etc.) since its establishment in 2011. AWOCA's core values are premised on collaboration, mentorship, and advancement. First, scholars engage in collaboration in the areas of research, grantsmanship, scholarly publications, creative activities, and conference presentations to disseminate knowledge and research nationally and globally. Second, scholars receive support from one another including guidance on the process of writing for publication and navigating the academy (i.e., challenges and opportunities of the academy as they pertain to unique issues for women of color). Finally, scholars aim to increase the tenure and promotion of women of color (i.e., assistant to associate; associate to full professorship) within and across institutions of higher learning, generating a legacy of success for future scholars and society-at-large.

CONCLUSION

Much of this chapter centered on my nontraditional journey into the teaching profession. However, my experience as a woman scholar of color depicts the ongoing struggle women from underrepresented communities encounter in the academy (Jean-Marie, 2006; 2012; Turner, González, & Wood, 2008). For women of color, the journey to the academy includes overcoming milestones at all levels, which sometimes encompass gender and racial barriers. A common attribute women of color share is their ability to triumph over challenges and barriers. Through mentoring relationships developed in a variety of contexts and across race and gender, women of color are able to overcome challenges and barriers that will help them build characters of strength, persistence, and resilience. These character factors become part of their repertoire on how to achieve success in their roles as faculty and administrators.

REFERENCES

Anderson, L. (2006). Analytical autoethnography. *Journal of Contemporary Ethnography, 35*(4), 373–395.

Baugh, S. G., & Scandura, T. A. (1999). The effect of multiple mentors on protege' attitudes toward the work setting. *Journal of Social Behavior and Personality, 14,* 503–521.

Bickford, D. M. (2008). Using testimonial novels to think about social justice. *Education, Citizenship and Social Justice, 3,* 131–146.

deJanasz, S. C., & Sullivan, S. E. (2004). Multiple mentoring in academe: Developing the professorial network. *Journal of Vocational Behavior, 64*(2), 263–283.

Diggs, G. A., Garrison-Wade, D. F., Estrada, D., & Galindo, R. (2009). Smiling faces and colored spaces: The experiences of faculty of color pursuing tenure in the academy. *Urban Review, 41,* 312–333.

Dunbar, P. L. (1993). The collected poetry of Paul Laurence Dunbar. In J. M. Braxton (Ed.). Charlottesville: University Press of Virginia.

Ellis, C., & A. P. Bochner. (2000). Autoethnography, personal narrative, reflexivity: Researcher as subject. In N. K. Denzin & Y. S. Lincoln (Eds.), *Handbook of qualitative research,* (2nd ed., pp. 733–68). Thousand Oaks, CA: Sage.

Freire, P. (2000). *Pedagogy of the oppressed.* (New Revised 20th-Anniversay Edition). New York: Continuum.

Gibson, S. K. (2006). Mentoring of women faculty: The role of organizational politics and culture. *Innovative Higher Education, 31*(1), 63–79.

Girves, J. E., Zepeda, Y., & Gwathmey, J. K. (2005). Mentoring in a post-affirmative action world. *Journal of Social Issues, 61*(3), 449–479.

Glazer-Raymo, J. (1999). Shattering the myths: Women in academe. Baltimore, MD: The Johns Hopkins University Press.

Greene, M. (1988). *The dialectic of freedom.* New York, NY: Teachers College.

Higgins, M. C., & Kram, K. E. (2001). Reconceptualizing mentoring at work: A developmental network perspective. *The Academy of Management Review, 26*(2), 264–288.

Holmes, S. L., Land, L.D., & Hinton-Hudson, V.D. (2007). Race still matters: Considerations for mentoring Black women in academe. *The Negro Educational Review, 58*(1–2), 105–129.

Holmes, S. L., & Terrell, M. C. (Eds.). (2004). Lifting as we climb: Mentoring the next generation of African American student affairs administrators [Special issue]. *National Association of Student Affairs Professionals Journal, 7,* 1–134.

hooks, b. (1994). Teaching to transgress: Education as the practice of freedom. New York: Routledge.

James, J. (1993). Teaching theory, talking community. In J. James & A. Y. Davis (Eds.), *Spirit, space & survival: African American women in (white) academe* (pp. 118–138). New York, NY: Routledge.

James, J., & Farmer, R. (Ed.) (1993). *Spirit, space & survival: African American women in white academe.* New York: Routledge.

Jarmon, B. (2001). Unwritten rules of the game. In R. O. Mabokela & A. L. Green (Eds.), *Sisters of the academy: Emergent Black women scholars in higher education* (pp. 175–181). Sterling, VA: Stylus.

Jean-Marie, G. (2011). "Unfinished agendas": Trends in women of color's status in higher education. In G. Jean-Marie & B. Lloyd-Jones (Eds.), *Women of color in higher education: Turbulent past, promising future* (pp. 3–20). Bingley, UK: Emerald Group Publishing Limited.

Jean-Marie, G. (2009). "Fire in the belly": Igniting a social justice discourse in learning environments of leadership preparation. In A. Tooms & C. Boske (Eds.), *Building bridges, connecting educational leadership and social justice to improve schools. Book series:* Educational Leadership for Social Justice (pp. 97–119). North Carolina: Information Age.

Jean-Marie, G. (2006). Welcoming the unwelcomed: A social justice imperative of African American female leaders at *Historically Black Colleges and Universities. Educational Foundations, 20*(1–2), Winter-Spring, 83–102.

Jean-Marie, G. (2005). Standing on the promises: The experiences of Black women administrators in historically black institutions. *Advancing Women in Leadership Online Journal, 19.* Available: http://www.advancingwomen.com/awl/fall2005/index.html.

Jean-Marie, G., & Brooks, J. (2011). *Mentoring and supportive networks for women of color in academe.* In G. Jean-Marie, & B. Lloyd-Jones (Eds.). *Women of color in higher education: Contemporary perspectives and new directions* (pp. 91–107), Volume 10, Diversity in Higher Education Series. Bingley, United Kingdom: Emerald Group Publishing Limited.

Jean-Marie, G., & Mansfield, K. (2013). Race and racial discrimination in schools: School leaders' courageous conversations. In J. Brooks & N. Arnold, (Eds.), *Educational leadership and racism: Preparation, pedagogy & practice* (pp. 19–35), Charlotte, NC: Information Age Publishing.

Johnston, S., & McCormack, C. (1997). Developing research potential through a structured mentoring program: Issues arising. *Higher Education, 33,* 251–264

McDemmond, M. (1999). On the outside looking in. In W. B. Harvey, (Ed.), *Grass roots and glass ceilings: African American administrators in predominantly white colleges and universities.* New York: State University.

McLaren, P. (1998). *Life in schools: An introduction to critical pedagogy in the foundations of education.* New York: Longman.
Noddings, N. (2002). *Educating moral people: A caring alternative to character education.* New York, NY: Teachers College.
Reissman, C. K. (1993). *Narrative analysis.* Newbury Park, CA: Sage.
Richardson, L. (2000). Writing. In N. Denzin & Y. Lincoln (Eds.), *Handbook of qualitative research* (2nd ed., pp. 923–948). London: Sage.
Rios, A., & Longnion, J. (2000). Agenda for the 21st century: Executive summary (Retrieved from http://www.umn.edu/women/wihe.html. Accessed on December 15, 2010). Minneapolis, MN: University of Minnesota, National Initiative for Women in Higher Education.
Ryu, M. (2010). *Minorities in higher education 2010: Twenty-fourth status report.* Washington, DC: American Council on Education.
Sorcinelli, M. D., & Yun, J. (2007). From mentor to mentoring networks: Mentoring in the new academy. *Change,* 58–61.
Tillman, L. (2001). Mentoring African American faculty in predominantly White institutions. *Research in Higher Education, 42*(3), 295–325.
Tuitt, F. A., Sagaria, M. A. D., & Turner, C. S. V. (2007). Signals and strategies in hiring faculty of color. In: J. C. Smart (Ed.), Higher education: Handbook of theory and research (Vol. 22, pp. 497–535). New York, NY: Springer.
Turner, C. S. V., Gonzalez, J. C., & Wood, J. L. (2008). Faculty of color in academe: What 20 years of literature tells us. *Journal of Diversity in Higher Education, 1*(3), 139–168.
van Emmerik, J. H. (2004). The more you can get the better: Mentoring constellations and intrinsic career success. *Career Development International, 9*(6), 578–594.
Van Manen,, M. (1990). *Researching lived experience: Human science for an action sensitive pedagogy.* Albany: State University of New York Press.
Walker, A., & Dimmock, C. (2005). Developing leadership in context. In M. Coles & G. Southworth (Eds.), *Developing leadership: Creating the schools cif tomorrow* (pp. 88–89). Milton Keyes: Open University Press.

CHAPTER 4

YOUNG, GIFTED, FEMALE, AND BLACK

The Journey to Becoming Who I Am

April L. Peters

> Well, son, I'll tell you:
> Life for me ain't been no crystal stair.
> It's had tacks in it,
> And splinters,
> And boards torn up,
> And places with no carpet on the floor—
> Bare.
> But all the time
> I'se been a-climbin' on,
> And reachin' landin's,
> And turnin' corners,
> And sometimes goin' in the dark
> Where there ain't been no light.
> So boy, don't you turn back.
> Don't you set down on the steps
> 'Cause you finds it's kinder hard.
> Don't you fall now—
> For I'se still goin', honey,
> I'se still climbin',
> And life for me ain't been no crystal stair.[1]

My career in education has been characterized by pioneering decisions and achievements. I have been the first, the youngest, and/or the first African American to achieve or to have certain experiences in some settings. These experiences have been rewarding and challenging. In the midst of pioneering my career, I acknowledge that I've depended upon and created support networks, navigated through unchartered territory, and developed a deeper understanding of myself grounded in my intersecting identities as well as my personal and professional goals. The poem above, *Mother to Son*, in many ways is a metaphor for me. I am able to be a pioneer because of the giants whose shoulders I stand upon. Specifically, because of the women (like the Mother speaking to her Son) in my life (and those who have come before me professionally) who have faced hardships and still kept "climbin" in spite of these challenges. And like these "Mothers," I too, have endured some profound challenges, and I, too, keep "climbin."

Breaking Into the All Male's Club (Mertz, 2009) helped me to make sense of some of my experiences, viewed through the lenses of women pioneers in the field of educational leadership, and several coauthored pieces (Sherman, Beatty, Crum, & Peters, 2010; Sherman et al., 2013) helped me to articulate these experiences in my own voice.

PRELUDE TO MY JOURNEY

Education has always emphasized to me the differences in our society along racial, gender, and socioeconomic lines. Educational attainment itself is a privilege often afforded only to those with privilege. I was raised in a household where extreme value was placed on education. My mother is an educator and a very brilliant individual. She taught my sister and me to read so that we were school ready. She attended school in a middle class community in the Northeast and was one of the first Black students to integrate the higher-level classes. My dad is a product of the segregated, rural, Deep South and experienced an early life punctuated by Jim Crow oppression. His mother was widowed with eight children at the age of 33. She had to work as a domestic in order to support my aunts and uncles. My dad taught us that society would view us as lesser based on race and gender. He often said, "You have two strikes against you, because you're Black2 and you're female." Because of this, he stressed education as a way to overcome the "strikes" against us. My parents often told me that I could not be "just as good" as my White peers; I had to be "better."

I learned the "you MUST be better" lesson early. I attended an all-Black private school during my formative years. However, in elementary school (fourth grade) I transferred to the local racially integrated public school in my community. I was educated during the age of tracking students according to "academic ability." I truly believe that I was placed in classes with other Black students who lived in my neighborhood because of my address (an indicator of socioeconomic status) and my race. Although I attended schools in a very middle class district, my immediate neighborhood was made up of working class and lower class families. My family was one of the few traditional family units in my neighborhood. I found the work in the classes I was in to be too easy and the behavior of the students to be contrary to what I knew was acceptable. I told my mom and she came to the school to investigate. We learned that I should have been administered placement tests to ascertain my reading and mathematic ability. I had been placed without being administered such tests. When I did take the tests, I was immediately moved into higher classes (I was moved from the lowest reading and math to the second highest reading and math classes). My mother taught me an interesting lesson at this time. Although I got one or two questions incorrect on the reading test, she did not insist I be moved into the highest reading class since I did not receive a perfect score. She told me that if I wanted to be in the highest classes, I could not be just as good. I had to demonstrate that I was the best by getting a perfect score. What a harsh lesson on the impact of race and socioeconomic status for a ten year old!

There were many such "fights" I experienced in proving my intellectual acuity and my right to be in advanced classes during my K–12 schooling. One other experience that stands out is a conversation I had with my guidance counselor in which he all but told me that I would not gain admission to Northwestern University, but that I would likely be admitted to two lesser schools to which I applied. Thank goodness he was not on the admission committee and I did not listen to him, because I did get accepted (and eventually graduated) into Northwestern.

HOW DID I GET HERE?
BECOMING AN EDUCATOR AND SCHOLAR

I became an educator in a very nontraditional (at the time) manner. I was a Teach for America teacher in my home state. I fell in love with teaching and fast tracked my career into administration. I have often had the experience of being the "youngest" teacher/administrator as a result. I was the youngest teacher in my school when I began teaching. I was the youngest sitting high school principal when I started. I found my age (along with my race and/or gender) often to be a blessing and curse throughout the journey of my career.

Journey to K–12 Leadership

I noticed the need for others to "validate" my credibility in my first administrative position in a charter school (one of the first charters in the state). I was part of a very small administrative team that consisted of two White males and me. At the beginning of the school year we held several parent meetings. The school was located in an urban inner city and the overwhelming majority of students were African American.

At each parent meeting, I was always introduced with my name AND credentials. One or the other of the coprincipals would say, "This is Miss Peters. She is our new Dean of Students and she graduated from Columbia University, an Ivy League school." I often wondered why they needed to validate my education and credentials to parents who should (in my opinion) connect to me racially. This was made even more poignant by the fact that we were ALL Ivy League graduates, but they never "outed" themselves. I learned quickly something that they both already understood: White masculinity is read as authority in ways that Black femininity is not. They had no need to prove their credibility given their subject position as White men. However, irrespective of the fact that the audience was almost always made of a majority of Black women, they implicitly understood that my authority would not be widely received without making my credibility transparent. This understanding was reified continually in my role in this school. I was often challenged by parents who would then openly accept the same communication from the White male administrator. These experiences made me extremely curious about race and power (and later in my journey I began to question the intersection of race, gender, age, and power, and in some measure influenced my subsequent doctoral dissertation work.

Journey to the PhD

My experience as a doctoral student helped me to understand myself and craft my agenda for scholarship and practice. I entered the doctoral program with the intention of studying the impact of classroom culture and school culture on student achievement (an area of research in which I still maintain interest). However, my experiences and courses helped me to understand myself; to question traditional notions of power, authority and leadership; and to interrogate the organizational structures in which I operated.

I was an anomaly as a student in that my intent was always to become a principal rather than a scholar. I planned to enter academia much later in my professional career, perhaps after retiring from the principalship. I was one of two African American students in my doctoral cohort. There were other African American doctoral students in the College of Education and across the university, and many of them became a significant part of my support network.

I came to my dissertation topic in the first quarter of doctoral study as a result of a class assignment. I decided to research race and school leadership. This topic eventually narrowed to race and gender in school leadership (specifically, African American female principals). I was intrigued to study the experiences of those racially similar to me who were practicing in the same field I intended to enter. I took courses across the university, specifically in Women's Studies, Sociology and African American/African Studies. These courses were wonderfully eye opening. There were scholars who dedicated their research to theorizing about race, gender, privilege, and hegemonic structures.

Initially, I resisted labeling myself a feminist, because I felt this term had negative connotations. However, eventually I came to understand myself as a Black feminist. I accepted this nomenclature as a way to understand my subject position as female AND Black. I ultimately embraced Black Feminist Thought (Collins, 1990), an epistemological position that represented my own thinking, experiences and attempts at meaning making and knowledge production. Throughout the course of my studies, I read many wonderful works that helped me to theorize about the double jeopardy (Doughty, 1980; Lerner, 2001), or multiple jeopardies (King, 1995), of intersections (Crenshaw 2000; McCall, 2005; Shields, 2008) of race, gender, and class. My experience of the world is not disaggregated from race or gender. Thus, identifying myself as a Black feminist fit. As I developed an understanding of the tenets of Black feminism, I continued to read works about Black women in school leadership (Alston, 2005; Dillard, 1995; Loder, 2005a; Loder, 2005b). This body of scholarship spoke to me as a Black woman intending to become a school leader, but also as a Black female scholar. So, my dissertation research was a qualitative case study of a Black female principal and has formed the foundation of my research agenda. This knowledge gave me language to understand what was happening in the charter school where my introduction as Dean of Students included my credentials. I realized that because I was "other" (Collins, 1998) in many intersecting ways (being Black, female, young, highly educated), I was being validated by those who occupied a stance of "authority."

The doctoral experience was a bit grueling for me. It was lonely and frustrating. I was researching a topic that did not have wide support in my program. I was a student intent on entering into practice enrolled in a program intent on preparing me for scholarship. I was often one of two Black students in my classes (unless I took courses in other departments such as African American/African Studies). I had an experience in a doctoral core course where a professor asked me what the Black perspective on a particular issue was. As one of two Black students in the class, I was highly uncomfortable and even more unqualified to respond on behalf of the entire race.

I did have the benefit of support networks I established outside of my department via a Black graduate student organization and other networks I cultivated. Research suggests that often Black women have to cultivate networks outside of the academy in order to sustain themselves inside the academy (Peters, 2011). It is this resilience and resourcefulness that have helped me to manage in the academy.

HERE I STAND: LIFE IN THE ACADEMY

I was the first African American faculty member hired in the program area (after the reorganization of the college). I was welcomed openly and my experience as an administrator was a plus in terms of my credibility with students. In general, my experience was positive during the first semester. However, there were a few incidents of note. In particular, I noticed certain faculty making note and commenting on certain things about me such as the style of my hair, the style of my dress, where I parked in the lot, how long I stayed at work, and how early I arrived to work. Patricia Hill Collins (1998) terms this kind of observation "surveillance," and defines it as being intensely observed by others within the organization. Needless to say this was very uncomfortable for me. I often felt alone and isolated in an environment where I was being watched.

As a faculty member of color, students of color tend to gravitate toward me (and others of color) for support and informal mentoring in navigating the academy. I am open to helping students, particularly students of color, as I understand the loneliness they experience in matriculating the academy and the unlikelihood of encountering many African American faculty members. The research literature suggests that although mentoring and other organizational support is elusive for Black women, they often seek to provide these kinds of support to others in need (Jean-Marie, 2008). Interestingly, I was approached by a White colleague early in my career who attempted to provide me some professional advice. She stated that she is colorblind, and then instructed me not to advise all the Black students. I thought this was interesting for several reasons. First of all, there is no such perspective as being colorblind, and her follow up statement evidenced this. To embrace the perspective of colorblindness and to engage with me through this lens is to render me invisible. That is, my experiences as a Black woman become negated through the lens of colorblindness (Shields & Sayani, 2005). If she were truly colorblind, then she presumably would not have noticed my race or the race of any of my advisees. Second, I have never heard a White colleague say that they were admonished not to advise all the White students. It is assumed that students and faculty advisors will select one another based on mutual interests and fit, which is my practice in advising students as well.

Doing Research and Developing an Agenda

I developed my research agenda as mentioned earlier as a result of my professional experience as well as my doctoral research. I have struggled in the academy to feel as though my research is validated. As the only tenure track scholar focused on school leadership in my program area, I have not received a tremendous amount of push back from program area colleagues regarding my research agenda, but I feel that I have deliberately downplayed aspects of my work that focus on race and highlighted those elements of my agenda that focus more on leadership and mentoring. I have questioned why I have not "labeled" some of my work as social justice or antiracist, given the emancipatory and advocacy nature of my research.

I recently published a case study of four African American female faculty in the field of educational leadership (Peters, 2011). One of the areas they discussed concerned the development of their research agendas. Several participants discussed the necessity of engaging in a research agenda with which they feel personally connected and is purposeful (Peters, 2011). Other studies about African American scholars suggest that Black scholars often undertake research that may not reflect mainstream scholarship, but is beneficial to the Black community (Fenelon, 2003; Jean-Marie, 2006; Stanley, 2006, Weems, 2003). I connected with these perspectives on research agenda development. It was in the course of conducting this study that I was able to answer the questions I have posed of myself regarding my research agenda. The idea of immersion in research to which I am connected personally and professionally is an imperative for me. I learned that I am not ready to be branded as a particular kind of scholar. I am continuing to become a scholar and I want freedom from the labels that place me in a particular box.

Teaching and Leading

Teaching has always been a rewarding aspect of my responsibilities. In higher education, in addition to being rewarding, it is a challenge. I have far more autonomy as a college instructor than I did in the K–12 environment. With autonomy comes responsibility. As a college professor, I teach people who are predominantly racially and culturally different from me. This is unique for me as an instructor. In my college, African American faculty often receive lower teacher ratings than their White colleagues. Each semester as I prepare for class, I am concerned that my teaching evaluations will reflect my subject position, rather than my knowledge, skill and care for my students. In addition to being racially different from my students, I often find myself younger than many of my students as well. I have spoken with several of my African American colleagues in academia who perceive their credibility to be challenged by their students because of their intersecting identities (race, gender, class, age, experience, or lack thereof, etc.). Therefore, I attempt to be proactive in my interactions with students by introducing myself in the way I want to be addressed, and sharing my educational and professional experience. It is my hope that this demonstrates my credibility and proactively prevents overt or implicit challenges to my authority.

Leadership, in general, and educational leadership, in particular, is a field characterized by a White, masculine canon responsible for knowledge production. As an African American female scholar, I (and many others) contribute to the production of knowledge in ways that depart from the traditional canon (Collins, 1998). When selecting course material for my courses, it is important to me to have a balance of materials that represent a wide range of thinking, and to always lead my students in the process of interrogating that which is advanced as knowledge in the field.

SUSTAINABILITY: FINDING AND MAINTAINING SUPPORT

Research indicates that women and people of color benefit from formal (and informal) mentoring structures within organizations, especially in positions where they are traditionally underrepresented (Crawford & Smith, 2005; Smith & Crawford, 2007, Turner, 2003). My experiences with mentoring (and particularly the lack of it) within my professional career have continued to influence my investigation of mentoring as part of my research agenda. From my first professional role as a sixth grade teacher to my work as a tenure track professor at a research university I have struggled to obtain appropriate mentoring. In each role, mentoring was indicated and there have been structures to provide a mentor, but on the whole the experience has been wanting.

Mentoring (Formal and Informal)

In particular, I chose employment in the district where I became principal, because they had a principal internship program designed to provide administrative aspirants support and mentoring that would equip them to lead their own schools. My experience with preservice leadership (prior to assuming the principalship) in this district did not particularly equip me with the necessary support, information or mentoring structures needed to succeed in the principalship. When I became principal, the district offered a mentor for a very brief time and then removed her to work with other schools. I experienced a total of four "mentors" in a calendar year period. Needless to say, this was counterintuitive and not at all helpful. Mentoring can be critical to professional success (Crawford & Smith, 2005; Turner, 2003). The mentoring relationship takes time to establish trust and rapport. Having a series of mentors, one of whom was completely subversive and had to be removed after a month, made the first year of the principalship inordinately difficult. It is this experience in particular that informed the strand of my research focused on mentoring and support for early career principals.

When I entered academia, I fully expected to receive mentoring toward success. It is the custom of some of the departments to provide formal mentoring to new assistant professors. My department chair assisted me in selecting the members of my mentoring committee. Initially, these meetings were helpful. However, they quickly began to feel like a re-enactment of my doctoral defense. Instead of receiving information that helped me to increase my productivity or improve my teaching, I often felt as though I was defending my presence in academia as justified by what I've been working on. I eventually learned that not everyone's mentoring committee meetings went this way. I attempted to "take back" the direction of these meetings, but ultimately, with the assistance of the department chair, the composition of the committee was changed. This helped immensely.

Over the course of my journey toward tenure, I have experienced a number of shifts on my mentoring committee. The genesis of these shifts have not always been positive. However, I have been able to cultivate some very important relationships with senior colleagues (within and outside of my department) invested in my success that have helped me progress toward tenure and promotion.

Conferences/Source of Support

"In order for African American female faculty to achieve success in academe, they must learn to adopt strategies of establishing support systems external to the work organization" (Peters, 2011, p. 150). Attending conferences has been an important source of support for me. I came to academia from the world of practice and realized that I needed to make connections to assist me in my career trajectory. I began attending conferences and attempting to make professional connections immediately. I didn't realize how painstaking the process would be, but ultimately it has been fruitful.

I have been able to develop personal and professional relationships with several other young women faculty, as well as with senior faculty well known in the field. These connections have provided me many opportunities to learn and grow as a scholar.

One significant connection that serves as tremendous source of support for me has been with other young African American female junior faculty. Nearly all of these women are part of the University Council for Educational Administration (UCEA) Jackson Scholars program. I think it is ironic that the program is so named. As a doctoral student, Dr. Barbara Jackson was a scholar whose work I admired greatly and referenced often, as she studied women in leadership. In addition to having the pleasure of meeting her personally, I have also enjoyed reading about her journey through academia in the *Breaking Into the All Men's Club* book (Mertz, 2009).

I graduated the semester before the Jackson Scholars Program was inaugurated at UCEA. However, I came to know several Jackson Scholars in the course of my journey through the academy. Several of these women have been school administrators like me. They are all university faculty now and we have shared many common experiences regarding intersecting identities, credibility from students and challenges in finding support. We often joke that we can call and "talk each other off the ledge." This support has been invaluable for me. I engage them as critical friends, peer mentors, scholarly collaborators and personal friends. My journey through the academy has been greatly enriched by having a support network of scholars who: look like me; have had similar experiences as me; and care for me personally and professionally. Their support has been pivotal and critical along my journey.

STAYING POWER: TENURE AND PROMOTION

It is difficult to write this piece as I am going through the tenure process currently. Tenure is often a challenge for scholars of color (Patitu & Hinton, 2003). Many of the African American faculty that I know have had difficulty with the tenure process either at the associate or the full level; despite the fact that they are highly productive and receive positive teaching evaluations. This makes one wonder if these decisions are racially motivated.

My third year review process went well. I worked with my third year review committee as well as senior faculty mentors to prepare my documents. The review was favorable and provided me with helpful feedback to progress toward tenure and promotion. I was encouraged in many ways. I came to academia from what one of my mentors called a "dead stop." I was a principal, thus I didn't have any projects in the pipeline. I began my career as a scholar from ground zero. I hit the ground running and had to keep sprinting to feel "ready" for tenure and promotion.

Somewhere along the way, the dynamics in my department shifted. There were personnel shifts and there were shifts in my mentoring committee, as was mentioned earlier. In my fifth year (which is traditional at my university), I put together my materials for an initial consideration vote for tenure. This process is a straw vote among senior faculty within the department to determine if the candidate is ready to request external review letters. My mentoring committee (as well as a retired faculty member well-renowned in the field) all supported me for going forward. They told me I was ready. I felt confident about submitting materials. However, somewhere between being told that my materials and productivity indicated that I was ready and the departmental straw vote, something went abysmally wrong. My committee seemed blindsided by the straw vote and ultimately, not even all of my mentoring committee members voted for me to move forward. I felt betrayed, embarrassed and angered. But, I view all life lessons as teachable moments, and I decided to use this experience as a way to learn what I needed to do to improve my dossier and go forward the next year.

I met with all the senior faculty in my program area and several in my department to gain input and advice about how to improve my materials. I also met with two senior faculty who encouraged me to go forward in spite of the straw vote. I truly appreciated their support and guidance. One senior faculty member from my department (a White male) met with me and tried to assure me that this decision was not racially motivated. I thought the sentiment was interesting, since I never brought up race during the discussion. Several African American senior faculty in the College of Education reached out to me to encourage and support me. I appreciated all of the gestures from these colleagues. By sharing their challenges toward tenure and promotion (all of which were attributed to race) they helped to normalize the experience.

Of all of the experiences I had in processing and learning from my failure to obtain the support of the senior faculty, I had one experience that was more upsetting than any other. I met with two senior faculty who initially seemed to be willing to support me. However, the meeting turned ugly quickly. One told me that they didn't think I would ever be able to demonstrate a line of research that would enable me to get tenure. This individual went on to tell me that I was "unmentorable," that I had upset several people in the department because I don't come to meetings (it is worth mentioning here that I actually do attend meetings—when I am unable to attend I let the convener of the meeting know. It is also worth mentioning that this individual rarely ever comes to meetings and in a one-on-one conversation about five months prior to this meeting, told me that meetings were not important and he/she doesn't bother to come). The other faculty encouraged me to seek employment at a teaching institution. To say the least, this was an uncomfortable meeting, filled with caustic directives (I just sat and listened). I have been bullied by both of these faculty members on several occasions, but this was uncharacteristically unhealthy.

Interestingly, as things continued to disintegrate in my department, several senior scholars told me that I should have received the tenure vote last year. Several also told me that they had tremendous respect for me for being professional during the entire next year after not receiving the vote. This experience taught me to strategize going forward. I met with my mentoring committee and used the feedback from the first straw vote to inform how we compiled and presented my materials the next year. We worked offense instead of defense. We planned who would present my materials and how they would be presented. One of the "complaints" about my work was that I wasn't published in the right journals. In particular, that some of the UCEA journals weren't rigorous enough. However, the specific journal being referenced has been published in by every faculty member in the program area (junior and senior). The department faculty (the department is made up of several different program areas) did not have this information the previous year, and so the mentoring committee strategized about how to make all of the necessary information transparent. In addition, I solicited feedback from three highly regarded full professors outside of my department in an effort to craft my materials effectively and to get additional feedback. They were incredibly helpful in their feedback and I believe this feedback helped make my materials stronger.

Ultimately, I learned to manage my process and to lead my own journey. I have been told that if I earn tenure I will be the first African American person to do so in this program area. This is in some ways a heavy burden but, simultaneously, it is a wonderful opportunity. I have had a career full of pioneering moments and this will be no different. I am young, female, gifted and Black. Because of who I am becoming and who I am, I am ready, and life (in the academy) for me, ain't been no crystal stair.

NOTES

1. Hughes, L. (1994). Mother to Son. *The Collected Poems of Langston Hughes*. Vintage Books.
2. The terms Black and African American are used interchangeably throughout this paper.

REFERENCES

Alston, J. A. (2005). Tempered radicals and servant leaders: Black females persevering in the superintendency. *Educational Administration Quarterly, 41*(4), 675–688.

Collins, P. H. (1998). *Fighting words. Black women and the search for justice.* Minneapolis: University of Minnesota Press.

Collins, P. H. (1990). *Black feminist thought: Knowledge, consciousness, and the politics of empowerment.* New York: Routledge, Chapman and Hall.

Crawford, K., & Smith, D. (2005). The we and the us: Mentoring African American women. *Journal of Black Studies, 36*(1), 52–67.

Crenshaw, K. (2000). *The intersectionality of race and gender discrimination.* Paper presented at United NationsRegional Expert Group Meeting, Zagreb, Croatia (November 2000).

Dillard, C. B. (1995). Leading with her life: An African American feminist (re)interpretation of leadership for an urban high school principal. *Educational Administration Quarterly, 31*(4), 539–563.

Doughty, R. N. (1980). The Black female administrator: Woman in a double bind. In: S. Biklen & M. Branningan (Eds.), *Women and educational leadership* 165–174. Lexington, MA: D.C. Heath and Company.

Fenelon, J. (2003). Race, research, and tenure: Institutional credibility and the incorporation of African, Latino, and American Indian faculty. *Journal of Black Studies, 34*(1), 87–100.

Jean-Marie, G. (2006). Welcoming the unwelcomed: A social justice imperative of African American female leaders at historically Black colleges and universities. *Educational Foundations, 20*(1–2), 85–104.

Jean-Marie, G. (2008). Social justice, visionary and career project: The discourses of Black women leaders at historically Black colleges and universities. In: M. Gasman & C. Tudico (Eds.), *Historically Black colleges and universities: Triumphs, troubles and taboos* (pp. 53–74). New York, NY: Palgrave Macmillan.

King, D. (1995). Multiple jeopardy, multiple consciousness: The context of a Black feminist ideology. In: *Words of fire: an anthology of African American feminist thought.* New York: The New Press.

Loder, T. L. (2005a). African American women principals' reflections on social change, community, othermothering and Chicago Public School reform. *Urban Education, 40*(3), 298–320.

Loder, T. L. (2005b). On deferred dreams, callings, and revolving doors of opportunity: African American women's reflections on becoming principals. *The Urban Review, 37*(3), 243–65.

McCall, L. (2005). The complexity of intersectionality. *Signs: Journal of Women in Culture and Society, 30*(3), 1771–1800.

Mertz, N. M. (2009). *Breaking into the all-male club. Female professors of educational administration.* Albany: SUNY Press.

Patitu, C. L., & Hinton, K. G. (2003). The experiences of African American women faculty and administrators in higher education: Has anything changed? *New Directions for Student Services, 104,* 79–93.

Peters, A. L. (2011). Black women faculty in educational leadership: Unpacking their silence in research. In G. Jean-Marie & B. Lloyd-Jones (Eds.), *Women of color in higher education: Turbulent past, promising future. Diversity in Higher Education, 9,* 147–67. Bingley: Emerald Group.

Sherman, W. H., Beaty, D. M., Crum, K. S., & Peters, A. L. (2010). Unwritten: Young women faculty in educational leadership. *Journal of Educational Administration, 48*(6), 741–754.

Shields, C. M., & Sayani, A. N. I. S. H. (2005). Leading in the midst of diversity. *The SAGE handbook of educational leadership: Advances in theory, research, and Practice* (pp. 380–402). Thousand Oaks, CA: SAGE.

Shields, S. A. (2008). Gender: An intersectionality perspective. *Sex Roles, 59,* 301–311.

Smith, D. T., & Crawford, K. (2007). Climbing the ivory tower: Recommendations for mentoring African American women in higher education. *Race, Gender & Class, 14*(1/2), 253–265.

Stanley, C. A. (2006). Coloring the academic landscape: Faculty of color breaking the silence in predominantly white colleges and universities. *American Educational Research Journal, 43*(4), 701–736.

Turner, C. S. (2003). Incorporation and marginalization in the academy: From border toward center for faculty of color. *Journal of Black Studies, 34*(1), 112–125.

Weems, R. E., Jr. (2003). The incorporation of Black faculty at predominantly white institutions: a historical and contemporary perspective. *Journal of Black Studies, 34*(1), 101–111.

CHAPTER 5

THE INVISIBLE OTHER

Ruminations on Transcending "La Cerca" in Academia

Azadeh F. Osanloo

> *I want to be welcomed, not just tolerated.*
> —Ward, Hajjar & Miller (Sparta), 2004

This chapter offers a critical autoethnographic account from an invisible other. As a young female Persian academician in educational leadership, it is incumbent I navigate the windy path of higher education, as well as consistently negotiate my gender and race within liminal spaces, in order to transcend the fence, "la cerca." Not only am I rendered "other" based upon my gendered and racialized status, I am further made "invisible" due to the lack of group, cultural, or affiliative identity within the field. As such, I am the invisible other—not visible, concealed, ignored, and not taken into consideration. This chapter uses Puwar's theory of space invaders, which details the interplay of race, gender, and space, to assist with cultivating a better understanding of my structurally ambiguous position in higher education. In essence, it helps make visible that which is unseen, and oft unspoken. After a discussion of Puwar's theory, I offer a brief account of Turner's views on liminality as they interconnect with the fecund ideas around space.

Moreover, I provide reflective thoughts on my journeys, in three phases from the fence. And lastly, I offer recommendations grounded in the values of mentoring, which is an imperative tool of navigation and negotiation for women in educational leadership.

SPACE INVADER—PARTY OF ONE

Grew up on a man made line,
That's left me warm,
Count your blessings, you're the lucky one.
—Ward et al., 2004

Puwar's notion of space invaders is a form of critical geography that can be used as the theoretical underpinning for understanding the necessity and complexity of creating spaces for women scholars of color within the professorate. She posited (2004) that "reserved" positions in society, most often found in government and professional positions, are saved for the ideal figure of modernity that does not yet include everyone (p. 33). "Thus different bodies belonging to 'other' places are in one sense out of place as they are 'space invaders'" (p. 33). When these space invaders enter the positions, they disrupt the "look" of the White consecrated places and create an "ontological anxiety" (p. 39) that results in dissonance and disorientation for the hegemony. She asserted (2004):

> While women and racialised minorities are still not totally of the world of professions, because it is predominantly White and male, the classed familiarisations have an impact on how they interact and feel at 'home,' as well as how others respond to them. There is no doubt that their bodies are conspicuous and marked as different entities which are noticed and that they are subjected to additional pressures and expectations because of their minority status. (p. 128)

Puwar's statement acutely underscores the "othering" that female scholars of color can experience in the professorate and addresses the somatic norm from the vantage of the othered. Within this conceptual reasoning, the aim should be to create safe familiar spaces for ideas and research, which are decolonizing so unheard voices can be unearthed and conspicuous bodies can rest. In an effort to understand the spatial static of bodies and dissonance, it is important to understand the relationship between space invasion and liminality as an obscured and obfuscated epistemological state, especially for academics.

Applying this theory to academia, Puwar (2004) commented on the disorientated bodies in this space as throwing institutional positionalities into disorder regardless of how seemingly inclusive institutions of higher education are of difference and diversity. This is partly due to the fact that racialized bodies are put into the position of "subject" as opposed to "object" when it comes to knowledge. This disrupts the "territorial demarcations" that underscore the hierarchical structuring of identity building within higher education (p. 45).

Integral to the discussion on the invasion of space is the notion of liminality. Relying on Van Gennep's (1960) three-part structure of rites of passage, Turner (1967, 1974) noted, "the subject of the passage ritual is, in the liminal period, structurally, if not physically invisible" (p. 95). That is to say, individuals in liminality are neither structurally or socially sound, but rather ambiguous. La Shure (2005) summed up liminality as: "one of the most visible expressions of anti-structure in society. It is a midpoint between a starting point and an ending point, and as such it is a temporary state that ends when the initiate is reincorporated into the social structure" (para. 15).

Integrating the two theories, I offer that Puwar's restless and conspicuous bodies are in a state of liminality, which causes discontent and struggle for the privileged and the other. For example, as a female faculty member of color in educational leadership (the invisible other), I am within the confines of the structure as a space invader, but occupy a liminal, transitory, and nebulous space—one in which I am not "seen" within the structure as an asset, but perceived as a danger and threat to privileged spaces, and those in charge maintaining the structure.

Emancipatory Method

Autoethnography is the research method used to examine and analyze the lived experience of this invisible other in a critical, objective, and analytical manner. According to Bennett (2004), autoethnography often describes the self in terms of the "other." This otherness is often times a cultural separation from society, however can also be gender based. Because the goal of autoethnographic research is to describe differences in oneself from the inside, it is written to an audience and not to oneself. Autoethnographers "ask their readers to feel the truth of their stories and to become co-participants, engaging the storyline morally, emotionally, aesthetically, and intellectually" (Ellis & Bochner, 2000, p. 745). Moreover, autoethnographic research acknowledges the researcher and audience as equally significant. As this research stems from personal exploration of the "invisible other" in academia, autoethnography is used to express the self from authentic, dialogical, and critical perspectives. This emancipatory methodological tool is used to better understand the migratory identity of the female scholar of color in higher education. Ellis and Bochner (2000) advocate for autoethnography, as a form of writing that "makes the researcher's own experience a topic of investigation in its own right" (p. 733) rather than "as if they're written from nowhere by nobody" (p. 734).

As an analytical account of a conflict of race, gender, and space, the autoethnography presented here can help provide other female scholars of color with resources for understanding and explaining differences from the inside. Expanding this idea, a reconstituted version of the autoethnographic method involves the use of collaborative approaches to writing, reflexive interchange, and critically analyzing personal stories of experience. Labeled "collaborative autobiography" by Lapadat (2009), this approach can be used not only in teaching, but also as a boon to creating bridges between academicians who share similar experiences and want to use their stories to help others. The stories presented in this body of work can serve as an example of collaborative autobiography.

The significance of this work can be explored from an epistemological perspective. It is important for scholars in the field to better understand the epistemological significance of knowing how female scholars of color interact and react to the racialized and gendered space(s) within the professorate. This type of investigation can help provide epistemological clarifications on how female scholars of color know how and strive to be successful in a field dominated by the culture of Caucasian men (Hackmann & McCarthy, 2011).

RUMINATIONS FROM THE "LA CERCA"

Grew up on a man made line,
That's left me empty.
—Ward et al., 2004

Looking Up at the Fence—A Child in Academic Clothing

I am not White. I am not American. I am not male. I am female. I am the "other." I became conscious of my peripheral status during my adolescence. The daughter of Persian emigrants, I was raised in the homogenous suburbs of Chicago where I felt like an outsider. As I aged, my identity manifested itself within the dominant American culture. As the first-generation daughter of immigrants I was grounded in academic pursuit, as the hopes of future prosperity resonated with successful scholastic endeavors. As I aged I became aware of my gendered, ethnic, and racial status within the tenuous spheres of acceptance I coveted. Although I felt embraced by the society in which I lived, a tangible void existed within me. I always felt like an outsider, someone on the periphery, peeking over, looking in. I did not look right, feel right, or speak right. My existence was shrouded in darkness, from my obvious skin and hair color to my unpronounceable name. Compounding the "otherness," my parents were not well versed in American teenage life, and I often struggled against their "old-world" will. I quickly became unsettled in the hierarchy of my gendered and racialized status, and sought to quell these injustices. Alienated by the signifiers of my existence, my pursuit for educational equity and social justice was made concrete.

My pursuit for educational equity and social justice began in the Bronx. My early career in teaching helped clarify the complex issues of identity I had struggled with all my early life. The experience of my students in the Bronx mirrored my own discontent with self and agency. Most tangible was the anger that had developed in us all; angry that the façade of visual self had dictated the construction of our identity. Needless to say, that *mis*-construction was not to our benefit. As a fire raged within, I furthered my pursuit of knowledge by working as a teacher in Harlem and obtaining a Master's Degree in Public Policy from New York University and doctorate from Arizona State University. These experiences not only helped to solidify my devotion and dedication to the study of education, they additionally expanded my knowledge of self with respect to power signifiers in the manipulations of race, gender, and space.

It is easy to imagine my younger self, looking up at the fence, wondering—to the point of intellectual schizophrenia—how I was going to surpass all these intangible chain-links. I did know one thing: education was a boon for me to help identify myself in a world in which I am not underrepresented, but unrepresented. Education and the pursuit of self-knowledge helped me overcome the negative constructions of my own identity. It helped me engage in struggle with others that have been marginalized, much like me. This early realized pursuit of educational equity and social justice was not just "work" for me; it was a matter of passion, opportunity, goals, and dreams. It was a matter of life. It was a matter of me. And it was because I am not White, I am not American, I am not male, I am female, and I am the "other." The invisible one.

Climbing Onto the Fence—Othering the Other

Othering the other: the processes, thought constructions, or experiments of someone with the self-selected, perceived, or pronounced status of "other;" othering another member of an already othered group (as defined by author). I am *here* now. I am on the fence—amongst you.

Shrouded in the revealing cloak of subjectivity, my life and academic experiences at this juncture as an Associate Professor, at a Hispanic-Serving Institution (HSI) in the southwest have culminated to render me in a state of academic schizophrenia. By academic schizophrenia, I offer that although I am a relatively young academician (37 years-old) with some accomplishments under my belt, the ever-pulsating knowledge of not fitting in and not belonging *here* wears on my conscience. I never thought of myself as a weak or naive person, however in the six, going on seven, years I have been *here*, my thin, worn skin and navigational naïveté have not only become situated in my own weary head, but have been repeatedly confirmed by those around me. My identity and the identity that others put upon have comingled to create this ugly third space that houses feelings of inadequacy, incompetency, and self-defeat. No matter where I go I know that I do not belong... *here*.

Again, you see, I am the daughter of immigrants. I am the first child born in the United States, who walks between two worlds and yet does not belong to either. I have one foot in thousands of years of steeped Persian tradition and the other in the White version of America, to which I have never belonged. I am brown, or at least some version of it. Specifically, I like to call myself cinnamon—mostly because it is sweet and spicy. I am brown, but not Black; brown, but not Hispanic; brown, but not Native; brown, but not Asian, or any other box that offers me the safe confinement of an already identified compartment. In the past, I would check the box marked "other" not knowing then what I know now. The irony is now not lost, now that I am *here*.

I naively thought that if I worked at an institution that championed minority causes and was designated as an HSI that I would feel a sense of belonging—a transnational version of feminist collusion and cohabitation that was global in scope, and encouraged women to unite, not further divide. However, I was totally wrong. I came here so innocent, thinking we were all fighting for the same causes, the disenfranchised student, the forgotten youth of tomorrow, and the returning adult learner looking to make sense of the world through a newly earned degree. However, I was totally wrong. I have come here to know and understand the othering of the other. I am a theorist; you think my thoughts and ideas are worthless. I am a Persian; I do not fit into any of your confines, and thus you dislike and distrust me even more. I am Middle-Eastern; and in the post 9/11 world your fear and disgust with regards to me are tangible; and most of all I am an invader of your space; I am sitting right next to you. Right *here*.

Looking around the room I see a lot of faces. None look like mine. I see lots of White, with white hair; I see Black skin, many of whom are sitting together. And I see brown faces. The Rodriguez's, the Gonzalez's, and the Lopez's who know and greet each other with a familial smile and sisterly handshake that alienates me even further. I see one of me. I see me—whose name is repeatedly mispronounced and whose position and tenure in this colloquial, difficult to penetrate circle, are questionable.

You see, now, they are required to invite me to the table, but do the people who circumnavigate around me think I belong *here*? Again, I am invisible. I am invisible, but I am *here*. I am invisible in my own cinnamon skin—why I am *here*? How do I get there?

Sitting Atop the Fence—Watching and Being Watched

I now sit atop the fence, having clawed my way up one side. I have made my way from a mere child yearning with an academic's mind to an academic in a liminal, restless space. I am not over this tall looming "la cerca," as there are still battles to be fought.

Watch Your Tone

"I want to talk to you about your tone," he said. "My tone?" I said. "Yes, *YOUR* tone," he said.

I learned that day that my tone is perceived as tough, aggressive, and strong. This is what the older White man told me in his fancy office. And he told me I needed to "watch it," because two White faculty members did not like "it." What he did not know was that my mother, whose will and strength mirrors that of the Gods of the Pantheon, taught all three of her daughters to be strong, to be intelligent, to be independent, and to be assertive. Intellectual prowess combined with verbal dexterity—that was her Persian recipe for raising her daughters.

I looked at him. He looked at me. I apprised him of my skillful mother's child-raising philosophies and reminded him that the cultural codes inherent in my family structure would not mirror those of the White faculty members to whom he was referring. I advised him that I would not succumb to or believe in hegemony of language, which allows a certain way of speaking (a White way) to be privileged over my way. As a woman of color, I was raised to speak carefully and with intelligence, knowledge, and assertiveness.

I looked at him. He looked away. Invisible again. Thank you for letting me invade your office, nay, *YOUR* space.

The Curious Case of Strength and Eros

It has interested me to know when the word "strong" became a pejorative in relation to women faculty members in education—whether the term is used in relation to dispositions, personality, or tone. I wonder, was there ever an option for a space invader, like me, to not be strong? Would I be sitting at the same table as you, watching you as you curiously watch me, if I were not strong? Pervasive sexist and racist systems perpetuated by the hegemonic exclusionary elite require strong action. It is this type of action that will help me push past the liminal space, into a more solid realm. I do not have the luxury to be passive. However, I am thankful for the liminal space. As La Shure stated:

> While in the liminal state, human beings are stripped of anything that might differentiate them from their fellow human beings—they are in between the social structure, temporarily fallen through the cracks, so to speak, and it is

in these cracks, in the interstices of social structure, that they are most aware of themselves. (para. 15)

I am aware of myself, and I am aware of how you perceive me.

Through self-reflection, I have learned the informal lesson that if you can't beat 'em, sexualize 'em. My experiences as a young woman of color in academia have intersected with the notion of eroticizing the exotic. That which is exotic or foreign to the structural power-keepers is confounding and causes "ontological anxiety" (La Shure, 2005; Puwar, 2004; Turner, 1967). When that invading body comes in the form of a strong brown woman it is morphed into the "exotic erotic." On more than one occasion my intellectual positionality, gendered language, and invasion of the academic space has caused tension with the White male body. For example, a conversation on White privilege with a White male colleague devolved into the following:

> **Me:** I don't think you are taking into account the tenet of White privilege. It is not a racist way of thinking about privilege and space.
> **Him:** (yelling) You're a racist.
> **Me:** I am not a racist. In fact, given structural and institutional oppression, I cannot be a racist. I am happy to discuss this further with you when you are not yelling at me.
> **Him:** (hand waving in my face) You're just a naughty little girl. Does daddy needs to tame this naughty little girl? Daddy does need to tame the naughty girl.

The intellectual dialogue was rendered moot with my mind becoming invisible and my body became sexualized, watched, observed, othered. As Puwar (2004) stated, "Somatic male speech finds it difficult to deal with women's bodies from a perspective that does not exotocise, fetishise, or ridicule them" (p. 88).

How do I get off this fence? Can I ever?

MENTORING AS A TOOL OF NAVIGATION AND NEGOTIATION FOR FUTURE SPACE INVADERS

> *Let's crash these gates and join the party,*
> *I want to be welcomed, not just tolerated,*
> *. . . In order to grow you must be open to learn.*
> —Ward et al., 2004

As a scholar of color in academe I endeavor to not only be successful in my own professional enterprises, but to also create spaces for the next generation of scholars of color to build upon and thrive. I view this research as a potential conduit for creating bridges between the gendered and racialized hierarchical systems in the professorate while encouraging new scholars of color to invest in academe, and invade space.

Whether informal or formal, mentoring women of color who aspire to or already are faculty members is imperative, to assist with informed navigation and negotiation of the educational leadership space. If racialized and gendered bodies can coexist, comingle, and collaborate in meaningful ways, the dissonance could potentially evolve into harmonious aligned action. Mentoring can be a potent instrument in academia for encouraging new scholars. It is important that we assertively mentor women minorities so we can cultivate transformational minority or ethnic leaders (hooks, 2003).

Integral to understanding these experiences are the demographic trends in the educational leadership professorate especially as they relate to gender, race, and age. While the gender composition in the educational leadership professorate has reached near parity, Caucasians still comprise the majority group employed. In fact, only 15% of professors of educational leadership are of minority descent (Hackmann & McCarthy, 2011). It is interesting to note that the field that serves some of the most diverse populations (as found in school and university systems) is far from heterogeneous. Moreover, the average age of educational leadership faculty continues to rise, from age 48 in 1972 to age 56 in 2008. As the mean age continues to steadily climb it calls into question how young scholars of color are being perceived and received in educational leadership. This calls attention to the importance of women professors of color mentoring other women professors of color as a way to sustain diverse bodies of representation within the field.

FINAL THOUGHTS

Many of my female colleagues and I often discuss the sad idea that we must consistently "prove" we should be in this space; that there is a burden of proof that does not rest in our accomplishments, research, teaching, or service, but rather in the eye of the beholder. I feel the constant ebb and flow of the liminal space in which I inhabit and the constant watchful eyes waiting for me to make a mistake. As Puwar pointed out:

> Due to the existence of a racialised form of surveillance, there is also a racialised reason for wanting to succeed. Knowing that they are in a precarious situation and that the most minor of mistakes could be taken as evidence of incompetence, women and racialised carry what might be termed the "burden of representation..." (p. 62)

My shoulders are heavy with the weight and spectacle of performance. However, I am still sitting atop the fence. I am extending a hand to those who are behind me, talking to those on the fence with me, and learning from those who have made it over. I am still the invisible other, the invader of space, the liminal nebula, but I am here, to stay. And I want to be welcomed.

REFERENCES

Bennett, S. (2004). Susan Bennett on autoenthography. Retrieved from http://www.humboldt.edu/compfac/autoethnography.html

Ellis, C., & Bochner, A. P. (2000). Autoethnography, personal narrative, reflexivity: Researcher as subject. In N. K. Denzin & Y. S. Lincoln (Eds.), *The handbook of qualitative research* (2nd ed., pp. 733–768). Newbury Park, CA: Sage.

hooks, b. (2003). *Teaching community: A pedagogy of hope.* New York, NY: Routledge.

Lapadat, J. (2009). Writing our way into shared understanding: Collaborative autobiographical writing in the qualitative methods class. *Qualitative Inquiry, 15,* 955–979.

La Shure, C. (2005). *What is liminality?* Retrieved from http://www.liminality.org/about/whatisliminality/

Hackmann, D., & McCarthy, M. (2011). *At a crossroads: The educational leadership professoriate in the 21st century.* Charlotte, NC: Information Age Publishing.

Puwar, N. (2004). *Space invaders: Race, gender, and bodies out of place.* New York, NY: Berg Publishing.

Turner, V. (1967). *The forest of symbols: Aspects of Ndembu ritual.* Ithaca, NY: Cornell University Press.

Turner, V. (1974). *Dramas, fields, and metaphors: Symbolic action in human society.* Ithaca, NY: Cornell University Press.

Van Gennep, A. (1960). *The rites of passage.* London, UK: Routledge.

Ward, J., Hajjar, T., & Miller, M.G. (2004). "La Cerca" [Sparta], On Porcelain [CD], EMI.

CHAPTER 6

MY TRANSITION TO THE ACADEMY

Lessons and Community

Karen Sanzo

The most important piece of advice I have received from anyone since being in the Academy is that my colleagues are not only those individuals I work with in my university—my colleagues are international in scope—and all I have to do is reach out. They are there, ready and willing to help. It is not that every person you talk to will be able to assist—that is reality, too. But many people are there to listen, give advice, and, at times when it makes sense, collaborate. Being in the Academy can be lonely, especially when you are a new professor in the tenure-track race, stressed out at every turn, and not sure what to do to achieve the mysterious promotion and tenure ring. This piece of advice has made the field less daunting and has expanded my horizons indefinitely. It gave me the confidence boost I needed at a time when I was questioning my place in the Academy.

In this chapter I share some of my experiences leading up to my transition from the public schools to working in higher education. I have also provided some of the experiences I have had in higher education I found to be difficult, challenging, and character-building.

BACKGROUND

I joined the Academy after working eight years in the public schools teaching middle school mathematics and serving as an elementary school assistant principal. However, I worked in the public schools for more than eight years starting out as an office aid at my school district's central office when I was sixteen. Those early years were invaluable to me. I received a view of the inner workings of school districts many people are not privy to having and made long-lasting and critical connections. I was also exposed to a number of strong, focused, and hard-working women who served in senior level administrative positions, including the woman who hired me. They have been a powerful influence on me throughout my career.

I lucked into the office aid job after stopping in one of the district office departments to apply for a high school summer program. The secretary was out and the director of the office was pretty harried with multiple grants, reports due, and general administrative activities (i.e., necessary busy work/paperwork). She asked me to answer the phone, make copies, and help out before I completed the application. While I did not get into the summer program, those twenty minutes helping out turned into a 6-year part-time job in multiple offices at the central office.

Working at the central office in that capacity enabled me to meet school leaders throughout the system, school board members, and teachers in the district. I visited schools for various reasons (dropping off materials, collecting information, helping out schools if they needed an extra hand), interacted with the public, and was provided increasing levels of responsibility. When I was twenty, I was put in charge of the final component of the triennial census (the federal survey cards) and had a staff (two people—but at twenty having any staff was pretty interesting and two seemed to be a lot at the time) I supervised.

This was the same school district in which I ended up teaching and serving as a school leader. I credit these early years at the central office with the foundation I needed to be an effective public school teacher and leader and I also think these experiences provided me the credibility I needed to be an assistant principal at a young age (twenty-five). While teaching in the district, I proposed to create the new teacher handbook for the school district as a part of a graduate course—at the time there was not a handbook—and this offer was accepted. As a teacher and later as an assistant principal, I provided in-service training to new teachers and new administrators on the handbook and various district policies and procedures. Those early years gave me credibility with the district leaders, which in turn increased their confidence in me to eventually become an administrator. This also gave me increasing confidence in my skills and abilities.

I taught full time and attended graduate school at the same time to receive my Master's degree and administrative licensure. After two years of teaching, I had earned my Master's degree. A few fortunate turns of events and working hard landed me my first adjunct position at a state university. I was hired to teach a foundations of education course aimed at teachers in the district's career switcher program and was by far the youngest person in the class, which, of course, was interesting. Having had the experiences I had early on in my career, this was not something new, but it still proved to be one of those challenges to make you stronger. I can still remember one man in his fifties (I was about twenty-four) with a handlebar mustache who definitely had an issue with my age and made that clear in the class (I looked younger than I am, which probably did not add to his level of comfort in the class). But, I held my ground and the course went well. I still have students from that course I run into in public who speak positively about the semester. I continued to teach graduate courses for a while in the district, but then transitioned to other universities as an adjunct once I received my doctorate.

Perspective is everything in life and, looking back, I can see the aforementioned male student was the oldest in the class and, as luck would have it, the youngest person in the class was the instructor. He was in an uncomfortable situation and he probably felt like an awkward fifteen year-old in a high school class—everyone is looking at him and feeling all of the pressure on his shoulders. This was really my first encounter with someone being uncomfortable with my age, but it was not the last in the school district. When you are an assistant principal at twenty-five, you are going to run into people you supervise who need to see you in that position for a while before they are willing to trust you and put their faith in you.

I began my doctoral program while teaching and was then promoted to assistant principal. I continued to work full time and adjunct while in my doctoral program and I never stopped the hectic pace and this continued into my work as an assistant professor. After having earned my doctorate, I applied for a university position and was offered the job. While it was tempting to stay in my district and become a principal, my dream was to work in higher education; so I enthusiastically accepted the position (the enthusiasm was also paired with trepidation, since this was a whole new world... and it was even more different than I had ever imagined coming from the PK–12 setting).

Of course, there are stories from my time in PK–12 that would be fitting to include, but we all have omitted stories when we retell the journeys of our lives. Sometimes we add them in, swap out stories, or remember ones once forgotten. I would be glad to share these stories later on, but will transition here to my time in the Academy.

THE ACADEMY

Higher education is vastly different than PK–12 schools. It is more political, I think, but generally much more subtle in how politics are played out. The pace is slower and it can take years before a policy decision is made and acted upon. This is not to say, at times, it is not a fast-paced environment (envision trying to pull a grant proposal together in just a few weeks—then everything moves fast), but generally the pace is much more sluggish than PK–12 schools. Everyone has adjustments to make when moving from one career environment to another, and my case is no different. I had to adjust to this different work atmosphere and I learned what was looked upon as a positive advantage in PK–12 (youth and gender) was now something, at times, a negative. I had not really experienced negative biases in PK–12 because of my age and gender and had not encountered some of the experiences I have read about from other women who first worked in PK–12 schools before moving to higher education. We are each different and bring to the table a milieu of experiences, and my previous work life had, in a way, "set me up" to expect there would not be any perceived problems by colleagues because of my gender and age. This was not the case.

EXPERIENCING "ISMS"

Unfortunately I have a suspicion those reading this chapter and this book have experienced a range of "isms" in their lives. In my case, the "isms," for the most part, have been sexism and ageism. I think it is one of those odd realities we have come to know and accept that we have these "isms," while at the same time deriding their existences. We talk so fervently about social justice in the public schools, but this does not always translate to practice in higher education. It is a conundrum I am still trying to figure out. The old guard (some faculty, not all—I am not trying to insinuate this is a pervasive practice and stereotype every veteran faculty. If I did, I would only be doing what I have condemned) is persistent in perpetuating these negative "isms" at times, and there seems to be the occasional new guard who takes on these "isms" and perpetuates them.

Ageism

I started my career as an assistant professor at the age of 29. I was hired as a tenure-track assistant professor by the university with eight years of public school experience, having served as both a teacher and an administrator. When I was hired, there was no hint my age and youthful appearance would have any bearing on how I would be treated and how colleagues would interact with me. There was no cautionary probation term set in my contract because of my age, no stipulations, and no other requirements because of my age (which of course would have been both ridiculous and illegal), yet some faculty colleagues felt they could still talk about it to me and to others as if it were an oddity and I was not as qualified as other people.

I often wondered what would happen if I brought up the age of those people who were being so cruel to me and making comments about my age in a negative light; if they would laugh at any jokes I could potentially make. Of course I never did and never would; that's not in my nature, but, all the same, I did think about it on occasion. I wondered if they would be as pleasant as I was when I "laughed off" yet another hurtful comment about my youth. These jokes were hurtful and embarrassing and often made in a large group setting, but I found no other way to handle these than to just listen, smile politely, and leave the situation if possible. I found it disturbing it was generally accepted as funny and normal to make derisive asides about my age and others would laugh along with the person who was making the negative comment "just in good fun." This contributed to my feelings of isolation previously mentioned.

Ageism and Sexism

One of the most concerning cases I experienced that combined both my age and gender was my promotion to associate professor and receiving tenure. I will abstain from digging too deeply into the details of this, but I want to share the generalities of this situation. I made the decision to "go up" a year early for tenure. While uncommon, it also is not unheard of at my university. Just the year prior another faculty member had been successfully promoted in the same situation.

What I found interesting, and perhaps a bit disturbing, was my promotion and tenure case had been discussed in whispers and behind closed doors between a few faculty members far before anyone on the actual School committee had the chance to review my materials. I was even approached by two male faculty members to discuss my "situation" (again, before anyone had read my promotion and tenure materials). They decided it was critical to "give me a talk" regarding what they felt was necessary for me to gain tenure. This was after I had submitted my materials, but before the School committee met (officially) to discuss the candidates who had submitted their materials for tenure. Readers should keep in mind that I was going up a year early, so I made sure that not only did I meet the criteria for tenure in every category, I exceeded every single criteria set forth as that is the expectation if you are going to go up early for tenure. It was an uncomfortable situation that felt negatively patriarchal and it was clear my gender and age were strong influencing factors in their level of discomfort with me going up for tenure. Their concerns had nothing to do with me meeting the tenure criteria. Both acknowledged I was fine in those areas. However, they did have a problem with my personality and communication style. While not overly vocal, I have no problem speaking my mind and making clear my thoughts on situations of importance. This was something they did not like. I have always made it a point to speak my mind. I could tell this made both of them uncomfortable—a young woman with a mind of her own—and they imposed on me they wanted me to "be seen and not heard" on future faculty issues. I was on "pins and needles" the whole time the actual School committee was reviewing my materials since I was concerned one or two voices that had problems with my age and youth would cause negative votes to be cast against me. However, this was not the case in what turned out to be, ultimately, a positive tenure and promotion decision. But, my point is this never should have been an issue. I am disappointed I had to have such a negative experience and will work hard to ensure no other person (female or male) has this same experience. We are supposed to be evaluated on our ability to meet standards set forth by our colleagues and not by biased opinions by others having nothing to do with our merit as faculty.

A Second Case of Both "isms"

One of the most exciting opportunities I have had while working in the Academy has been with the United States Department of Education School Leadership Program (SLP) grant. I became the Principal Investigator for the grant I wrote for the SLP program in 2008. As PI and Director of the program at my university, I coordinate all aspects of the grant initiative. The SLP's are five-year grants designed to provide training to aspiring and/or current school leaders (in this case I designed an aspiring leadership program with a partnering school district that also providing ongoing professional development for current school leaders).

Around 2009, the university initiated a new public relations campaign. Different programs and faculty were asked to be featured in a multi-media campaign that included website features, post cards, and even billboards around the area. My co-PI and I were featured on one of the billboards, which was pretty exciting. You don't drive down the interstate everyday and look up and to see your face, along with a coworker's, on the billboard supporting and promoting your university. I think, though, I have had enough billboard exposure to last a lifetime.

We were asked for an interview to be included in a few of the university publications. One of the men who worked in the university's public relations office set up a time to meet with my co-PI and I to "dig into" the various nuances of the grant. When the public relations man arrived to my office, my co-PI was running late, so he and I began the interview. It seemed to be going well, and I was very excited to share the details of the grant, the benefits to the school district and to the university, and some of the plans for the upcoming years related to the grant. About fifteen minutes into the interview conversation, my co-PI walked in (who is a male) and the gentleman interviewing me looked right at me and asked "So he is your boss?", to which my colleague and I looked at each other and started to laugh, which clearly confused the person interviewing me. My colleague then said "no"—that I was the grant Director and Principal Investigator, not him. The man looked even more confused because it did not make sense to him that I was the one running the grant. We both knew this man assumed that my colleague was my boss simply because he was a man older than me and it was just "natural" that my colleague was in charge. It was a striking reminder ageism and sexism is alive and well in higher education.

My experiences in the public schools were very different than my experiences in higher education. I never had anyone question my ability to accomplish something in PK–12 because of my age or gender. This has not always been the case at the university setting and is something difficult to endure. I found with promotion and tenure, this changed somewhat (or maybe I am just looking older now!) and I can only hope it continues to improve. Often, I have I found solace in the interactions with my colleagues at conferences and external organizations, as this is never an issue. It is a curious juxtaposition.

A REALIZATION OF COMMUNITY

In Fall 2007, I went to Alexandria, Virginia for the University Council for Educational Administration's (UCEA) Annual Conference. This was my second year as an Assistant Professor and I was very nervous. I cannot remember my presentation schedule, but I think I had the wildly unrealistic number of paper presentations non-tenured faculty often do (somewhere around 4 or 5) at the conference. (Advice as an aside—*don't do that*. Enjoy the conference experience. Definitely present a couple of papers—but take the time to learn from your colleagues. Having that many papers to present prevents you from enjoying and learning from the sessions you attend, the conversations you have, and the informal networking opportunities. You will focus too much on too many different papers you have "to do"—which in turn makes the presentations and papers not as good. Quantity does not necessarily equal quality.) In my mind, I was constantly ticking off the boxes needed to achieve tenure. I had the sleepless nights, the worry-filled days, and the constant examining of where I had been, where I was, and where I wanted to go in my career.

While I had met the "minimum publication" requirements for my first year at my university, I was still unsure about my place in the higher education world. I felt isolated in my job and concerned about my future. To me, those were the biggest issues, honestly. Isolation and uncertainty. I had two little children (one was 2 years old and the other was 10 months old), the second being born during the January of my first year as an Assistant Professor (I did not take maternity leave) and I was exhausted, stressed, and worried about the various requirements to make tenure. My focus was torn between my children and my career (probably functioning on about three hours of sleep a night did not help the situation).

We are each solely accountable for our performance in the Academy and the choices we make. Our careers rest on our own individual shoulders and when you finally receive your letter at the end of your assistant professor term (generally five or six years) about the rest of your career at the university you work at, it is your own actions that make you responsible for that outcome. In saying that, though, our work is not individual. While some of us may always work alone in terms of research and writing, I really do not know of anyone that does not rely on the feedback, insight, and expert opinions of others. Our professional responsibility is to provide that to others. And we should expect that of others in the Academy if we are to continue to be professionals and help school leaders, teachers, and districts help students achieve positive educational outcomes.

At the UCEA convention, I had a fortuitous conversation with a colleague and friend who gave me the sage advice I shared at the beginning of this chapter. Essentially, I am not alone and my academic world is larger than my College of Education building. In fact, it comprises of all of those in the field and all I need to do is reach out. I had the realization I was, indeed, a part of a community reaching far beyond the scope of my own university.

When I worked in PK–12, I had a sense of community from the beginning. I had been raised in the PK–12 world (both my parents worked in the public schools for 30+ years) and started working in the public schools at 16. I had known most of the people in the school system I worked in before I started and I had a high level of comfort, understanding, and knowledge about how to navigate PK–12. I finally, then, understood the community in the Academy and that has made all the difference in my career.

FINDING BALANCE

One of the ongoing conversations I have had with some of my close colleagues at my institution, as well as with others while talking at conferences, has been the ongoing struggle to find balance between work and personal life. This job provides more flexibility than most other professions I know. However, I work more now than I ever have in any other job and my hours constantly change. Sometimes it seems I am performing an intricate dance to make sure I get all of my work done, my children are taken care of and I meet all of their needs, and I manage to get some time to myself to recharge a little.

I do not have a 9:00 to 5:00 job spanning Monday through Friday. Sometimes I will work on email at three in the morning, other times I will be at a coffee shop at 6:30 am working on an article, I will teach until 10:00 at night, and facilitate weekend professional development sessions related to a grant. It is difficult to find time for myself between making sure I am the best mother I can be to my wonderful boys and ensuring I am meeting not only the standards and expectations set forth by my institution, but the standards and expectations I continually set (and increase all of the time) for myself.

Previously, I shared I did not take maternity leave with my second son (I barely took any time with the first, but I was an eleven month employee at the time in the PK–12 schools as an administrator and had my child in the summer, so it was not as stressful). I did not know I could ask to have the tenure-clock stopped if I took maternity leave and was too worried about the unknowns of higher education to consider taking leave. And no one told me I could have the clock stopped. It could be argued that someone, anyone, should have advised me (or at least told me my possibilities) when I was hired (I had made it clear from the onset I was pregnant and was concerned about how that would impact my job), but it could also be argued I should have sought out better guidance on this issue.

My first son developed a health condition requiring me to take him to the local children's hospital frequently (about once or twice a week for six months and then about every week for the next six) my first year as an assistant professor. I know if I had been an administrator in the public schools, I would not have been able to do this and probably would have taken medical leave to attend to my son. Having my faculty position enabled me to take him back and forth for his various doctor appointments, tests, and other medical activities necessary at the time. This lasted for about a year and I was the only parent taking him to all of the medical visits. All of this was going on while I had a baby, was working full-time, and was essentially solely responsible for my children.

I have heard and read some women have had negative interactions with their colleagues regarding their young children and the issue of having more children while faculty members. For me, this has not been the case. My major challenge was not knowing I could stop the tenure clock if I took maternity leave. I am not sure if I would have done what I did again if presented the opportunity to go off the clock for a few months, but it has worked out for the best in my situation. However, it was incredibly exhausting and stressful and left little time for anything other than work and making sure my children's needs were met. I would never recommend it to anyone, but if someone decided it was the best option for her, then I would support it.

Many of my colleagues have had children, although currently not many have young children like me. What I have found is there has been support for my role as a parent and there have not been any questions when I have to miss the occasional meeting for a doctor's appointment or a sick child. In fact, there is an air of understanding and I really appreciate this. My colleagues have expressed concern when one of my boys is sick, and just ask randomly about how they are doing. I do not think they realize how important an occasional question about them is to me and it is nice to work with people who are like this.

I have tried to strike a balance between my work and my family in terms of being able to really convey to those outside of the Academy what it is we do on a daily basis. If you are not in the field, it is pretty difficult to explain what we do (or at least difficult for others to really process what we do). Mainly, people think that I teach a few classes a year and have to write a couple of "things" that are published. When I started this job, I tried to explain to my family it is perfectly legitimate to stay at a coffee shop for 8 hours working on a manuscript and to come home with one page written (and to be proud of the effort). I realize I have always felt, in some ways, I need to show I am working hard and demonstrate that I am doing well to family and friends. But, with this job, I have had to let go of that need and just accept that I am doing the best I can.

MOVING THE CONVERSATION FORWARD

My work on women's research in educational leadership makes some people at my institution pretty uncomfortable. I feel I have to have a couple of other areas of research to balance out this one particular research interest because it is not considered by some (not all, but at least some) to be a legitimate field of study. Women and men alike are visibly uncomfortable with the research topic. A few vocal colleagues have told me this is an area of research that has been exhausted and there is nothing more to learn. And I have occasional colleagues who quietly shake their heads when I talk about this line of research, or start surfing the internet or flipping through a book while trying to avoid making eye contact to somehow de-legitimize the topic are the ones I find difficult to understand. I do not question what they do, so I am not sure why it is sanctioned to question this line of work.

Most of what I have shared in this chapter has focused on some difficult experiences I have encountered in higher education. I do not want to leave readers thinking everything I have experienced has been bad. In fact, I love my career, working in higher education, and have flourished at my institution. I have been provided a plethora of opportunities I know I would not have had at other institutions and have been provided invaluable resources furthering my research and work in the field. I have been able to work in turn with amazing PK–12 educators to help further their skills as leaders and teachers to positively impact students. What I have tried to do in this chapter is to shed light on some of the persistent and pervasive problems I have experienced with hope others will not have to encounter the same challenges.

There are a number of dialogues we need to have at our individual institutions about race, gender, and age. I am not sure how we do this, and perhaps these would be good sessions to have at conferences to discuss how to engage in these conversations. What I do know, right now, not enough is being done to overcome these issues. There is an abundance of interest in engaging in these conversations at UCEA, AERA, and NCPEA, among other organizations, and, perhaps those are the forums we need to begin with (although saying begin with implies we have not been doing this, which is not the case. Perhaps, rather, to say we continue with these conversations but with more emphasis and dissemination of our discussions.) We are not always going to agree, and there may be a few heated discussions, but that is important if we are to find ways to break down the barriers continuing to be present around the "isms" us, as women faculty, experience.

CHAPTER 7

HAVING IT ALL

Wait, What Does "All" Mean?

Jennifer K. Clayton

INTRODUCTION

Higher education and the academy found me. I never aspired, nor even thought of the possibility of becoming a professor in educational leadership, or in any field of study for that matter. It has become clear to me, however, that this field and the world of research and publishing are exactly where I belong. The path that led me to this space and understanding has been one that has more closely resembled a traffic circle than the linear style of most highways. As I learn which lane to drive in to reach my desired destination, I make wrong turns and have to redirect. These detours, however, have often resulted in some of the most interesting experiences, rich dialogues, and important colleague interactions.

Entry Into the Field of Education

My upbringing most certainly helped pave the road for me in terms of goal setting, educational attainment, and high expectations. My parents communicated the importance of education for my two sisters and me from a young age. Despite being heavily involved in competitive swimming, the emphasis in our home was always on school and, thus, our schoolwork was a priority. While I do not have recollection of discussions around Master's degrees or doctoral degrees, I certainly recall my parents communicating that I could accomplish whatever I set my mind to when it came to education. That message was echoed by supportive teachers I encountered throughout my educational journey. I recognize the privilege of having such an upbringing and that my experience is not reflective of the experience of others, including many of my peers.

My entry into work as an educational professional began at James Madison University in Virginia where I majored in History and minored in Secondary Education and Sociology. Through my undergraduate degree and student teaching, I came to understand the diverse needs of students at the high school level and how critical it is to have teachers who not only have the ability to provide quality and engaging instruction, but to connect with youth on a personal level. I found it frustrating that upon graduation, teaching jobs for Social Studies teachers were challenging to find. After my May graduation, I had no employment prospects until October when I received a call and subsequent interview for my first teaching position. My expectation was that I would have a wonderful job teaching U.S. History (which I loved) to high school students. The first of my detours, however, was that this position was for a Physical Education teacher at a private high school, where I would largely work with all boys' classes of seventh and eighth graders. To say this was a challenge for a new teacher who was just 21 years old would be a gross understatement. However, this experience provided necessary classroom management skills that all new teachers need.

My next positions at both private and public schools in Atlanta, Georgia, Richmond, Virginia and Virginia Beach, Virginia helped create a patchwork quilt of experiences that would allow me to work as a high school and middle school Social Studies teacher. Several of my department chairs and principals during my tenure in these positions commented that they saw a future for me in school leadership. With so few years of teaching experience, it was not on my radar, but the repetition of the message from several sources made me pause and consider this opportunity. When I arrived to teach in New Jersey, I quickly understood that I was required to obtain a Master's degree within five years of my initial contract. The gift hidden in this language, however, was that my district would fully cover all tuition costs for any courses where I maintained a B or better. The cost of tuition had been an obstacle for a newly married couple just beginning their life together. As I explored graduate programs, in consultation with my new department chair, I heard again the echo of my potential as a school leader. The encouragement from myriad supervisors finally pushed me to explore a Master's degree in Educational Administration at Rutgers University.

Experiences as a Graduate Student: A Tale of Two Degrees

My tenure as a graduate student occurred at two different times in my life, at two different institutions, and for two very different reasons, yet the experiences were similar. At both Rutgers University and Old Dominion University, I felt fully supported by my professors and peers. In both cases, however, there was always a seed of self-doubt about my potential and capacity for success. For someone who never struggled in school, this was not a question of intellectual preparation, but more an internal nagging that questioned "Am I good enough?" In my first degree, a master's in Educational Administration, I always wondered if I had enough teaching experience to fully benefit from the program and contribute in a meaningful way in dialogue. With my doctoral degree, as I began, I always had a sense that others around me were more capable to analyze, understand, and make meaning of our readings and papers.

My master's degree was a wonderful experience, as it allowed me the chance to see schools from a systemic lens and to realize the impact educational leaders can have on student success, regardless of the measure. My supervisor and principals gave me several opportunities to serve in leadership capacities and to work extensively as an intern during my degree program. These opportunities included building level leadership and decision-making, curriculum supervision and development, professional development of new and experienced teachers, and working through our district's budget and political process. While my experience was positive, I witnessed other aspiring administrators in my district who were not as fortunate. There was no racial or gender trend to the access granted, but rather a system of identification of leadership potential. This system presented a conundrum for me. What was it that I had and a few others had or demonstrated that our supervisors deemed important or valuable? As I have worked through my own research, it is clear that often leadership identification is a process of recognition of one's own qualities in another. Ten women and one man comprised the central office staff of this district, including a female superintendent and female assistant superintendent. Clearly, this composition is not now, nor was it then, common for central office staffs. I have often wondered if my life path would have been different were it not for the composition of these women and the opportunities they gave me at this important juncture.

My decision to pursue doctoral studies was in part due to seeking a balance between my personal life and my professional aspirations. My two children were born between my Master's program and doctoral program, and my husband and I made a decision that I would stay home with them. In my life, this was the best decision I ever made and one for which I have no regrets. My commitment to education, however, did not diminish and I saw further graduate work as a door that would allow me to pursue my own educational goals, further prepare me for K–12 administrative work, and strike a motherhood balance to be home with my children. When I began my doctoral work, I was a mother of two amazing children, ages three and one. There are not many three year olds that know what a dissertation is, but my daughter learned very quickly. I was not employed outside of the home during my doctoral studies; a badge I quickly learned was not valued by many peers. I endured many comments about the large amount of time I must have had to dedicate to doctoral work and how much easier it would be for them if they were not working. There will likely be a persistent debate for generations to come about the value of work done by men and women in the home in the care of children. Through my experience, I can only say that my choices were viewed as second class by many of my peers.

The experience of my doctoral work and graduate assistantship, nonetheless, was inspiring, challenging, and life-altering. My passion for research, both as a consumer and producer of knowledge, was almost immediately ignited. Outstanding professors, like Dr. Whitney Sherman and Dr. Karen Sanzo, both authors in this book, were inspiring and generous with their time. I continued to work with Whitney from a distance after she left Old Dominion University and, in fact, my first experience presenting at a conference was due to encouragement from Whitney to present work from a class project at the University Council for Educational Administration (UCEA) conference in Alexandria, VA. This mentoring was not clearly seen to me at the time, but, reflection is a gift, and I now see that experience as a tipping point in my academic life. Karen was a perpetual presence for me during my doctoral studies and was generous with her time and in her willingness to include me in her own ongoing research. This was clearly an entrance for me to begin to establish my own research agenda in higher education. This also may serve as an example of where the road was paved more readily for me than for some of my peers. It is interesting to me even now that along with these opportunities came a sense of guilt about my own privilege.

Experiences in the Academy

I must begin this section by stating I am still an early career professor. I am not clear on when that changes or what circumstances eventually allow you to feel experienced. Is it years of experience, a profound research study with important implications, a publication in one of the top-tier journals, or the affirmation afforded by achieving tenure? I will have to wait for answers to those questions. In my relatively short career, I have had experiences that I know will continue to shape my development as a researcher and professor. I have held two positions as an Assistant Professor. My first was as a Visiting Assistant Professor at Old Dominion University. I worked as an adjunct and then transitioned into the aforementioned role for one year. At that time, I accepted a position as an Assistant Professor in a tenure line at The George Washington University.

My work at Old Dominion University, although brief, was an important foundation in my transition to higher education faculty life. First as a student and then as a colleague I was fortunate to have Karen Sanzo as a mentor who "showed me the ropes." Her mentorship included more than just helping me navigate the administrative world at one university; she also provided entrance into myriad opportunities and working groups at UCEA and through a School Leadership Program grant. While our mentoring relationship was not a formal one, it was critical to curing my naiveté about higher education and in helping me gain footing in the world of research and publication. Part of this naiveté had to do with my lack of knowledge about institutions preferring not to hire their own graduates. As the picture became clear that my work at ODU would have a time limit, I began to pursue full-time positions with other universities. As my husband had worked more than a decade to build a small business, I was geographically locked into my regional area. In a detour that I consider paved with good fortune, I was offered and accepted a position with The George Washington University.

My work with GWU has been filled with supportive colleagues who challenge my work as a researcher and instructor in fulfilling ways. My interaction with my own program and our Research Methods faculty has both helped me refine and increase my expectations of my own work and that of my students. One challenge I face is geographic isolation. As our main campus is in Washington, DC and my office is based three hours away, I feel a constant tension between my personal and professional obligations in my area and the opportunities, committees, special events, and daily interactions that occur in DC. Before I began my work at GW and during the interview process, I was reminded that I would need to make a conscientious effort to "see and be seen" in DC. This pressure is ever-present in my mind as I also work to balance the needs of the students served by the satellite campus and my own personal life. The corridor of Interstate 95 provides a gateway to many opportunities on the main campus, but also provides a minimum of six hours of idle time in the driver's seat. For an early career professor working toward tenure, this valuable time is difficult to spend in the car.

Balancing a dissertation advising load, completing administrative responsibilities, teaching, engaging in service on internal and external committees, and conducting research have provided me with a full plate and one that my tenured colleagues advise is too full. The challenge comes in how to go about reducing the load in a culture where everyone works equally as hard. Working with so many dedicated professionals does not allow one to retreat into her office and focus entirely on research. While this isolating type of culture exists at many institutions, it is not part of the fabric of GW. This challenge is actually one of the most inspirational aspects of working with GW.

The Path to Tenure: A Dimly Lit Road

Even as I write this chapter, I question the wisdom of sharing my experiences while I am still working toward tenure. The horror stories told by those for whom the process was very political echo in my mind, despite consistent reassurances that this is a transparent and equitable process, My current university has provided clear and consistent expectations in both written and verbal formats from my first days in the position. Additionally, both formal and informal mentors have provided specific and constructive feedback about my research, teaching, and service. Given this sense of support, one would expect that I would feel confident in the process and clear on expectations. Even under these best of circumstances, however, the path to tenure seems dimly lit and blurred in the distance. Perhaps it is the high-stakes nature of the tenure process. This path is one that not only results in viability at the institution, but that follows an early career professor if she attempts to change universities after a failed effort.

The most daunting challenge for me in this process has been one of time allocation. The balance of publication, teaching, and service and what to emphasize varies based upon the focus of the stakeholder I ask. For example, students at the Master's level are not particularly interested in my publication record; they are far more concerned with my teaching and the teaching of my peers. The old adage of publish or perish, however, does seem to rule. Despite what appear to be rhetorical references to a university wide emphasis on teaching; those tasked with tenure decisions have described teaching and service as gravy. The implication is that these other categories are used to confirm the ultimate decision, which is based mostly on publication records. With this in mind, I have attempted to allocate my time as such, but with heavy administrative loads, I do fall short.

Student Interaction

Recent discussions with a colleague reminded me that one aspect of my professional work that has never caused me insecurity is my teaching. Hearing from colleagues for whom this is less natural and who have to diligently prepare just to deliver basic instruction in their content area helped me realize how fortunate I was to come from a K–12 instructional background. My years as a high school teacher gave me a foundation in curriculum and instructional design that has translated into instruction in higher education. Additionally, my work in leadership and adult learning has provided me a basis for understanding the unique developmental needs of the adults with whom I work. While I certainly have worked with some students who seem uncomfortable with my age (for now, I am considered young), I think this is often more about their own insecurities and need to feel confident when faced with a younger professor. In my experience, most students, regardless of age or experience level make a determination about credibility based upon the knowledge and competence demonstrated by their instructor. I also have typically heard the references to age or how long "they've been doing this" when the students are faced with a failure on their part to complete an assignment or to work to their potential. In other words, it becomes a defense mechanism and reason not to heed feedback, rather than a true statement about age and experience level.

Work/Life Balance: Can Women Have it All?

The greatest challenge I have faced in my life as a student and professor has been the ever evasive trial of balancing professional obligations and aspirations with the joys and challenges of being a mother and wife. The societal debate which surfaces around the possibility of this balance existing seems to be ever present, with the most recently publicized visitation happening just this past summer with an article by Anne-Marie Slaughter (2012). On the one hand, my work as a professor has provided me with a quality of life balance unparalleled by my colleagues who work in other fields. For example, if one of my children has a performance at school, Kindergarten graduation, or athletic event, I usually can tweak my schedule to be there. Management of one's own time is a gift. It is true, however, that at the end of the day, those trying to strike this balance sometimes feel as though they have pleased no one and that both home and work have concurrently been underserved.

I have networked with other mothers of young children who are also professors and it seems there are several themes which we experience. Two such themes include a unique schedule and the extraordinary support of spouse/partner/family members. I do not pretend to speak for all mothers of young children in the professoriate, but rather can only speak to my own experience. The first theme of a unique schedule includes some specific nuances about work hours, conference attendance, and professional development opportunities. I have discovered that I work very different hours than my colleagues, often reporting to work hours ahead of the general crowd, leaving hours before, and working late into the evening after my children have gone to sleep. This leaves me often feeling that others might not be aware of the work I do as it is not measured always by an open office door. The time stamp on emails to and from my students demonstrates the late nights that often occur in my home. While I wait at a doctor's appointment with a child, I am constantly checking email and responding to student inquiries. Conference attendance, similarly, usually entails me flying in just as the conference begins and leaving on the earliest possible flight at its completion. Often, I have to look at the presentation schedule and miss a day of a conference. This results in fewer networking opportunities and more leisurely travel schedules than some of my colleagues enjoy. Finally, many of the professional development opportunities occur at times or on days that conflict with my availability. If I were to ask my family, they might say I miss a large number of events and am "always teaching or with students," whereas my work colleagues might report my lack of presence in evening hours at my office. This is a further example of trying to please all, while pleasing none.

In balancing this schedule, I would have failed before I began were it not for the support of my husband and family. My husband has supported my educational and professional endeavors at every turn and has helped me work with him to find a family/life/work balance for both of us. He has a career that requires long hours and intense professional obligations as well, but our first priority has always been and will always be our children and each other. I have been told by colleagues who have not yet, but may someday consider having children, that I must have an extraordinary husband because of my travel schedule for the basic school and department meetings that require nights away every month in the academic year. As I continue to find ways to achieve this elusive balance, I do not expect to be "given a pass" or treated differently because I have young children. I know, however, that I am different than those not raising young children. It falls to my shoulders, not those of my administration or colleagues, to determine how I will strike the balance. I am grateful, though, in knowing my experience is not unique and that at all stages of life, we encounter balance challenges, whether it is caring for children, aging parents, ill friends or family members, or in balancing our own health challenges. The work of many colleagues such as the recent book *Juggling Flaming Chainsaws* edited by Joanne Marshall gives us an opportunity for our own unique reflection.

Breaking Into the All Male's Club: Have We Broken Barriers?

As I reflect on the groundbreaking women who shared their stories in *Breaking into the All-Male Club: Female Professors of Educational Administration*, I am struck by the roads they paved for generations to come. While issues of gender persist, the stories I read of their early experiences do not reflect my daily interactions with my colleagues. Perhaps what we see more currently are series of micro-aggressions. When I read the stories of veteran women academics such as Diana Pounder and Martha McCarthy that occurred 20–30 years ago, the experiences they endured would be considered "smoking guns", so egregious as to require a response. Now, we see examples of smaller decisions, side comments, joke telling, and what seem to be harmless commentary that actually cause women to second-guess their own worth, qualifications, and sense of belonging. It leaves me knowing that we clearly have traveled a great distance into an esteemed status for women in the professoriate, but we have many miles to travel to reach a true sense of equity and equality.

Final Reflections

I will continue to struggle with questions of self-doubt, a concern about a balance for me and my family, questions about how I define success, and a perpetual need not to disappoint anyone. Is this due to my status as a woman, mother, contemporary professor, or some other demographic category ascribed to me? I am not sure I will ever fully have an enlightened answer to this. As the title of this chapter indicates, I am certainly not clear on what the "all" is in having it "all." For me, that changes with each chapter of my life. What I valued ten, five, or even one year ago seems to have changed with the tide.

I have taken several key lessons from my early years in higher education. These are likely not new themes, but, nevertheless, were not clear to me when I began.

A Mentor is a Must. Women in higher education must seek and cultivate relationships with formal and informal mentors. For me, the journey would have been a short trip were it not for the mentoring efforts of several of my early professors and colleagues. While I think I would have figured out a path eventually, I am not confident it would have been in the short time clock of tenure. We also must remember to pay it forward by offering our own guidance and advice to others who enter the field, and particularly to graduate students who have potential for or who express an interest in the professoriate.

Balance is Vital, but Not Permanent. In my second year with GW, I have done a better job at learning how to balance the often-competing needs of my doctoral students, Master's advisees, colleagues, publishers, and administrators. My family and I have adjusted to what life looks like for me as a professor and my children have the benefit of a vernacular in higher education. My husband has come to quote the theorists and colleagues that I enthusiastically share with him. This balance, however, can seem to change as the weeks pass. Despite my Type A personality style of scheduling, I cannot always plan for when doctoral students will submit chapters, when reviews will be returned, and when demands for special projects will intensify. One week I might feel like everything is in a Zen-like state, but the next it is though I have been punched by chaos. Part of the sense of balance in this second year has been the acknowledgement that there is no light at the end of the tunnel for the constant seeking of equilibrium. This struggle will continue. As long as I am not trying to reach a destination that is constantly moving, much of the frustration for that type of world has diminished.

Voice is a Gift. Finding one's voice is a venture unto itself. In many aspects of my life, my voice has tremendous clarity. I have a set of values that govern the decisions I have made for of my life. Voice as a professional, though, is a work of construction. As an early professor, my voice was often designed to avoid confrontation, attain approval, and join the "majority" chorus. I have realized through my second year, however, that what is valued is not saying what some might want me to say, but rather lending my voice to the range within the chorus. There is a reason that the most beautiful songs possess a range of talent and ensemble of voices. I am ever cognizant, however, that many before me did not have their voice valued or their diversity esteemed. This is why it is clear that voice is a gift.

Writing this chapter has been cathartic and challenging. As I acknowledged my existent self-doubt, I found myself again wondering whether anyone will care or be interested in my story and my journey. I leave this for the reader to decide.

CHAPTER 8

STILL I RISE

An Early-Career African-American Female Scholar's Told Truths on Surviving Academia

Cosette M. Grant

Little research exists on young female scholars' experiences in the academy (Sherman, Beaty, Crum & Peters, 2010), especially African-American women. Specifically, there is limited data which currently inform the literature about the doctoral preparation experiences of African-American female doctoral students for progression toward tenure-track faculty careers at predominantly White institutions (PWIs) and the connection to their successful transition to faculty in educational leadership programs at PWIs (Grant, 2012; Grant & Simmons, 2008). This article is an attempt to fill that void. Using scholarly personal narrative (Ellis & Bochner, 2003), an early-career African-American female tenure-track faculty in educational leadership, shares her doctoral preparation experience for entry into the professoriate at a PWI. Findings from the experience narrative are situated in critical pedagogies and link mentoring to successful progression from doctoral student to tenure track faculty in educational leadership at a PWI.

Strategies are offered to aid African-American women with successful entry into the academy (Grant, 2012; Grant & Simmons, 2008).

THE TABLES ARE TURNING

You may write me down in history
with your bitter, twisted lies.
You may trod me in the very dirt, but still like dust, I'll rise.

—*Still I Rise* (Angelou, 2011)

Many predominantly White Institutions (PWIs) have failed to recognize and value African Americans contributions to the field of education (Henry, 1994; Henry & Nixon, 1994, p. 54). Notwithstanding, a genesis of the achievements of early trailblazers (i.e., Black individuals, few in number) who broke through historical barriers by earning doctorates and joining the ranks of faculty at PWIs during unpopular times (Jackson & Johnson, 2011) is the remaining legacy of exclusion and struggle for access and equity for African Americans in U.S. higher education. Mainly, African-American women, have occupied marginal positions in academe for an extended period (Collins 1990, 1998, 2002).

Researchers have documented a multitude of barriers encountered by African-American female students, faculty and administrators (Bonner & Thomas, 2001; Gordon, 2004; Gregory, 2001; Henderson, 2005; Hughes & Howard-Hamilton, 2003; Nichols & Tanksley, 2004; Robinson, 1996; Simpson, 2001; Thomas & Hollenshead, 2001). Specifically, some research findings have indicated a co-occurring discrimination related to race and gender (Zamani, 2003), lack of support systems and networks (Patton & Harper, 2003), an unwelcoming, insensitive, and isolative environments (Watt, 2003). African-American female faculty in PWIs, more specifically, are less likely to gain access to networks and organizational systems in order to advance their agenda (Gibson, 2006; Tillman, 2007). This lack of inclusion of African-American women in faculty and leadership posts has limited their access to influential academic positions (Collins 2002). Very little has changed in recent years (Grant, 2012).

Nonetheless, as more African-American women are entering academic environments, they are challenging traditional notions of research, disrupting structural barriers, and defining their voices in these environments (Glazer-Raymo, 2008; Harley, 2008). Likewise, the lived experiences of African-American women mark a continuum of efforts to have a dominant voice in their respective academic environments, while advancing perspectives that traditionally have been marginalized (Grant, 2012; Jean-Marie & Lloyd-Jones, 2011). African-American women are resilient and have been able to make great progress toward attaining their rightful place within academia (Gregory, 2001).

Therefore, the impetus of this article is two-fold: (a) to fill a void in the nascent literature on the experiences of African-American women in educational leadership in PWIs, with emphasis on doctoral student preparation experiences for advancement towards early career tenure-track faculty; and (b) to provide narrative experiences from an African-American female early career-track educational leadership professor's perspective that speaks to issues critical to social justice and equity in educational leadership programs at PWIs. Experience narratives (Grant & Simmons, 2008) are highlighted to shed light on layers that typically don in PWIs, that speak directly to experiences of African-American women as emerging scholars and academicians who traverse many historic barriers and systemic boundaries to confront issues of inequity and marginalization commonplace in the academy.

Drawing from real-life occurrences of a young African-American female early career scholar's daily struggles of advancing nontraditional, yet, relevant scholarship, balancing scholarship, teaching and serving in a PWI, earning the respect of colleagues and students as a young, Black and female scholar, pedagogies and strategies are imparted. By sharing these specific experiences, critical theoretical insights—Black feminist thought (BFT) and critical race theory (CRT) are provided as thought-provoking issues critical to a young African-American female early career scholar's transcendence and survival in PWI settings. The use of Black feminist thought allows for the utilization of personal narratives to shed light on the doctoral preparation for advancement towards the professoriate as well as early career experiences as a tenure track faculty member in a PWI, in order to examine something larger than my individual story (Ellis & Bochner, 2003).

Further, the use of CRT in this study permits counter-storytelling to gain a more in-depth understanding of the transitioning experiences of an African-American female faculty in educational leadership at a PWI. CRT is based on five prominent tenets: (a) counter-storytelling; (b) the permanence of racism; (c) Whiteness as property; (d) interest convergence; and (e) the critique of liberalism (DeCuir & Dixson, 2004). For the purposes of this study, counter-storytelling and the permanence of racism are the tenets of CRT that are the most critical for gaining a better understanding of the experiences of an early career track African-American female faculty in educational leadership's transition into a PWI. Counter-storytelling is the "voice" (Ladson-Billings, 1998, p. 14) component of CRT. Through the use of counter-stories, people of color have the opportunity to tell of their experiences (1998).

This article concludes with outcomes that can be addressed in future research and in efforts to strengthen policies that support the academic success and entry of African-American women in educational leadership departments at PWIs.

REDEFINING OUR SPACE IN A DISCURSIVE PLACE

> *Does my sassiness upset you?*
> *Why are you beset with gloom?*
> *'Cause I walk like I've got oil wells*
> *Pumping in my living room.*
> —*Still I Rise* (Angelou, 2011)

As a young, African-American female early career tenure-track professor in educational leadership who is actively engaged in social justice research and discourse, namely the experiences and advancement of African-American women in PWIs, I have come to the realization that reflection of my own experiences has been compromised. This was more realized as I identified similar research by and about young female scholar experiences, including African-American female faculty in educational leadership, as well as in open and informal conversations with similarly situated female scholars in the field. I compared and contrasted my lived experiences in academe to that of White and women of color female faculty in educational leadership programs at PWIs. I learned though their lens that "enormous amounts of time had been spent pushing limits for women study participants they were researching, yet failing to do the same for themselves" (Sherman, Beaty, Crum & Peters, 2010, p. 1). Not only could I relate, but it also became apparent in research literature and in the discussions that additional commonalities in experiences related to ageism and sexism persists for women faculty. For example, I can relate to the following narratives shared by Sherman, Beaty, Crum & Peters (2010):

> While I enjoyed my graduate program, I do not feel that it did a good job, or even a mediocre one, in preparing me to work in higher education. If I had not been ambitious and sought out experiences on my own to better prepare me, I would not have been able to secure a position. (p. 10)

While I received great content knowledge on courses taken throughout my doctoral preparation experience and was supported by my doctoral program to participate in an educational leadership mentoring program for students interested in the professoriate, no faculty member within my doctoral program offered crucial insider knowledge essential to the process for preparation and successful transitioning and first time entry into the professoriate. Sherman et al., (2010, p. 10) indicate this as "hunting and gathering" in leadership education, hence looking outside of the "clan" so as not to starve as seminal to their preparation process. As such, similar to the some of the study participants in the Sherman et al., (2010) study, I had to go outside of the academy to receive specific guidance and preparation support.

> My doctoral program offered a strong core of both leadership and research training, mentoring relationships from senior scholars/faculty established in mentoring programs helped me to gain "insider" knowledge from faculty willing to engage in on-going dialogue with me. This provided me with better preparation than coursework and further with survival tools to "prioritize work—publish, teaching, and service should follow in this order" and "come out of the starting blocks right" immediately upon arrival. I would have been at an obvious disadvantage if I had not had this type of constructive intervention from a seasoned scholar/mentor in the educational leadership field.

However, there were varying degrees of social class, race, and identity differences that were more salient in the outcomes for these women in the Sherman et al., (2010) study. It was at this juncture that I began to differentiate the experiences of African-American women faculty in educational leadership at PWIs as different from that of overall female faculty experiences, although it can't be generalizable.

Understanding why the experiences of African-American women faculty in educational leadership at PWIs are different from those of White women is steeped in a historical progression and ideology of African-American women in the United States (Grant, 2012). In this regard, it is important to contextualize the historical milieu of African-American women in society and in education in order to situate the experiences of African-American female faculty in educational leadership departments at PWIs.

In the early nineteenth century, for example, African-American women were confined to domesticated roles (Guy-Sheftall & Bell-Scott, 1989; Payton, 1985). Educational attainment was not intended for persons of color—particularly African-American women, who were considered less than human. However, for those African-American women who entered the educational arena, they were relegated to jobs as elementary and secondary school teachers.

That said African-American women faced multiple challenges to education during this era. First, they had little experience in public or community affairs; second, they had internalized traditional beliefs about women's roles due to a gender-bound upbringing; and third, they had adopted a self-defeating perspective on life (Guy-Sheftall & Bell-Scott, 1989). One can argue that very little has changed for African-American women in higher education in present times (Grant, 2012). This unfortunate historical reality carries over to present day perceptions of White peers towards their ideals of an African-American female faculty's place in a PWI.

In paraphrasing Carroll (1982), "African-American woman in higher education face greater risks and problems now than in the past" because she is in a place previously occupied by the dominant group, and the numbers are growing in academic environments—she is becoming more "visible" (p. 115). This new reality creates formidable roadblocks for African-American female scholars and their devaluing as they continue efforts to gain entry and ascend the ranks in PWIs. Allow me to share my personal experiences in this regard. I am the only African-American female faculty in my program. I am one of two tenure-track faculty producing scholarship in my program and with graduate faculty status, which has allowed me a direct line of access to leadership equal to the program coordinator and support unavailable to other peers and the program coordinator. This has caused some backlash from White peers as a result. For example, in an email inquiry addressed to School of Education Leadership and that included my program coordinator (who was copied on the correspondence) my professionalism was questioned and thereby attacked. Below is an example of the email exchange. For the purpose of anonymity, pseudonyms were used. I sent an email to school leaders with a carbon copy to the Program Coordinator as follows:

> I am writing to solicit your recommendation to how best handle a time sensitive matter regarding travel support for doctoral students for an upcoming conference. Two students expressed financial limitations that limit their ability to pay for the conference (e.g., lodging and airfare costs). Are there any additional or emergency funds to help these students? I seek your thoughts, guidance, mentoring on the best course of action. Thanks so much.

Program Coordinator responds:

> Kozet, this is one of those conversations with which I could have been helpful up front, as a colleague and program coordinator. When the coordinator is not consulted in these types of situations, there is a loss of respect and subsequent influence for said coordinator in future situations. I prefer conversations in advance to problem solving after the fact. Have a great weekend.

My response:

> I thought in this instance it would be easier to go to the source.... This issue preceded your appointment as coordinator... I understand the School Director approves budget allocations and not the coordinator... If you have or know of additional funds, then let me know. If there is another source, let me know. Thanks. See you Tuesday.

Program Coordinator response:

> You did and you skipped one...The issue is one of professional courtesy. That's it. Have a great weekend.

This speaks volumes about an important, persistent, and under-researched social problem in the United States, hence PWI settings: racial microaggressions. Scholar Solórzano (1998) recognizes microaggression as subtle insults (verbal, nonverbal, and/or visual) directed toward people of color, often automatically or unconsciously as "put downs" of Blacks by "offenders" (Pierce, Carew, Pierce-Gonzalez, & Wills, 1978, p. 66). They further maintain that these "offensive mechanisms used against Blacks often are innocuous" and that the "cumulative weight of their never-ending burden is the major ingredient in Black-White interactions" (p. 66). Additionally, Davis (1989) defined racial microaggressions as "stunning, automatic acts of disregard that stem from unconscious attitudes of White superiority and constitute a verification of black inferiority" (p. 1576). This classic example of microaggression described above is an aspect of CRT that deals with the centrality of race and racism and their intersectionality, with other forms of subordination and how they influence the collegiate racial climate.

KEEPING MY EYES ON THE PRIZE

> *Just like moons and like suns,*
> *With the certainty of tides,*
> *Just like hopes springing high,*
> *Still I'll rise.*
>
> —*Still I Rise* (Angelou, 2011)

I spoke earlier of my doctoral preparation experience as overall positive. I was mentored within and outside of my doctoral program, I had peer support inside and outside of my program, I presented at national conferences and I published—all said to be precedents to successful entry into the professoriate.

However, my transition into a tenure-track faculty position was not automatic and met with ambiguities, twists and turns, before I gained successful entry. Upon graduating, I sought opportunities to adjunct in my former degree program, so that I could gain additional guidance and support to better prepare myself for successful entry in the professoriate at a PWI, but was met with some resistance. I figured that I had the chance to coteach a course during my doctoral preparation, that this would be a natural progression. NOT! I was told that my interest was not aligned with any of the available courses in the department and that I was perceived to be higher administration focused, since I was working in an administrative capacity at the time. I found this to be peculiar, and full of obscurity, especially from the same degree program that granted my degree, the same degree where I invested a good fortune to attain the highest academic achievement and the same institution that is expected as a result to support my endeavors. There were hints that I was doing too much, too fast and that I was too aggressive. Concurrent to this process, not one, or two, but three of the adjunct opportunities in the department were afforded to three of my classmates—two Black males and one White male, who were not interested in the professoriate, but needed the extra money. When I raised issue, the response was that they were a better fit.

Surprisingly, it was a young African-American female scholar behind the scenes blocking my opportunity to adjunct. She was new to the program, yet a decision-maker who chose to entertain negative stereotypes of African-American women, the same ones bestowed on her, that often times deter our advancement into PWIs. Patton and Harper (2003) assert that African-American women would be served best by other African-American women because they would "understand the complex intersection of race and gender in the academy and society" more than others from other racial backgrounds (p. 71). However, this is not always the case, as per my experience. While there are a number of African-American women who played an integral role in my doctoral preparation progression toward academe, there were just as many countering my progress. Sherman et al., (2010) speaks to a similar occurrence. One of the study participants stated the following:

> As a graduate student, I had mentors. However, I found that when some of those same people came to feel threatened by my performance and aspirations, some of those "mentors" turned quickly into obstacles. (p. 12)

For this participant, a sense of caution was gained regarding the process of mentoring. There was a general question whether the competitive nature of higher education of gaining entry and consequent tenure in the profession, led to this breakdown and relational shift. Nevertheless, I moved on. I continued working in administration and taught two courses as an adjunct professor in an interdisciplinary department within the university as well as at another institution. I also maintained an active research and publication schedule and continued to present at national conferences. Staying active in scholarship was my strategy for gaining successful entry. It seemed as though I had done all of the right things that I had been prepared to do, yet the opportunities remained bleak.

As I began to share my challenges and frustration to obtaining a faculty post with those closest to my process—my advisor, committee members, former professors—I was discouraged by some. Surprisingly, I was advised to "slow the pace down," perhaps pursue a teaching position at a junior college, take a few years off and to do other things. I was two years out and I could not fathom why someone I trusted, regarded as a mentor, and relied on for professional support, would provide such advisement. This same trusted source also failed to provide job leads and politely refused to write any recommendations, claiming to be too busy during the times asked. Further shocking to me was that this resistance, lack of support, discouragement and failure to assist, came from an African-American female senior scholar who understands, (or should at least know and/or be sensitive to) the challenges and obstacles many African-American women face often in PWIs, especially as we attempt to gain entry. I am reminded here that not only must a young African-American emerging scholar (Generation X) confront systemic barriers and the pervasive racisms that persist generally in PWIs, but that we must also deal with intergenerational conflicts from older female (Baby boomer) colleagues. For example, "Many younger women feel that older female colleagues aren't helpful, and women of the baby boomer generation are uncomfortable helping a woman who might get her job next" (Zaslow & Martinez-Beck,2006).

As such, I took on a different strategy approach in order to gain entry. My support base had grown, particularly in my mentoring and professional networks outside of my doctoral program and institution. I had two years of proven success as an adjunct professor and in my on-going research and publications. Witnesses to that process were thereby able to serve as resources and were proactive in endorsing me for successful entry as a tenure track professor into an educational leadership program. So, two years and three publications later, after graduating, I made my formal debut into the professoriate.

THE TIES THAT BIND US

Did you want to see me broken?
Bowed head and lowered eyes?
Shoulders falling down like teardrops.
Weakened by my soulful cries.

—*Still I Rise* (Angelou, 2011)

Even though I looked forward to the anticipation of the academy—teaching, working with students, collaborating with colleagues, researching and writing, I had to realize, though, that racism and sexism is omnipresent in the academy, especially as there is an underrepresentation of African-American female faculty in educational leadership in PWIs. While this may seem to be a pessimistic and defensive posture, the reality of it all is that there are indeed significant challenges oftentimes inherent in small numbers coupled with institutional racial and gender inequality. This has prompted African-American women in academia to employ a variety of coping strategies that have been integral to their academic and professional advancement (Bagilhole, 1994; Thomas & Hollenshead, 2001).

Specifically, African-American women connect with mentors within their academic discipline, establish supportive networks of colleagues in and outside of their departments and institutions, work to achieve high visibility in their communities, and rely on their personal contacts to create useful professional alliances (Gregory, 2001). Central among these intermediaries of goal attainment are all forms of connecting and forming mentoring networks, especially with other African-American women faculty, to bridge the physical gap on campuses caused by lack of a critical mass and to lessen the impact of racism. Support systems in the lives of African-American female faculty in PWIs have been found to be important because of these women's needs for guidance, strength, and encouragement to help them negotiate academic settings that are often unfriendly and isolating (Grant, 2012; Grant & Simmons, 2008; Tillman, 2001), as well as disparate.

Mentors also have been found to nurture a sense of belonging for women of color in the profession (Tillman, 2001). Many studies confirm that mentoring programs can provide greater access to resources for research, advice, and collegial networks, which can often lead to greater academic productivity and a faculty position (Gasman et al., 2008; Grant, 2012; Grant & Simmons, 2008; Tillman, 2001). Mentoring support for me during my doctoral preparation for advancement toward the professoriate was a critical factor for my entry into the professoriate in educational leadership at a PWI. In particular, mentors within my mentoring network served as staunch supporters and advocates in my candidacy process by way of writing letters of support, as well as making phone calls to endorse me for the faculty position and confirm my qualifications. Similarly, Dixon-Reeves' (2003) study examined the experiences of recently minted African-American PhD recipients in the field of sociology and confirmed in her study that recent degree earners reported receiving more mentoring that resulted in career enhancement.

Further, Grant and Simmons' (2008) study, although nongeneralizable, claims that mentoring is most essential to the advancement success of African-American female doctoral students in educational leadership in PWIs, who are interested in the professoriate in educational leadership at PWIs. For example, I participated in a mentoring program that helped prepare students of color interested in the professoriate in educational leadership for a faculty position. In specific, I had peer reviewed publications, participated in peer-reviewed scholarly presentations at international and national conferences and service outcomes that help ready me for my first tenure-track position I believe that my engagement in such scholarly activities made me a viable candidate immediately upon degree completion. I also believe that these scholarly attributes combined with the one-on-one mentoring and extended mentoring networks are primary factors that landed me my first tenure-track faculty post. These findings are consistent with literature indicating that the probability of one's success in graduate school and beyond is clearly connected to mentoring (Johnson & Huwe 2003).

While several success strategies have been proposed to help African-American women navigate the treacherous conditions in which they commonly find themselves, the effects of systemic racism and lack of critical mass intertwine to make connecting with one another difficult in some cases, and virtually impossible in others. Because of this dynamic, many African-American women faculty are, unfortunately, left with no choice but to navigate the race and social dynamic issues, hence sociopolitical complexities of the PWIs in isolation (Grant, 2012, 2014). However, I have been fortunate to have access to many African-American women senior scholars and other professional peers in educational leadership. We are a small network, but the few that are present, have made themselves available. As such, formal and informal mentoring have indeed played a direct role in attaining my former and present faculty position. It was also a combination of cross-race/gender (Grant, 2012; Grant & Simmons, 2008; Jean-Marie & Brooks, 2011) as well as same-sex/gender mentoring (Tillman, 2001) that aided in my success toward attaining a tenure-track faculty position in educational leadership at a PWI.

I am the only African-American female tenure-track professor in my department; however, there are a few African-American women faculty in other departments in the college in with whom I have been able to connect and receive additional mentoring. Though my immersion into my department has been relatively smooth and I have made beneficial connections with White peers, I have experienced some instances of ostracism from White colleagues and superiors. I was the only African-American female hire in my cohort, yet my White peers were provided with mentoring support upon entry into their various departments or programs. Many were assigned a university mentor along with a mentor from within the college. Upon recognizing the potential or deliberate oversight 18 months into my position, I formally requested a mentor within the college. I requested a senior colleague of color with whom I had established great rapport and was granted that individual 18 months into my position. In some other cases, I have been excluded from informal social networks, silenced in meetings, had exaggerated performance expectations, and have been relegated to miniscule while at the same time overburdening tasks unrelated to my research, scholarship and professional agenda—which detracts from the tenure process. For example, as the only African-American female faculty with graduate faculty status in the department (i.e., allowed to chair dissertations), I have been overburdened with requests to chair and/or serve on dissertation committees. As well, I have been told, yet misguided, by some tenured peers, the same peers who will eventually vote on my tenure status, that I am obligated to chair or serve when asked by students. Herein lies the challenge of deciding on how to strike a balance in serving the needs of doctoral students, entertaining the suggestions of colleagues related to serving students, while focusing on publications in order to achieve tenure status. Mentoring from both White and Black peers, helped play a critical role in my decision to say "NO" to chairing dissertations during my first year on the job as a newly minted professor, and to align all work and activities with preparation for successful publications.

Although my experiences are real and well documented, I am not comfortable disclosing my sentiments of racism with a White peer for fear of being viewed as *playing the race card, complaining, being paranoid or angry*. And after all, these are experiences unique and specific to the mere status of being the only African-American woman faculty member in an educational leadership department functioning in a PWI. Grant's (2012) article speaks to this matter directly. The African-American female participants in the study believed that a White male or female mentor could not relate to the depth of experiences unique to African-American women in predominantly White settings.

> Another African-American female would understand their tears, their failures, and their triumphs, both in graduate school and outside academe...She could share advice and offer observations from her own experiences to help me avoid pitfalls and blunders. (Grant, 2012, p. 11)

In particular, the participants were not willing to disclose to their White peers, specific issues because of fear that it would reinforce negative perceptions of weakness or incapability of handling rigorous circumstances, when in fact they were dealing with race issues.

> I could not in reality go to a white mentor and complain about racial undercurrents from white professors and peers—like "Why are you researching on Black people and issues...you will have a hard time finding a job if you use Black feminist theory or critical race theory...Your work needs to be more mainstream in order to graduate and/or get hired at a PWI..." I would be seen as a troublemaker if I complained and uncooperative to constructive criticism. Therefore, I don't share too much with them, especially on a personal level, just strictly focused on concerns related to the educational leadership program, and that's about it...That may not be a real relationship, but I'm not comfortable telling them everything...I've cried on the phone with

my Black mentor, but I would never cry about these issues with a white mentor... Crying is a sign of being emotional and unstable and weak—they may label me as such—and so I would never let them see me upset... but a Black female mentor would understand and could relate. (Grant, 2012, p. 12)

Similar findings have also been reported on comparable issues of African-American females in academe (Bell, 2004; Henry and Glenn, 2010).

One vexing issue that emerges when considering the impact of the lack of critical mass African-American women face in PWI's is the scarcity of other African-American women to serve as role models, mentors, peer advisors, and confidants. However, I entered into academe with mentors, but have also have sought additional relationships with other African-American women outside of the department and outside of the institution in order to gain support, given the lack of diversity in my department. Hughes and Howard-Hamilton (2003) provide evidence that supports this assertion and contend that many African-American women faculty are forced to look outside of their academic discipline for support. In their conclusion, they verify the physical isolation that is the result of the low numbers and dispersion of African-American women in academia, which causes us to connect sporadically and haphazardly (2003), and become one of the ties that bind us in PWIs.

TAKING A LICKING AND KEEP ON TICKING

Does my haughtiness offend you?
Don't you take it awful hard
'Cause I laugh like I've got gold mines
Diggin' in my own back yard.
—*Still I Rise* (Angelou, 2011)

African-American women in academia grapple almost daily with an overwhelming lack of support and respect that persists from the dominant culture's elitist attitudes and exclusionary practices (Bagilhole, 1994). Evidence of this devaluing can be observed in almost every type of interpersonal encounter in which the African-American woman engages within PWI settings (i.e., superiors, colleagues and students). Therefore, I have had to take a licking and keep on ticking. I have particularly found the sense of diminishing to be the case in various instances with superiors, colleagues and students. I have a specific example regarding a student, during my first year of teaching. I sent an email to a White female student as follows:

> I appreciate your involvement in the planning and implementation of the student symposium and think that it has gone over pretty well. Thanks for your

> input and participation. However, I wanted to point out to you an observation of references made during the symposium. In particular, you referred to my colleagues as Dr. X, Y, and Z and to me by my first name. I would appreciate the same courtesy given to me that was given to my other colleagues in this setting. Thanks for the courtesy moving forward.

The student responds:

> Dr. Grant. Absolutely! I can see it means a lot to you and will do so from now on. I'm also looking forward to one day carrying the title, so I very much appreciate the hard work and struggle it must have taken you to get there. Please don't take offense to my familiarity. Prior to you joining our session yesterday, I noted our discussants without title and generally do so within the university setting. It comes from my years as an administrator. For instance, Ron, the provost and I hold that familiarity. See you later on this morning. You're doing a great job!

You see, I was facilitating the symposium and asked this doctoral student to participate in order for her to network and gain national experience. You would think from the email exchange, that she was in charge— "Prior to you joining our session..." However, I was disrespected and devalued from a student, the same student of whom I afforded an opportunity, who as a thank-you to me, demonstrated blatant bias. This is further demonstrated by the student in the following:

> I can see it means a lot to you to be called Dr..." "I very much appreciate the hard work and struggle it took you to get there..." "I generally note without title within the university setting... It comes from my years as an administrator..."

In the words of Piece (1974), "the subtle, cumulative, miniassault is the substance of today's racism..." (1974, p. 516). Despite my defined leadership role, not only in action, but in print, the students' White privilege and entitlement caused her to ignore the reality and persist with her sense of perception, while defaulting to her normal state of believing in her hegemony. CRT in this regard, has enabled me to offer insights, perspectives, methods and pedagogies that guide one's efforts to identify, analyze, and transform the structural and cultural aspects of education that maintain subordinate and dominant racial positions in and out of the classroom (Matsuda, Lawrence, Delgado, & Crenshaw, 1993; Tierney, 1993; Tierney & Rhoades, 1993).

Following this email exchange, the student the following morning calls out to me—"Well, Good Morning DOCTOR Grant." I shared with her that it is not necessary to be formal at all times, only when all are referred by title. The student quickly responds, "Uh, I prefer to be formal at all times..."

To this day, this student refuses to speak or acknowledge me in any setting. This student now has her doctorate. Right after the notice of her dissertation defense date went out, her business cards were already ordered, her office name plate had been changed to Doctor and everyone was calling her doctor. I suspect that she has not had to deal with the disrespect and racism from a student that had shown to me. As shown in the above experience, and also reflected in Harris' (2007) study, this was a "precarious position of defining and defending [my] professional identity because of [my] race" (p. 57). Like Harris (2007), I have insisted since the beginning of my career in academia on being addressed by my professional title, Doctor Grant, to deal with the lack of respect within and outside of the classroom—places where my "intellect, authority, and credibility" (p. 59) as a professor are questioned.

Hughes and Howard-Hamilton also (2003) reported further that evidence of systemic racism can be found in the classroom when students question, query, challenge, and dismiss the intellectual ability of an African-American faculty member. In all of these situations, no amount of experience is enough to prove that I am highly capable when the group comprises people who do not look like me (p. 99). I had a situation in a class where I provided weekly agendas of readings, questions and specific discussions before classes; however a student indicated in her evaluation of my course, that I was not thorough and failed to expound on the readings. These are readings I had provided, questions and discussions I had developed in advance of class; however, I am reduced to not being thorough.

Additionally, Crouthers (2002) contends that when the grade point average of some White students is threatened by a grade lower than an "A," from a woman faculty of color, there can be problems to include unfavorable faculty evaluations. Here is one example—Student, in response to receiving below an A in the course sends an email to me stating:

> Could you please give me your reasons for giving me below an A in the class? I need to understand what I did not do in your class that would warrant the grade I got. There was never a rubric given for the project, so I am not sure what to gauge your grade upon—please help me understand.

In agreement with Crouthers (2002), Solórzano and Yosso (2002) posit "a critical race methodology in education that challenges this White privilege scenario" (2002, p. 26). Furthermore, CRT offers insights, perspectives, methods, and pedagogies that guide efforts to identify, analyze, and transform the structural and cultural aspects of education that maintain subordinate and dominant racial positions in and out of the classroom. (Solórzano et al., 2000, p. 63).

BFT also can be used in this regard to explain the unique experiences of African-American women faculty in educational leadership at PWIs. BFT in essence allows African-American women to possess a unique standpoint on, or perspective of their experiences and to share those experiences (Collins, 1990). The student scenario above is one case of multiple experiences felt by African-American women faculty in dealing with majority White students in PWIs. Despite, the increasing numbers of African-American women beginning to occupy important positions of authority and prestige in academe, there are forces at work today as in the past that tax the physical and emotional stamina of African-American women, undermine their authority, compromise their competence, limit the power that they might conceivably exercise (Dumas,1979, p. 205).

BEATING THE ODDS

You may shoot me with your words,
You may cut me with your eyes,
You may kill me with your hatefulness,
But still, like air, I'll rise.

—*Still I Rise* (Angelou, 2011)

Finding and applying commonly-accepted concepts and theoretical constructs that are appropriate for explaining and understanding the experiences of African-American women can be challenging. Traditional theories used to explain the status of women in academe, for example, are very general, are from a predominately, if not exclusively, White male perspective and, therefore, might miss important issues encountered or attributes embodied by women, especially African-American women. Current research continues to reveal that issues of racial and gender inequality remain extremely salient features within American Higher education for African-American women (Hughes & Howard-Hamilton, 2003). Given this, the systemic racism that African-American women face in the academy may be observed from a wide variety of lenses/angles. As such, conceptions that use race and gender constructs and explores how the intersectionality of race and gender (Crenshaw, 1990) inform and influence the theorizing conceptions of African-American women scholars in educational leadership today.

Findings, in part, will be situated in the foundation of critical race theory (CRT) to support the assumption of the social creation of realities and the intersection between daily-lived experiences and methods for which individuals negotiate those experiences (Crenshaw et al. 1995). Critical race theory (Delgado & Stefanic, 2001; Villalpando & Bernal, 2002; Smith, Altbach, & Lomotey, 2002) was developed in response to racial oppression in society and seeks to "deconstruct [the] racialized content" (Howard-Hamilton, 2003, p. 22) of institutional practices, curriculum, and research. It takes a stand against avoiding issues of race and history through colorblindness and a historicism. In particular, critical race theory deeply values the knowledge of people of color that is grounded in their daily life experiences. This theory is centered on the transforming empowerment experienced by people of color that is the result of examining the various contexts that construct their identities. Deconstructing and analyzing the socially-constructed realities and experiences of African-American women scholars helps others to understand the struggles and positionality of African-American women in society, and empowers us to affirm, redefine, reinterpret, and reclaim the value of own experiences and aspirations as voice to express hopes for ourselves. Within this theoretical framework, an African-American female scholar shares her experiences, also referred to as "counter stories" in an open, welcoming counter space (Hughes & Howard-Hamilton, 2003, p. 101). Additionally CRT is employed to transform Eurocentrism, paternalism, and classism of the U.S. higher education community (Grant & Simmons, 2008). This approach is particularly well suited for documenting African-American women's stories because the methodology itself models education as a "practice of freedom" (Freire, 1976).

I have recounted throughout this article, specific accounts of racial indignities experienced, whether intentionally or unintentionally initiated, that other women similarly situated and face on an almost daily basis. This has especially been evident in some of my experiences as the only African-American female in the department. I have often been isolated from conversations and informal events—happy hours, office talk, and lunches, for example. I also find that my peers inform me of important decisions after the fact or during a meeting, leaving me little time to respond, react or formally comment. On the other hand, upon arrival to a new environment, there had been this rush to curiosity. I was immediately invited to join the dominant group of colleagues for lunch and expected to respond to the line of inquiry pertaining to my family background, marital status, age, neighborhood of residence, the car I drive, whether I rent or own a home—all things to help reaffirm or defy their negative stereotypes and perceptions of African-American women. Soon after, they have learned (or not learned) all there is about me, it's back to business as usual—being ignored, uninvited and/or unacknowledged and left alone to navigate the cumbersome confines of academe. This is not to say that at all times I am left out of lunch invites in every academic environment. In my current department, I am often asked to join the guys for lunch off campus or in the faculty lounge or in the lunchroom.

Additionally, African-American women faculty in PWI's, continue to experience alienation from their colleagues and superiors (Patitu & Hinton, 2003) and even students. For example, in some department meetings, collaboration on documents, or when there is discussion about policies and guidelines, I have found that when I respond or offer suggestions, my suggestions are ignored and dismissed. Here is an example. The Program Coordinator writes:

> We have tried to include your edits that we have received to date into the "Draft" that we will be forwarding to the Dean later... We will also send you a copy of that draft to you to facilitate further edits...

My response:

> The in-depth edits I provided took time to provide, so I hope they are considered and included in the final outcome of the document style, especially the grammar, punctuation, spacing, and citation corrections, that were provided. Here are my edits once again... I also have cc'd the School Leader so he/she is aware of my edits.

School Leader's response to Program Chair

> Helpful corrections to style issues were suggested throughout the document by Dr. Grant... Therefore, I will work off of her draft...

Program Coordinator's Response as a result of the School Leader's Response:

> Thanks for your hard work on this... Your edits are very helpful...

Scholar Collins (1990, 1998, 2002) recognizes this marginalization, as the "outsider within status" (Howard-Hamilton, 2003, p. 21), in which African-American women in PWIs have been invited into places where the dominant group has assembled, but they remain outsiders because they are still invisible and have no voice when intellectual dialogue and/or collaboration commences. This use of Black feminist thought (BFT) is suggested as an appropriate framework most applicable to the needs of African-American women in higher education (Howard-Hamilton 2003). BFT centralizes and validates the intersecting dimensions of race and gender uniquely experienced in the lives of African-American women in educational leadership (Grant, 2012). BFT was therefore employed as a theoretical framework in this study to better situate my experiences that were empowering, and as feminist practice—"promoting women, people of color, and others who are less favorably positioned within the academy and assisting them in negotiating the relations within the academy" (Moss & Debres, 1999, p. 413).

Race and gender are often internalized in ways that contribute to a significant portion of one's worldview (Smedley, 2007; Zamani, 2003). As members of two groups—African Americans and women—who have been historically oppressed and marginalized, my unique voice offers important insight into the needs and aspirations of African-American women faculty at PWIs (Collins, 2004; Simien, 2006), specifically educational leadership (Grant, 2012, 2014; Grant & Simmons, 2008). Applied in PWI settings, Black feminist thought is significant in assisting African-American women to successfully deal with the wide array of microaggressive acts (i.e., racists attitudes and behaviors) encountered in their daily campus experiences (Howard-Hamilton, 2003). Moreover, telling the story of my transition into academe in a PWI, through scholarly personal narrative can offer insights and solutions on ways to increase African-American women faculty in educational leadership at PWIs (Grant, 2012; Grant & Simmons, 2008; Shealey, Watson & Qian, 2011), while beating the odds against attrition. It is my hope that my narrative provokes new ways of thinking about supporting current and future African-American female faculty, challenges the status quo, and illuminates the research that already exists on African-American women in the academy.

I'M A SURVIVOR...

Does my sexiness upset you?
Does it come as a surprise
that I dance like I've got diamonds
at the meeting of my thighs?

—*Still I Rise* (Angelou, 2011)

These underlying and perpetual oppressive conditions are the interrelated global obstacles of systemic racism and the lack of a critical mass, especially at predominantly White institutions (PWIs) (Bagilhole, 1994; Henry, Thompson & Richards, 2006). For example, Howard-Hamilton (2003) noted that one of the issues that African-American women face when participating in higher education, is that they are confronted with a multitude of "conscious, unconscious, verbal, nonverbal, and visual forms of insults [that] are directed toward people of color, [which] are called microaggressions" (p. 23). This phenomenon was mentioned earlier and I also deal with it through a spiritual dimension as well.

Consequently, reliance on my spirituality has played an integral role with coping with challenges, impediments and oppression as they come. I have been fortunate not to have too many obstacles, but then again, I am new to the academy and have not gone through promotion and tenure. There has been some resistance however in my formal leadership role. In particular, I was appointed by leadership to direct a National Center and when a colleague found out, there was objection and a request for the appointment to be rescinded. When that attempt was unsuccessful, the colleague then proceeds in the following weeks during a program meeting with an attempt to dismantle the center, asking "Do we as a faculty want to be involved in supporting a center, I for one don't want to be involved." However, the other faculty did not support this attempt. This same faculty member has attempted throughout my tenure to undermine every appointment of service bestowed on me, but has been unsuccessful at all levels. Staying the high ground despite the blatant efforts and hint of racism has proven favorable. To this end, Spirituality has been documented as useful in helping African-American women combat "the everyday struggles that come with living in a socially and politically oppressive system" (Watt, 2003, p. 29).

Furthermore, some researchers have defined the role of faith and spirituality as a coping mechanism (Constantine, Miville, Warren, Gainor, & Lewis-Coles, 2006; Thomas, 2001), a point of psychological resistance (Brookins & Robinson, 1995; Robinson & Howard-Hamilton, 1994; Robinson & Ward, 1991) and an identity construct that is emphasized in the African-American woman's plight to develop a positive identity (Stewart, 2002; Watt, 1997). Accordingly, "the search for an integrated identity is intense for African-American women who exist in a culture where being female and being African-American are devalued," (Watt, 2003, p. 32). In essence, the unique intersectionality of the constructs of race and gender contributes to the formation of African-American women's developmental and social identities (Howard-Hamilton, 2003; Stephens & Phillips, 2005). From this perspective and within the common context of African-American female underrepresentation in PWIs, spirituality is useful/used/ important as a strategy to overcome the issues of isolation, marginalization, overt racism sometimes experienced in my PWI settings. I have and continue to pray, attend church, talk to a spiritual advisor and others who are part of my spiritual circle, as a means to survive, and, thus overcome challenges as they occur. I am a survivor! I use my spirituality to re-energize, since there is no single or isolated incident of challenges for African-American women in PWIs, but rather on-going, yet sporadic vituperations.

KEEPING MY HEAD TO THE SKY

Out of the huts of history's shame
I rise
Up from a past that's rooted in pain
I rise
—*Still I Rise* (Angelou, 2011)

African-American academicians often experience isolation from their White peers (Smith, 2000; Tillman, 2001; Simmons, 2007) because of their seemingly controversial research interests (West, 1993; Wilson, 2002). In research pursuits, Thomas and Hollenshead (2001) labeled the result of the widespread lack of support that African-American women experience, "a feeling of invisibleness" (p. 166). These researchers suggested that even in one of the most highly regarded academic activities within the academy, scholarly research, African-American women faculty oftentimes find little support for their research, especially if they are interested in studying issues that affect or pertain to people of color. Coincidentally, my research is focused on social justice research and praxis and advancing scholars of color in academe. I do not apologize for my research agenda. I have been successful at publishing and presenting my research in peer-reviewed settings. Yet, I have been asked my White peers, in particular, (who have no recent publications by the way) on a number of occasions how does my research get published, since it is nontraditional.

Furthermore, many African-American women academicians believe that their research is not valued, their opinions regarding research ideas do not matter to colleagues (Thomas & Hollenshead, 2001), and that they are less likely to be asked by a senior White faculty member to be a coauthor on a publication (Patitu & Hinton, 2003). I have not been asked to collaborate on publications with senior colleagues within my department or institution. However, when the conversation of my research and publications do take place, I am reminded more often than not through subtleties, that expectations of me are lower. I am further reminded of double standards, persistent stereotypes, exclusion from interdepartmental networks, and devaluation and marginalization of my scholarship (Alfred, 2001; Brayboy, 2003; Gregory, 2001; Hendrix, 2007; Holmes, Danley, & Hinton-Hudson, 2007; Moses, 1989, 1997; Patitu & Hinton, 2003; Rockquemore & Laszloffy, 2008; Stanley, 2006; Turner, 2002) that often times can detract from publication success. In one instance, I reported out on the number of publications I had in process and the overwhelming response from around the table was "That is unheard of in one year"... "how do you manage all of that? ..." "that's an aggressive agenda..." "how did you get that work into a major journal like that?..." Well after all, I am qualified to be here, RIGHT?! And I hired here in part to publish, RIGHT?! Yet, when my White counterparts reported on similar amounts of publications in progress, they are referred to as "superstars" It is these types of subtleties that add particular stressors, unique to the experiences of an African-American female scholar in PWIs and can affect your emotional well-being. But don't let it! Keep your head to the sky!!!

AND STILL I RISE...

I'm a black ocean, leaping and wide,
Welling and swelling I bear in the tide.
Leaving behind nights of terror and fear
I rise
Into a daybreak that's wondrously clear
I rise

—*Still I Rise* (Angelou, 2011)

In examining the current status of African-American female faculty, researchers contend that although major gains have been made in the numbers of African-American women working in higher education, they remain severely underrepresented and have not yet obtained the same levels of participation as their White male and female counterparts (Gregory, 2001). African-American female faculty represent 4% of female faculty and total faculty employed at degree-granting institutions (U.S. Department of Education, 2010). At the Assistant Professor level, African-American female faculty numbers are 5,438, with only 1,986 employed as Full Professors.

Today there are more than 33,000 African Americans teaching full-time at colleges and universities in the United States. Nevertheless, the progress into faculty ranks is so slow that, at the current rate, it will take about a century and a half for the percentage of African-American faculty to reach parity. This is based on the current percentage of Blacks in the nation's population. As recent as 2009, some 7% of college and university faculty were African American—95,095 (African American) and 1,078,392 (Whites) out of 1,439,144 (Aud. et al., 2011; NCES, 2011). African-American professors nationally have dropped to 4% or the total number of professors (JBHE, 2010). African-American women females currently account for only 6.8% of all female faculty and 2.9% of all faculty, with their tenure rate and full-rank reflected even lower and as the lowest rate among White males and females and African-American males. The preceding data suggest that African-American women continue to be severely underrepresented in both faculty positions within the academy and their ability to overcome the obstacles that result from systemic racism is greatly hampered by this underrepresentation.

It must be stated that many of the challenges faced by African-American women faculty at PWIs require methods that extend beyond the traditional components of mentoring that I described earlier. Past and recent accounts of barriers and challenges confronting African-American female academicians, including my shared experiences, illuminate the uniqueness of mentoring needs, especially at PWIs. There are two challenges identified in this study based on empirical data: (a) limited numbers of tenured

African-American females within the U.S. professoriate; and (b) the lack of African-American female faculty in educational leadership working at PWIs, thus perpetuating the limited numbers of African-American female mentors for early career and emerging African-American female scholars in educational leadership (Gay, 2004; Grant, 2012; Grant & Simmons, 2008).

These unfortunate realities point to the need for strategic recruitment and retention policies that consider the cultural differences and needs of these women. Further, Academicians need to grapple with and articulate the passionate commitment that propels African-American women in educational leadership, specifically academe, (Grant, 2012). In particular, enhanced mentoring programs at PWIs in Educational Leadership programs across the country should be in play in order to help majority environments more adequately accommodate the myriad of needs of, interests of and barriers for African-American female faculty in educational leadership (Grant & Simmons 2008).

REAPING THE HARVEST

Bringing the gifts that my ancestors gave,
I am the dream and the hope of the slave.
I rise
I rise
I rise

—*Still I Rise* (Angelou, 2011)

African-American women have been extremely resourceful in using their position of marginalization to resist the oppression they have encountered within the academy and society at large despite the enduring history of disenfranchisement they have faced (Thomas & Hollenshead, 2001). In order to maintain this position of resistance, African-American women in the academy must pool their collective energy and continue to proactively identify and participate in formal and informal mentoring relationships; they must pursue both conventional and unconventional connective opportunities. For example, the use of social media (specifically computer-mediated communication mechanisms for networking) is an innovative approach that institutions may employ in helping African-American women manage the challenges they face due to the lack of critical mass and systemic racism they face within the ivory tower. Email correspondence, skyping and on-line instant messaging with mentors have been a value-add to getting quick and immediate strategic advisement and affirmation. Gregory (2001) noted the lack of opportunity that African-American women have to reap the benefits of professional support networks while Phelps (1995) reported that African-American female faculty considered it essential to "have access to others who could validate their experiences, welcome their input, and critique their work" (Gregory, 2001, p. 130).

This article has focused some attention toward the success and challenges of African-American women faculty in educational leadership at PWIs, yet a great deal more qualitative and quantitative research is needed to determine effective ways to assist them in overcoming some obstacles. Research exploring the use and effectiveness of mentoring, spirituality, and involvement in professional networks, as well as creating and maintaining engagement opportunities for African-American women professionals in higher education should be conducted and can expand our knowledge base of additional strategies that can aid in more favorable outcomes and experiences for African-American women in PWIs. All of these acts for African-American women in PWIs to identify, establish, cultivate and maintain relationships will empower them for ultimate success in the academy.

REFERENCES

Alfred, M. V. (2001). Success in the ivory tower: Lessons from Black tenured female faculty at a major research university. In R. O. Mabokela & A. L. Green, *Sisters of the academy: Emergent Black women scholars in higher education* (pp. 56–80). Sterling, VA: Stylus.

Angelou, M. (2011). *And still I rise*. Random House.

Aud, S., Hussar, W., Kena, G., Bianco, K., Frohlich, L., Kemp, J., & Tahan, K. (2011). The condition of education 2011. NCES 2011-033. *National Center for Education Statistics*.

Bagilhole, B. (1994). Being different is a very difficult row to hoe: Survival strategies of women academics. In S. Davies, C. Lubelska, & J. Quinn (Eds.), *Changing the subject: Women in higher education* (pp. 15–28). Bristol, PA: Taylor & Francis.

Bell, D. (1990). Brown and the interest-convergence dilemma. In D. Bell (Ed.), *Shades of Brown: New perspectives on school desegregation* (pp. 90–106). New York Teachers College Press.

Bell, D. (2004) *Silent covenants: Brown vs. Board of Education and the unfulfilled hopes for racial reform*. New York, Oxford University Press.

Bonner, F. B., & Thomas, V. G. (2001, Summer). Introduction and overview: New and continuing challenges and opportunities for Black women in the academy. In F. B. Bonner & V. G. Thomas (Eds.), *Black women in the academy: Challenges and opportunities* [Special issue]. *Journal of Negro Education, 70*(3), 121–123.

Brayboy, B. M. J. (2003). The implementation of diversity in predominantly White colleges and universities. *Journal of Black Studies, 34,* 72–86.

Brookins, C. C., & Robinson, T. L. (1995). Rites-of-passage as resistance to oppression. *Western Journal of Black Studies, 19*(3), 172–179.

Carroll, C. M. (1982). *Three's a crowd: The dilemma of the black woman in higher education.* New York: The Feminist Press.

Chronicle of Higher Education Almanac (2006). Employees in colleges and universities by racial and ethnic group, Fall 2003. Retrieved July 3, 2008, from http://chronicle.com/weekly/almanac/2006/nation/0102602.htm

Collins, P. H. (1990). *Black feminist thought: Knowledge, consciousness, and the politics of empowerment.* Boston: Unwin Hyman.

Collins, P. H. (1998). *Fighting words: Black women and the search for justice.* Minneapolis: University of Minnesota Press.

Collins, P. (2000). *Black feminist thought: Knowledge, consciousness, and the politics of empowerment.* New York: Routledge.

Collins, P. H. (2002). Learning from the outsider within: The sociological significance of Black feminist thought. In C. S. Turner, A. L. Antonio, M. Garcia, B. V. Laden, A. Nora, & C. Presley (Eds.), *Racial and ethnic diversity in higher education.* Boston: Person Custom.

Collins, P. H. (2004). *Black sexual politics: African Americans, gender, and the new racism.* New York: Routledge.

Constantine, M. G., Miville, M. L., Warren, A. K., Gainor, K. A., & Lewis-Coles, M. E. L. (2006). Religion, spirituality, and career development in African-American college students: A qualitative inquiry. *The Career Development Quarterly, 54*(3), 227–241.

Constantine, M. G., Wilton, L., Gainor, K. A., & Lewis, E. L. (2002). Religious participation, spirituality, and coping among African-American college students. *Journal of College Student Development, 43*(5), 605–613.

Crenshaw, K. (1990). A Black feminist critique of antidiscrimination law and politics. *The politics of law: A progressive critique, 195.*

Crenshaw, K. (1993) Beyond racism and misogyny. In M. Matsuda, C. Lawrence, & K. Crenshaw (Eds.), *Words that wound.* Boulder, CO: Westview Press.

Crenshaw, K. (1995). Mapping the margins: Intersectionality, identity politics, and violence against women of color. In K. Crenshaw, N. Gotanda, G. Peller, & K. Thomas, (Eds.), *Critical race theory: The key writings that formed the movement* (pp. 357–383. New York: The New Press.

Crouthers, L. A. (2002). Results matter: When the other teacher teaches English in the bluegrass state. In L. Vargas (Ed.), *Women faculty of color in the White classroom* (pp. 219–236). PeterLang: New York.

Davis, P. (1989). Law as microaggression. *Yale Law Journal, 98,* 1559–1577.

DeCuir, J. T., & Dixson, A. D. (2004). "So when it comes out, they aren't that surprised that it is there": Using Critical Race Theory as a tool of analysis of race and racism in education. *Educational Researcher, 33,* 26–31.

Delgado, R., & Stefancic, J. (2001). *Critical race theory: An introduction.* New York: New York University Press.

Dixon-Reeves, R. 2003. Mentoring as a precursor to incorporation: An assessment of the mentoring experience of recently minted PhDs. *Journal of Black Studies 34*(1), 12–27.

Dumas, R. G. (1979). Dilemmas of Black females in leadership. In L. Rodgers-Rose, (Ed.), *The Black woman.* Beverly Hills (pp. 203–215). CA: SAGE Publications.

Ellis, C., & Bochner, A. P. (2003). Autoethnography, personal narrative, and personal reflexivity. In N. K. Denzin & Y. S. Lincoln (Eds.), *Handbook of qualitative research* (2nd ed.) (pp. 733–768). Thousand Oaks, CA: Sage.

Freire, P. (1976). *Education, the practice of freedom*. London: Writers and Readers Publishing Cooperative.

Gasman, M., Hirschfeld, A., & Vultaggio, J. (2008). Difficult yet rewarding: The experiences of African-American graduate students in education at an Ivy League institution. *Journal of Diversity in Higher Education, 1*(2), 126.

Gay, G. (2004). Navigating marginality en route to the professoriate: Graduate students of color learning and living in academia. *International Journal of Qualitative Studies in Education, 17*(2), 265–288.

Gibson, S. K. (2006). Mentoring of women faculty: The role of organizational politics and culture. *Innovative Higher Education, 31*(1), 63–79.

Glazer-Raymo, J. (Ed.). (2008). *Unfinished agendas: New and continuing gender challenges in higher education*. Baltimore, MD: Johns Hopkins University Press.

Gordon, M. (2004). Diversification of the faculty. In F. W. Hale (Ed.), What makes racial diversity work in higher education: Academic leaders present successful policies and strategies (1st ed., pp.183–198). Sterling, VA: Stylus.

Grant, C. (2014). From chair to podium: A narrative experience of an African American female emerging scholar's entry into the academy. In G. Jean-Marie, C. Grant & B. Irby (Eds), *The duality of women scholars of color: Transforming and being transformed in the academy*. Charlotte, NC: Information Age.

Grant, C. (2012). Advancing our Legacy: A Black Feminist Perspective on the significance of mentoring for African-American women in educational leadership. *International Journal of Qualitative Studies in Education, 25*(1), 99–115.

Grant, C., & Simmons, J. (2008). Narratives on experiences of African-American women in the academy: Conceptualizing effective mentoring relationships of doctoral student and faculty. *International Journal of Qualitative Studies in Education, 21*(5), 501–517.

Gregory, S. T. (2001, Summer). Black faculty women in the academy: History, status, and future. In F. B. Bonner & V. G. Thomas (Eds.), *Black women in the academy: Challenges and opportunities* [Special issue]. *Journal of Negro Education, 70*(3), 124–138.

Guy-Sheftall, B., & Bell-Scott, P. (1989). Finding a way: Black women students and the academy. *Educating the majority: Women challenge tradition in higher education*, 47–56.

Harley, D. A. (2008). Maids of academe: African-American women faculty at predominantly white institutions. *Journal of African American Studies, 12*(1), 19–36.

Harris, T. M. (2007). Black feminist thought and cultural contracts: Understanding the intersection and negotiation of racial, gendered, and professional identities in the academy. *New Directions for Teaching and Learning, 110*, 55–64.

Henderson, C. E. (2005, December). *When and where I enter: Black women in the academy. Diverse*. Retrieved August 7, 2006, from http://www.diverseeducation.com/artman/publish/article_5266.shtml

Hendrix, K. G. (2007). She must be trippin': The secret of disrespect from students of color toward faculty of color. *New Directions for Teaching and Learning, 110*, 85–96. Retrieved August 23, 2008, from Academic Search Premier database.

Henry, M. (1994). Ivory towers and ebony women: The experiences of Black women in higher education. In S. Davies, C. Lubelska, & J. Quinn (Eds.), *Changing the subject: Women in higher education* (pp. 42–57). Bristol, PA: Taylor & Francis.

Henry, W. J., & Glenn, N. M. (2010). Black women employed in the ivory tower: Connecting for success. *Advancing Women in Leadership Journal, 25*(1).

Henry, W., & Nixon, H. (1994). Changing a campus climate for minorities and women. *Equity & Excellence in Education, 27*(3), 48–54.

Henry, W. J., Thompson, G., & Richards, E. (2006). *African-American women in the academy: Best practices for winning the game.* Southern Association for College Student Affairs (SACSA) Conference, Jacksonville, FL.

Holmes, S. L., Danley, L. L., & Hinton-Hudson, V. D. (2007). Race still matters: Considerations for mentoring Black women in academe. *The Negro Educational Review, 58*(1–2), 105–129.

Howard-Hamilton, M. F. (2003). Theoretical frameworks for African-American women. In M. F. Howard-Hamilton (Ed.), *New directions for student services. Meeting the needs of African-American women* (Vol. 104, pp. 19–28). San Francisco, CA: Jossey-Bass.

Hughes, R. L., & Howard-Hamilton, M. F. (2003, Winter). Insights: Emphasizing issues that affect African-American women. In M. F. Howard-Hamilton (Ed.), *New directions for student services. Meeting the needs of African-American women* (Vol. 104, pp. 95–104). San Francisco, CA: Jossey-Bass.

Jackson, S., & Johnson, R. G. (Eds.). (2011). *The black professoriat: Negotiating a habitable space in the academy* (Vol. 6). New York, NY: Peter Lang.

Jean-Marie, G., & Brooks, J. (2011). Mentoring and supportive networks for women of color in academe. In G. Jean-Marie, & B. Lloyd-Jones (Eds.), *Women of color in higher education: Contemporary perspectives and new directions* (pp. 91–107), Volume 10, Diversity in Higher Education Series. Bingley, United Kingdom: Emerald Group Publishing Limited.

Jean-Marie, G., & Lloyd-Jones, B. (Eds.) (2011). *Women of color in higher education: Contemporary perspectives and new directions*, Volume 10, Diversity in Higher Education Series. Bingley, United Kingdom: Emerald Group Publishing Limited.

Johnson, W., & J. Huwe. (2003). *Getting mentored in graduate school.* Washington, DC: American Psychological Association. *Journal of Blacks in Higher Education* (2010). Wealth and access to higher education: The double whammy of race and gender. No. 67, 40–41.

Ladson-Billings, G. (1998). Just what is critical race theory and what's it doing in a nice field like education? *International journal of qualitative studies in education, 11*(1), 7–24.

Matsuda, M., Lawrence, C., Delgado, R., & Crenshaw, K. (1993). *Words that wound: Critical race theory, assaultive speech, and the First Amendment.* Boulder, CO: Westview Press.

Moses, Y. (1989). *Black women in academe: Issues and strategies.* Washington, DC: Association of American Colleges and Universities.

Moses, Y. T. (1997). Black women in academe: Issues and strategies. In L. Benjamin (Ed.), *Black women in the academy: Promises and perils* (pp. 23–37). Gainesville, FL: University Press of Florida.

Moss, P., & K. J. Debres. (1999). Toward mentoring as feminist praxis: Strategies for ourselves and others. *Journal of Geography in Higher Education, 23*(3), 413–427.

National Center for Education Statistics (2008). NAEP 2008 trends in academic progress. http://nces.ed.gov/nationsreportcard/pdf/main2008/2009479_1.pdf

National Center for Education Statistics. (2011). *Digest of Education Statistics, 2010* (NCES 2011–015) Table 199.

Nichols, J. C., & Tanksley, C. B. (2004, October). Revelations of African-American women with terminal degrees: Overcoming obstacles to success. *The Negro Educational Review, 55*(4),175–85.

Patitu, C. L., & Hinton, K. G. (2003). The experiences of African-American women faculty and administrators in higher education: Has anything changed? In M. F. Howard-Hamilton (Ed.), *New directions for student services. Meeting the needs of African-American women* (Vol. 104, pp. 79–93). San Francisco: Jossey-Bass.

Patton, L. D., & Harper, S. R. (2003). Mentoring relationships among African-American women in graduate and professional schools. In M. F. Howard-Hamilton (Ed.), *New directions for student services. Meeting the needs of African-American women* (Vol. 104, pp. 67–78). San Francisco: Jossey-Bass.

Payton, C. R. (1985). Addressing the special needs of minority women. In N. J. Evans (Ed.), *Facilitating the Development of Women: New Direction for Student Services, 29*, 75–90. San Francisco, CA: Jossey-Bass.

Phelps, R. E. (1995). What's in a number? Implications for African-American female faculty at predominantly White colleges and universities. *Innovative Higher Education, 19*(4), 258–259.

Pierce, C., Carew, J., Pierce-Gonzalez, D., & Wills, D. (1978). An experiment in racism: TV commercials. In C. Pierce (Ed.), *Television and education* (pp. 62–88). Beverly Hills, CA: Sage.

Robinson, T. L., & Howard-Hamilton, M. F. (1994). An afrocentric paradigm: Foundation for a healthy self-image and healthy interpersonal relationships. *Journal of Mental Health Counseling, 16*(3), 327–340.

Robinson, T. L., & Ward, J. V. (1991).A belief in self far greater than anyone's disbelief: Cultivating resistance among African-American female adolescents. *Women and Therapy, 11*(3/4), 87–104.

Rockquemore, K., & Laszloffy, T. (2008). *The Black academic's guide to winning tenure—without losing your soul.* Boulder, CO: Lynne Rienner Publishers.

Shealey, M. W., Watson, A. L., & Qian, Z. (2011). Your story is my story: Examining the research literature on Black women in teacher education. In G. Jean-Marie & B. Lloyd-Jones (Eds.), *Women of color in higher education: Turbulent past, promising future* (pp. 127–145). Bingley, UK: Emerald Group Publishing Limited.

Sherman, W. H., Beaty, D. M., Crum, K., & Peters, A. (2010). Unwritten: Young women faculty in educational leadership. *Journal of Educational Administration, 48*(6), 741–754.

Simien, E. M. (2006). *Black feminist voices in politics.* Albany: State University of New York Press.

Simmons, J. M. (2007). Life notes about the dual careers of a black female: Race and gender politics in public school administration and higher education professorship. *Advancing Women in Leadership Online Journal, 22.* http://www.advancingwomen.com/awl/winter2007/JSimmons.htm.

Simpson, B. (2001). *"Can't You Lighten Up a Bit?" Black women administrators in the academy.* Paper presented at the Annual National Conference of the National Association of African-American Studies and the National Association of Hispanic and Latino Studies (Houston, TX, February 21–26, 2000), pp. 1–25.

Smedley, A. (2007). *Race in North America: Origin and evolution of a worldview.* Boulder, CO: Westview Press.

Smith, D. G. (2000). How to diversify the faculty. *Academe, 86*(5), 48–52. Retrieved January 6, 2008, from http://www.aaup.org/AAUP/pubsres/academe/2000/SO/Feat/smit.htm?PF_1

Smith, W. A., Altbach, P. G., & Lomotey, K. (2002). *The racial crisis in American higher education: Continuing challenges for the twenty-first century.* New York: State University of New York Press.

Solórzano, D. G. (1998). Critical race theory, race and gender microaggressions, and the experience of Chicana and Chicano scholars. *International journal of qualitative studies in education, 11*(1), 121–136.

Solórzano, D., Ceja, M., & Yosso, T. (2000). Critical race theory, racial microaggressions, and campus racial climate: The experiences of African-American college students. *The Journal of Negro Education, 69*(1/2) 60. Research Library Core.

Solórzano, D., & Yosso, T. (2001). Critical race and LatCrit theory and method: counter storytelling. *Qualitative Studies in Education, 14*(4), 471–495.

Stanley, C. A. (2006). Coloring the academic landscape: Faculty of color breaking the silence in predominantly white colleges and universities. *American Educational Research Journal, 43*(4), 701–736. DOI:10.3102/00028312043004701

Stephens, D. P., & Phillips, L. (2005). Integrating Black feminist thought into conceptual frameworks of African-American adolescent women's sexual scripting processes. *Sexualities, Evolution, and Gender, 7*(1), 37–55.

Stewart, J. L. (2002). *Factors related to students' decision to remain in band.* (Doctoral dissertation). Available from ProQuest Dissertation and Theses Database. (UMI No. 3110589).

Thomas, D. A. (2001). The truth about mentoring minorities: Race matters. *Harvard Business Review, 79*(4), 98–112.

Thomas, G. D., & Hollenshead, C. (2001, Summer). Resisting from the margins: The coping strategies of Black women and other women of color faculty members at a research university. In F. B. Bonner & V. G. Thomas (Eds.), Black women in the academy: Challenges and opportunities [Special issue]. *Journal of Negro Education, 70*(3), 166–175.

Tierney, W. (1993). *Building communities of difference: Higher education in the twenty-first century.* Westport, CT: Bergin & Garvey.

Tierney, W. G., & Rhoads, R. A. (1993). *Faculty socialization as cultural process: A mirror of institutional commitment* (ASHE-ERIC Higher Education Report No. 93-6). Washington, DC: George Washington University, School of Education & Human Development.

Tillman, L. C. (2001). Mentoring African-American faculty in predominantly white institutions. *Research in Higher Education, 42*(3), 295–325.

Tillman, L. C. (2007). Halls of anger: The (mis)representation of African-American principals in film. In D. Carlson & C. P. Gause (Eds.), *Keeping the promise: Essays in leadership, democracy and education.* (Vol. 305, pp.) New York, NY Lang Publishing.

Turner, C. (2002). Women of color in academe. *Journal of Higher Education, 73*(1), 74–93.

U.S. Department of Education, National Center for Education Statistics, (2010a). *Conditions of education 2007-2008*, Indicator 23 (NCES 2010-028) Retrieved from http://nces.ed.gov/fastfacts/

U.S. Department of Education, National Center for Educational Statistics. (2010b). *Digest of education statistics, 2009* (NCES 2010-013), Chapter 3. Retrieved from http://nces.ed.gov/fastfacts/

Villalpando, O., & Bernal, D. D. (2002) A critical race theory analysis of barriers that impede the success of faculty of color. In W. A. Smith, P. G. Altbach, & K. Lomotey (Eds.), *The racial crisis in American higher education: Continuing challenges for the twenty-first century* (pp. 243–269). Albany: State University of New York Press.

Watt, S. K. (1997). *Identity and the making of meaning: Psychosocial identity, racial identity, womanist identity, self-esteem, and the faith development of African American college women* (Doctoral dissertation, North Carolina State University.).

Watt, S. K. (2003). Come to the river: Using spirituality to cope, resist, and develop identity. In M. F. Howard-Hamilton (Ed.), New directions for student services. Meeting the needs of African-American women (Vol. 104, pp. 29–40). San Francisco, CA: Jossey-Bass.

West, C. (1993). *Prophetic reflections: Notes on race and power in America*. Common Courage Press.

Wilson, S. J. (2002). Retention in the New Zealand Diploma in Business. *New Zealand Journal of Applied Business Research, 1*(1), 195–206.

Zamani, E. M. (2003, Winter). African-American women in higher education. In M. F. Howard Hamilton (Ed.), New directions for student services. Meeting the needs of African-American women (Vol. 104, pp. 5–18). San Francisco, CA: Jossey-Bass.

Zaslow, M., & Martinez-Beck, I. (Eds.). (2006). *Critical issues in early childhood professional development*. Baltimore: Brookes.

CHAPTER 9

NAVIGATING MY CAREER AS A TRAILING SPOUSE

Melanie C. Brooks

I started my career in higher education as a trailing spouse—a following, dragging, straggling, lagging, shadowing, stalking, pulling, and bringing-up-the-rear wife. As many dual career couples know, finding a workplace that accommodates and supports the careers of both spouses is akin to finding the proverbial needle in a haystack. It took my husband Jeff and I four years and three universities before we were offered tenure-track and tenured positions at the same institution. The toll was high. Moving was difficult on our finances, marriage, and children. More challenging, though, were the many unwelcomed opportunities to learn about the dark side of academe: the politics; dishonesty; backbiting; misconduct; carelessness; sexism; and mismanagement that were common in each workplace (Pounder, 2009). As I transitioned from one clinical-level position to the next while Jeff took on tenure-track and tenured positions, I slowly began to put the pieces of the puzzle together. By the end of this time, I had no illusions. I could count on very few people. I found that promises tied in any way to a budget are empty unless they are in writing, however, things are *rarely* (if ever) put in writing. Having said that, while my path was not the one I expected to take, I did finally make it into a tenure-track position where I feel that I fit. I recently completed my first year as an assistant professor and am relieved to be moving forward.

When I reflect on my path to the professorate, I am not indignant or incensed. Upon reflection, having experienced the dark side of academe was a worthy education that gave me the chance to work on skills I will need in order to be successful. I hope that my candor will help others who may face similar experiences, whether as a trailing spouse or simply working to find their own way in academe. Before I discuss my experiences as a new assistant professor, however, it is best to take you along my journey from the beginning including my training for the professorate, the positions that were offered to me as a trailing wife, and the choices we made as a family because of the lack of accommodation and consequential work dissatisfaction, frustration, and disappointment we suffered before finding a good situation. In writing this chapter, I decided to use pseudonyms for the universities where Jeff and I worked previously because what follows are my experiences told from my perspective.

BEGINNING WITH THE END IN MIND: BUT EXPERIENCING A MESS IN THE MIDDLE

I completed my PhD at University 1 in Educational Leadership and Policy Studies (ELPS) with an emphasis on Sociocultural International Development Education Studies (SIDES) in 2009. At the time, I was employed full-time as an education subject specialist librarian at University 1 because I previously earned a master's in library science and worked as a high school librarian. Jeff was an assistant professor in ELPS and, although our workplaces overlapped, we approached my role as a student and his role as a professor with a respectful distance. It wasn't until right before I graduated that we felt the weight of being a dual career couple.

Working at University 1's main library was difficult. It was not my goal to be an academic librarian. I wanted to start my tenure-track career as quickly as possible in international education, policy studies, or a related field. My fears at the time were that life was passing me by, career and research opportunities were slipping away, I would forget my newly developed research skills, and the field would become increasingly inaccessible as I missed annual conferences and opportunities for networking. Additionally, I wanted to leave the dysfunctional culture of the library. I was hired as an education subject specialist. My position required me to be the research and instruction librarian for the college of education. My immediate supervisor and I had a good relationship; however, the department also included two female colleagues who were constantly at odds. They took turns complaining to me about something the other said or did. I did my best to listen and offer modicums of advice, but I did not know what to do to solve the underlying issue of noncompatibility. Coupled with the stress of arguing and disgruntled colleagues, I learned that even though I was the education specialist, the College of Education was somehow another librarian's territory. She was a veteran of the library and said in frank terms that I was to work only with the departments and programs she did not have a strong relationship with. This left me to work with educational psychology, kinesiology, and special education. With this informal job revision, my full-time employment amounted to working with 1/3 of the college, and in areas where I had little expertise. I explained this to my supervisor and he refused to discuss this with the veteran librarian or lead any change. This was the first of many experiences I was to have with what I came to feel was "conflict-avoidant leadership." The upside was that I had a lot of free time. I decided to use this to my advantage and worked to complete my dissertation and begin writing a few manuscripts.

Close to the time when I expected to finish my degree, Jeff approached the dean of the College of Education to request my relocation from the library to a position of some kind in the college, preferably a tenure-track position. The dean valued Jeff's work, as evidenced through a pay raise and increasing responsibilities. Yet, when responding to Jeff's inquiry concerning his wife transferring to the college, the dean responded: "Sometimes you are going to have to leave. I had to leave. But, then I came back." The dean told Jeff that the college does not hire its own graduates, but Jeff and I knew that several of the faculty he worked with everyday earned their terminal degree from University 1. University 1 could bend policies, but with both of us being relatively new to academe, we did not fully understand how to 'be political' to get things done. In hindsight, I wonder if the outcome might have been different had I talked to the dean. I question now why I left it to Jeff to have this conversation? Would going over the dean's head and talking to the provost have changed the outcome? We will never know because we took the dean's advice at face value. We felt that in order for me to have a tenure-track appointment, we would have to relocate to another university.

The Grass is NOT Greener on the Other Side of the Fence

Jeff and I accepted positions at University 2. We built a house and began that August with the idea that we were committed to staying and raising our young family close to the university. Part of our excitement for this opportunity was the promise from the dean of the college of education that I would be able to transition into a tenure-track appointment; however nothing was put in writing. My position was unusual for University 2. I worked

60% of my time in the library and 40% of the time coordinating international programs.

Only a month into our work, we began to recognize systematic barriers that would make it impossible to build successful careers at University 2. I was the first faculty member with a joint appointment between the college of education and the library. My supervisors, both in the library and at the college, did not know how to accommodate my appointment. Mondays, Wednesdays, and Thursdays I worked in the library. I sat at the reference desk when required and taught freshmen library instruction sessions. Tuesdays and Fridays I was expected in the college of education. Although this was a schedule arranged by my library supervisor, the fact that I missed every-other Friday morning caused a huge problem for her and the staff. Time sitting at the reference desk was rotated; twice a month reference librarians were required to sit an extra hour. My supervisor expected me to sit at the reference desk on those Fridays. Yet, my schedule had me in the college of education every Friday. I refused to come into the library and use my college of education time to work at the reference desk. This incensed administration and staff and exacerbated already widening rifts in our workplace relationships.

Library administrators frequently used bullying and intimidation to assert their authority (Tehrani, 2004). One example of this type of bullying I experienced was a direct scolding I received from my supervisor (Gumbus & Lyons, 2011). She asked me into a conference room and as soon as I sat in a chair, she stood above me and pointed her finger in my face. She waved her finger, her face bright red, and yelled at me for not showing enough deference to her or, in her opinion, to anyone in the library. This came as a shock to me. I left the building early that day, crying. I could not see how I had done anything wrong. My job was different, but I still met my responsibilities within the parameters of the joint appointment. Another new librarian confided in me about her experiences with intimidation and bullying, and how she felt she was being set up to fail. There was no collegiality. My supervisors would see me (and other new librarians) and would not acknowledge us or offer a greeting. I dreaded working in this hostile environment (Monahan, 1999; Pounder, 2009). A colleague confided in me after I left University 2 that during my interview for the joint appointment, the search committee relayed that they expected me to fail. Some went so far as to ensure that I did fail. In the end, I guess they got what they wanted.

The situation was similar in the College of Education. My 40% responsibility was to help coordinate international student teaching for undergraduate students. The climate was narrow-minded and prejudicial. In meetings with professors, they were outwardly hostile to the idea of students doing a portion of their internship abroad. One male social studies professor insisted that if he were to let his students go abroad, the collaborating foreign teachers would have to be trained by him and the students would have to complete two semesters of internship, one stateside and the other abroad. Another professor asserted that teachers in other countries were not highly skilled and therefore could not train U.S. teachers. As I identified the problems facing the internationalization of the college and brought these to the administration, I was taken aback when they offered me no support and chose not to get involved. I faced another systemic barrier that I could not overcome. Even though the college joined a consortium to expand international opportunities for students, and hired me to coordinate these opportunities, there was a genuine lack of understanding about the benefits to international travel, teaching and research and I questioned why I was even hired.

Another example of a systemic barrier to my success was the manipulation of power by my associate dean. The importance of writing grants was stressed throughout the college. I took it upon myself to collaborate on an international grant with a faculty member in the college of agriculture, merging the concepts of information access and water safety. When it was time to obtain the correct signatures from the associate dean for research, I received a reprimand for not acquiring his permission before I worked on the grant. He refused to sign the documents until I added soft money to help support an additional administrative assistant for the dean's office. The administrative assistant would have no role in the grant, however. Not only was he not supportive of my grant writing effort, he was dooming me to fail by adding an unneeded and unjustifiable line item in the budget. With this extra position in the budget, we submitted, but did not win the grant. Like in the library, my job as the international education coordinator seemed doomed to fail from the beginning.

Jeff experienced abuse and intimidation from administrators as well and our situation quickly became untenable. I discussed my situation with the dean of the college of education, but she was very slow to change the joint appointment. Nearing the end of the first year, Jeff and I decided as a couple and as a family we were too miserable to continue at University 2 and both accepted positions "back home" at University 3. The impetus behind our decision to relocate was twofold: (a) we both were originally from the state and had graduated from the university; and (b) we were given assurances by several influential administrators within the college that a tenure-track position was a real possibility for me in the near future. I guess I did not learn my lesson the first time, and we moved on a promise. We sold our house for a huge loss (due to the banking crisis of 2010) and moved, once again, and planned to stay at our new location. This state was our home and we put faith in the assurances of the administrators. I went so far as to promise our children that we would stay until they graduated from high school. I regret this promise because, in the end, it was one I did not keep.

Smelling Something Fishy the Moment I Stepped Into the Water

When I arrived at University 3, I was met with a surprise. My contract was not for the three years as previously agreed to, but for a nine month temporary position. I spoke with the individual I negotiated the position with and explained that I would not have taken the position if I had known it was temporary. His response was an uncaring, "It is a step down, that is true." I was angry, but I tried to not let it show. I knew that showing anger would not help solve the problem. I reminded him of our prior conversations and he did change the contract after I was able to produce an email in which he had offered me a three year appointment (Note to readers: when negotiating, keep *everything*). Interestingly though, I was given a very large professional development account, so I wrote up a detailed proposal for a research project focused on libraries in the Philippines. The administrator immediately declined my request stating, "This is just geography. In fact, some people waste their whole careers comparing one country to another." I was taken aback by his ignorance and hubris. After several refusals to access this professional development money, it became clear to me that the tens of thousands of dollars in this account was for reasons that had more to do with hiding the money in a "creative place" than for my "professional development." This was a frustrating education for me in the manipulation of university budgets.

At University 3, I worked hard. I was required to teach a minimum of 180 students a year, all online. It was a demanding workload, but I received good teaching evaluations and many thank you emails from students. Yet, within my department, my contributions, and potential contributions as a scholar, were not acknowledged. They did not care about me as a scholar and were not concerned with my instruction as long as they didn't receive any complaints. When a tenure-track line opened, I was a finalist but the committee called a failed search. They reopened the search, quickly hired someone else, and spent the rest of the year ignoring my contributions to the program. No one ever spoke to me about the outcome of the search, other than my supervisor saying that I would never be qualified because my terminal degree was not in library science. This was a very different view than his original reassurances of my line becoming a tenure-track position. Additionally, the dean would not make accommodations to transfer my line to another department and we were told again, "Well, you just might have to move." Jeff also spoke to the people who had given him assurances about my position and its move to a tenure-track line. One "friend" in particular said he would fight for us, and would do everything he could to keep us at University 3, but, in the end, he did nothing and he himself left the university. It was a sad time because the people who did not step up to help were the same people who, during the recruiting process, promised to be our advocates. This was the first time I sought mental health therapy. I was depressed. I felt stuck. I did not see a future for myself, or a way to achieve the career that I could so easily see at the beginning (Namie & Namie, 2004). We knew as a family that something needed to change. So, once again, we were on the job market. My children were angry, frustrated, disappointed, and scared. They were getting older and moving every other year was becoming a huge burden in their lives. Jeff and I could feel this unrelenting pressure and we desperately wanted to find a place where we fit.

TENURE-SEEKING ASSISTANT PROFESSOR: STILL BEING THE "OTHER HALF"

Iowa. I never visited Iowa before my interview. I knew it as a place that was flat and filled with corn. But, as Jeff and I drove to Ames that day, we were surprised by Iowa's beautiful rolling hills, charming old barns, and the serene fields filled with cows, horses, and tulips. I was offered a tenure-track position as an assistant professor. We celebrated, but also had the unfortunate task of telling our three daughters that we were moving, again. When we sat down after dinner one night to share the news, tears flowed from their eyes. Our oldest stood up and stomped her foot, mad that we would renege on a promise. Our middle daughter cried a deep sobbing cry. They had friends. They were in girl scouts. They liked their lives, and, once again, we were uprooting everything they knew. It was a time of hurt feelings, but, in spite of the pain I was inwardly excited. I was headed now on the path I worked so hard to find. This time, it would be different. Mom would be happy.

Wife, Mom, House, Pets... and Where's My Career?

As a dual-career couple navigating academe, we both stated fervently that our marriage did not conform to typical gender norms—most of the time. Jeff cooked and bathed the baby. I did yard work and hammered nails. Yet, as September turned into October and colder weather brought sick kids home from school early, it was me who stayed home. We quickly slipped into the gendered role of wife taking care of the children, house, doctor appointments, scheduling, grocery shopping, and the day-to-day unforeseen events, and husband taking care of his work. Why did I so willingly take on the household responsibilities? Was it my gender? Was it because society expected the mom to be home? Was it more my responsibility than his? Was it due to our different career stages? Maybe it was all of the above? It was frustrating for me. Jeff was insistent that he was too busy to stay home. He was firm on this issue. I also had a new career to attend to, but I had to set it aside frequently to take care of unforeseen family events. The straw that broke the camel's back was Jeff's travel schedule in the spring of 2012. He went away for six weeks straight at different points in time. Just as we were back into a routine, he would catch another flight. I felt that I missed the whole months of March and April. I was frustrated. Irritated. And, I let him know. We had to find a better balance. Yet, as I write this, we are still working on finding this equitable balance. It is not easy. The homemaker role continues to be largely my responsibility, and I really don't see much of a way around it other than trying to work with life's demands (Brooks, 2012).

Colleagues, Research, Teaching, Service....and Where's My Identity?

Germinal scholars such as Barbara Jackson, Martha McCarthy, and Norma Mertz emphasized the significance of finding and developing strong mentoring relationships. For me, my husband is my mentor. He is a critical friend and his insights and our discussions have been and continue to be invaluable to me as I navigate the political complexities of a career in academe. For several years I struggled working in professional positions that were not a good "fit" and this caused us to dialogue about the importance of identifying and fighting the right battles and to thinking first, and acting later (if I am needing to act at all) (McCarthy, 2009). My ability to identify political quagmires and issues related to rank and hierarchical power has improved through conversations about the complexities of working in higher education (Pounder, 2009). Stated simply, I have learned not to tilt at windmills, thanks to these discussions.

As a result of my husband's connections and having navigated difficult situations before, I was able to start my career a step ahead and without much ambiguity about what I had to do to be successful. Jeff and I have a network of scholars who are a great and valuable source of support for both of us. McCarthy (2009) emphasized the benefits of networking, especially with other young female professionals, both nationally and internationally. On the flip side, although my network has grown out of my husband's, I cannot rely on his professional network for my future. I am focused on and working toward establishing my own identity as a scholar. I am aware that there are people who will find reasons to believe why my success is not legitimate—there are people who question the success of every scholar, for various reasons. In my case, this may be grounded in my marriage, the content or methods of my research, friendships, acquaintances, gender, race, and/or privilege. However, while I am mindful of the various kinds of privilege I enjoy and constantly educating myself about and reflecting on them, I also recognize that I cannot work in a state where I am constantly defending who I am or the work that I do. But, in response to these issues, I feel it is important to approach my work reflectively and in a manner that benefits others (Pounder, 2009).

The Clinical Professor and the Research-Professor Divide

I am a professor of educational administration, but I have not worked as a school principal. I taught English and was a high school librarian. To some, I am not fit to teach in an educational administration program. Much like Nelda Cambron-McCabe experienced when applying for admissions to begin her graduate work in educational administration in the 1970s, there still exists a divide between those who were administrators and now teach and those whose work is focused on research. This gatekeeping criterion—"experience as a school administrator" is alive and well and I experienced it during meetings, personnel decisions, and discussions concerning curricula and programming. But, rather than it coming from tenure-track scholars, the downward gaze comes from clinical faculty who feel that the world of research is separate from the "real world" of schools and principal practice (Bueschel & Cambron-McCabe, 2009, p. 53). I have found these tensions to be like an elephant in the room about which no one will speak. As a young scholar, I feel that this is not an issue for me to address head-on at my university (too politically hazardous). However, I experience the downward gaze frequently, both because I am a woman and because I have not been a school leader. Yet, I have to remind myself that my knowledge and background is of value and what I contribute does improve the education of future school leaders who, in turn, influence thousands of children. I would not do this work if I didn't believe this to be true.

Slowly Moving from Half to Whole

Having shared the circuitous route that has led me to my present career stage, it is important to note that I still have a long way to go and, in many ways, I am only at the beginning. I still see myself as "the other half," but, a "half" that is working hard to become a "whole" separate and independent scholar. Unlike being the nontenure track spousal hire, trailing wife, or spousal accommodation, I am now in control of my future as a scholar. I am content with the pressures this entails—problems, politics, and all. As I reflect on where I have been and the path that I am on now, it is surprising to me that the quote I picked for my high school yearbook is still germane to my current life. It is the last stanza of *Invictis* by William Ernest Henley. Maybe it will ring true for readers as they navigate their own circuitous routes:

> It matters not how strait the gate,
> How charged with punishments the scroll.
> I am the master of my fate:
> I am the captain of my soul.

As I started out on the path toward a tenure-track assistant professor appointment, I would never have guessed how difficult it would be to navigate the world of nontenure track positions. While I worked on my doctorate, I received no mentoring or socialization into the field from my professors or committee members (Mertz, 2009). The opportunities I did have were generated by Jeff's expanding network of scholars. Without his help and willingness to be a critical friend and a mentor, I do not think I could have found a way to survive the bullying, intimidation, hostility, and maliciousness that plagued my young career. What I learned along the way is that I am worthy of respect as a scholar. We decided as a family to not settle for mistreatment and to not allow systemic barriers to mar our chances of success. We are the first to say that the dual career path in academe is difficult, but, with effort, both 'halves' of the couple can find a place to be 'whole.' It just takes time and sometimes you have to walk uphill through many individual and institutional barriers before you get to where you wanted to go all along. The key is to not give up, believe in yourself, and persevere.

REFERENCES

Brooks, M. C. (2012). myworklifebalance.edu. In J. Marshall, J. S. Brooks, K. M. Brown, L. H. Bussey, B. Fusarelli, M. A. Gooden, C. A. Lugg, L. C. Reed, & G. Theorharis', (Eds.), *Juggling flaming chainsaws: Faculty in educational leadership try to balance work and life*. Charlotte, N.C.: Information Age Publishing.

Bueschel, E. V., & Cambron-McCabe, N. (2009). Traversing the fault line. In Norma T. Mertz's (Ed.), *Breaking into the all-male club: Female professors of educational administration*. Albany, New York: State University of New York Press.

Gumbus, A., & Lyons, B. (2011). Workplace harassment: The social costs of bullying. *Journal of Leadership, Accountability and Ethics, 8*(5), 72–90.

Henley, W. E. (1893). Invictus. *Book of verses*. New York: Scribner.

McCarthy, M. (2009). Breaking through. In N. T. Mertz's (Ed.), *Breaking into the all-male club: Female professors of educational administration*. Albany, New York: State University of New York Press.

Mertz, N. T. (2009). Framing the stories. In N. T. Mertz's (Ed.), *Breaking into the all male club: Female professors of educational administration*. Albany, New York: State University of New York Press.

Monahan, D. M. (1999). Brutal bosses and their prey: How to identify and overcome abuse in the workplace. *International Journal of Conflict Management, 10*(1), 85–88.

Namie, G., & Namie, R. (2004). Workplace bullying: How to address America's silent epidemic. *Employee Rights and Employment Policy Journal, 8*(2).

Pounder, D. G. (2009). Goodness of fit. In N. T. Mertz's (Ed.), *Breaking into the all male club: Female professors of educational administration*. Albany: State University of New York Press.

Tehrani, N. (2004). Bullying: A source of chronic post-traumatic stress? *British Journal of Guidance and Counseling, 32*(3).

CHAPTER 10

REFLECTIONS ON PERPETUAL LIMINALITY

Katherine Cumings Mansfield

lim·i·nal·i·ty
noun *Anthropology.*
The transitional period or phase of a rite of passage, during which the participant lacks social status or rank, remains anonymous, shows obedience and humility, and follows prescribed forms of conduct, dress, etc.

While revisiting Norma Mertz's book, *Breaking Into the All-Male Club* and pondering the title of Whitney Newcomb's book, *Continuing to Disrupt the Status Quo?*, I was struck by how on the one hand change *has* taken place in academe. There are more women studying and earning advanced degrees than ever before. On the other hand, however, the huge growth of female graduate students and the modest visibility of women professors has not, in and of itself, allowed an immediate and thorough overhaul in the reign of the status quo in the Ivory Tower. I was reminded of some of the literature I read while completing a doctoral portfolio in Women's and Gender Studies concerning the concept of liminality—or what I call, "outsiderness"—and how women may be *allowed* in the so-called club, but still struggle for full membership with the rights and responsibilities that come with it.

The purpose of this chapter is to define liminality as well as reflect on both the negative and positive aspects associated with the liminal state. Following Sherman, Beaty, Crum, and Peters (2010) who used biographical narrative inquiry in their study of young women educational leadership faculty, I share what the literature on liminality calls, "formative thresholds" to allow readers a window into my life and how liminal space was used in my identity formation as a woman in academe. It is also a story of being "betwixt and between" and my failure to fall in line with prescribed forms of conduct and my resistance to those who would hold me back from living my authentic self. I follow with a discussion of how my experiences coalesce or diverge from other studies on liminality and conclude with recommendations for educational leadership departments in schools of education.

THE PROMISES AND PITFALLS OF LIMINALITY

The concept of liminality has both negative and positive connotations and appears mostly in anthropological works studying the rites of passage amongst a variety of cultures beginning with Arnold Van Gennep's (1909) seminal work, *Les rites de passage*. Gennep's ideas were then further developed by Turner (1967) who focused on the change process of identity formation; especially the period of time whence a person is between identity constructions. Thus, liminality takes on the meaning of a person's identity being "betwixt and between." Within this state, the liminar has few rights, is expected to obey the "elders" and must take a non-questioning, non-threatening stance. And since then, these ideas have been translated across a variety of fields including organizational studies, education, religion, and medicine.

For example, Beech (2011) described liminality as a "state of in betweenness and ambiguity, as it applies to identity reconstruction of people in organizations." Identity work is viewed as coconstructed between neophyte workers (outsiders) and the managers (elite insiders). Researchers study the interplay between the attempts of the elite to "manufacture subjectivities" and the ways people resist or succumb to managerial pressure to produce a "work-imposed identity" or an "authentic self" (p. 285). There is an "agency-structure dialectic" whereby the outsider "constitutes and is constituted by their social setting and the discourses available to them and those around them" (p. 286). So, while an outsider still possesses agency, members of the elite work to restrict personal agency to ensure stability or maintenance of the status quo.

Ziegenhals (2011), writing from the perspective of a seminary scholar, views liminal space as a crucial, formative period that can be used in two important ways: as a traditional sabbatical for seasoned pastors and scholars and as a purposefully-derived protective space for new faculty. According to Ziegenhals, "in order to be fully creative, [established leaders] must let go of what is safe and predictable and spend some time in a liminal space. And during this time, they need to be supported, both institutionally and personally" (¶2).

While individual productivity is essential to institutional integrity, it should also be acknowledged that the "publish or perish" mentality robs individuals of the opportunity to

> process what they've done in the past and clear a space for what they will do in the future. When we are always required to produce, we often lose the needed hours to take stock of where we are and where we might go. We lose the opportunity to brainstorm freely, without a goal or objective in mind. (¶9)

In addition to supporting seasoned faculty, Ziegenhals (2011) advocates the practice of a "liminal year" for new faculty to enable them to find their "footing and voice in a new work environment" (¶10). The liminal year protects new faculty from serving on committees or having other institutional responsibilities. That way, they might focus on honing their teaching skills and organizing their research agendas. Obviously, these practices require strong institutional support and supportive colleagues willing to take on additional responsibilities to afford others a period of temporary liminality.

Cook-Sather and Alter (2011) studied a specific program that was designed to challenge the traditional expectations and responsibilities between faculty and students in higher education settings. Their findings add to our understandings of the promises and pitfalls of liminality. Cook-Sather and Alter view the liminal state as something that can be very powerful in that it has potential to challenge the status quo. But they also acknowledge that the liminal state is dangerous because those who dwell there are "never secure: their position is never fixed but, instead, constantly shifting and vulnerable" (p. 38).

Cook-Sather and Alter (2011) found that to be successful, it was essential for liminars to "sit with the discomfort" of being in an unclassifiable situation. They also found that liminars who took advantage of the liminal space by inviting others to dwell with them there to envision "what is and what can be," where better positioned to challenge traditional hierarchies between student and faculty (p. 48). They also found that the some student participants were able to overcome the "negative feelings of being overwhelmed that can come with existing in an in-between space" and were able to develop unique skills and abilities that enabled them to "act as a bridge between multiple communities" (p. 50). This bridging work was made possible by the fact that the student participants were dwelling in a liminal space and not expected to conform and perform as either student or faculty, but somewhere in between as consultants.

Liminal Practices

Liminality is the phenomena of being on the threshold of something, while liminal practices describe some of the ways liminals cope within this liminal space. Beech (2011) found that liminal practices often include: experimentation, reflection, and recognition. *Experimentation* is akin to a person trying out versions of the self similar to shopping and trying on clothing to see what "fits" the individual's body and perceived image as well as attempting to find what might be "presentable" to the elite. During this stage of identity development, a person may entertain contradictory or paradoxical identity elements as they "move towards a desired identity" or "resist the imposition of an unwanted identity" (p. 289).

In addition to experimentation, the act of *reflection* is an important liminal practice. During this period, the individual participates in active self-questioning and either absorbs or reacts to external influences and perceptions. After reflection comes *recognition* or understanding which can come suddenly as a type of epiphany or more slowly as a gradual "dawning" of their relationship with the new society and arrival at new identity construction (Beecher, 2011). These recognitions are sometimes referred to as, "The Formative Thresholds" or "triggering events" that act as a "jolt" of learning for a person during identity work (Beecher, 2011).

Communitas

Within this space of identity formation, often appears a phenomenon Turner (1969) named, "communitas." Communitas, a Latin noun, refers to an unstructured community or the spirit of a community of people. Communitas can be experienced by fellow liminars who are experiencing liminality together within which exists an intensity of camaraderie and solidarity despite the fact that they may have nothing else in common but their liminality. Yarnal (2006) described communitas as "being apart together" that does not usually occur outside of liminal space due to the inflexibility of everyday life. Mascia-Lees, Sharpe, and Cohen (1987) interpreted Turner's ideas on communitas as

> experienced by individuals who, by virtue of their shared participation in rites of passage or their shared position as marginals or outcasts, are jointly liminal. It is an experience analogous to a state of grace, a state of communion among liminals. (p. 108)

Importantly,

> *communitas* does not merge individual identities. People from different walks of life may form strong bonds because they are removed from the social and cultural constraints of daily life, but the gifts of each person are alive to the full. (Yarnal, 2006, p. 56)

Communitas can also describe the experience of the entire community—liminars and elders—as they share a common rite of passage. This shared heritage acts as empathizer and equalizer: No matter where one is in the organizational hierarchy, all have dwelled in liminality and have at one time or another accomplished the common rite of passage (Beech, 2011).

Reassimilation and Extended Liminality

While liminality is often understood to be a temporary transition during which identity is reconstructed, it can also be considered a long-term state of ambiguity and in-between-ness. This extended liminality, marked by a disrupted sense of self, can be damaging to a person's psyche (Beech, 2011). According to Beech (2011), in order for reassimilation to be complete, the liminar must understand, and have a clear picture as to the specific phases of, the liminal period and must be supported during this time of change by the elders. This is best accomplished by providing supportive mentorship accompanied by specific, anticipated rituals that mark the plebe's progress toward full integration with the society. A lack of mentoring, or a process devoid of rituals that mark out the liminar's progress toward full membership, can be injurious to the individual and ultimately, the organization or society.

While extended liminality has its negatives, Gloria Ladson-Billings, in her seminal piece, "Just what is critical race theory and what's it doing in a *nice* field like education?" (1998) wrote about the power of being a "permanent outsider" who "call[s] into question the rules" of American society (p.19). She speaks of the need for educational researchers to *purposely assume* a liminal position as outsider in order to disrupt the status quo. Likewise, she also lamented the fact that most educators regard themselves as "permanent residents in a *nice* field like education" who never will venture into liminal space with the outsiders because it is uncomfortable, even dangerous, work.

Mascia-Lees, Sharpe, and Cohen (1987) took ideas on liminality and applied to women's position in the academy and determined that women could be automatically assumed to dwell in a type of extended liminality since they had been historically marginalized. Furthermore, black women, being neither male nor White dwelled in a type of "double liminality" that, on the surface, may seem to be a prostrate position, when in fact, the liminality of women generally, and double liminality of black women in particular, could be used in a powerful way to usurp the status quo.

> Historically, both as subject and as researcher, women's position in the academy has been marginalized. While this is a fact that feminists have traditionally

decried, more recent work in feminist scholarship has begun to recognize the liberating potential of this position... to raise substantial challenges to traditional "truths" that have defined what women are and can become, but also to raise epistemological challenges to the underlying assumptions and methods of those disciplines. Responding to our marginalization and questioning the traditional competitive nature of the academy, many feminist scholars have turned to collaborative research efforts, finding the strength in community with other women scholars to envision insights challenging to the academy. Furthermore, feminist scholars' unifying focus on women's oppression had demanded interdisciplinary approaches, which by their very nature are "betwixt and between." Thus, from the position of marginality...feminist scholars have produced powerful new insights into women's realities and into the constraints and biases of mainstream thinking and institutions. (pp. 101–203)

Thus, while liminals (women) are outsiders in terms of normative structure and "betwixt and between the interstices of culture," Mascia-Lees, Sharpe, and Cohen (1987) view liminals (women) as "imbued with a tremendous magical potency" (p. 104). They also point out that Turner's (1969) ideas on communitas emphasized the existential and the subjective. Thus, women experiencing the power of communitas transcend the individual sense of self to a community identity that creates a sense of bonding and sharing that is potent and positive. Their "otherness" is perceived as *what they can become*, rather than couched in what they are not.

FORMATIVE THRESHOLDS

Following Sherman, Beaty, Crum, and Peters (2010) who used biographical narrative inquiry in their study of young women educational leadership faculty, the following description of formative thresholds also allow readers a window into my life. In the interest of time and space, these formative thresholds are only brief snap shots to convey important learning experiences that acted as "jolts of learning" in my identity formation and in my understanding of my positionality in academe.

"Only Wealthy WASPs Welcome"

At fourteen, my mother told me I was smart and that I needed to go to college in order to make something of my life. I was not sure how to go about accomplishing this, so I made an appointment with the school counselor to discuss my academic future.

After introducing myself to the counselor, I asked, "What do I need to do to go to college?" Laughter immediately ruptured the silence. I waited for her words, but none were forthcoming. I repeated my question, to which she shook her head and chuckled again. I asked, "Did I say something funny?" She answered, "Well, you aren't exactly college material." I felt ashamed of my ragged hand-me-downs and her gape that named me *white trash*. My cheeks were aflame as I realized she must know about the verbal taunts. The punching. The kicking. How the echoes of high heels crescendoing on concrete sent them scurrying like roaches sensing impending light. This was the first of many times that desperation held shame captive long enough to audibly hear my voice interrogate that which could never be bound.

"How would you know I'm not college material? You don't even know me." She answered, "For one thing, people who go to college take at least two years of foreign language." She raised her eyebrows when I told her I already had three years of French and planned to graduate from high school with six years of foreign language on my transcript. She retorted argumentatively, "Well, have you had chemistry yet? I bet not!" I had to admit that I had not had chemistry yet, but immediately added, "But, that is why I am here. To find out what I need to do to go to college." I asked her to please write down all the classes I needed to take for the rest of my high school years in order to make that happen. I tried to hand her a piece of notebook paper and a pen. She raised her palm in a "stop right where you are" gesture, and then stated in a dismissive tone that she did not believe I would ever go to college. I left angry but undaunted and brought the matter up again at my third high school.

The first week of school, I went to the counselor's office and asked the same question: "What do I need to do to go to college?" But now, I'm a junior. This is when most people have taken their college entrance exams and are already applying to the very best schools for early acceptance. The counselor was meeting with someone, but the secretary offered to help me. The first question she asked me was what my GPA was. "What's a GPA?" was my answer. She seemed surprised, but said calmly, "Hmm. Well, let's find out!" And she dug in this giant file cabinet for my "permanent record" and found that my current GPA was a 2.6. A slight shadow cast over her face and I asked, "Is that bad?" And she said, "To be honest, most colleges look for at least a three-point-oh, but don't you let this get you down! This is something you can change. It is not too late."

She got out her bulky calculator and figured out what I needed to get as far as grades in order to raise my current GPA to a 3.0 by the end of my senior year. She made me a list of courses that I had to take in order to have a solid course of study. Her only concern was getting in the foreign language requirements at such short notice. She was surprised and delighted to learn that I had already taken four years of French and had earned all "A's" in that. She then made me promise that I would study harder and turn all my work in. She also made me promise I would come and visit her after every marking period each quarter to see how I was doing and to get a pep talk.

And I did. I visited her every quarter. And every quarter she would praise me for my good grades and get out that old, giant calculator and figure out what my current cumulative GPA had become. Every quarter, it went up. And she would rejoice with me. One quarter, during my senior year, I got a 4.0 and she literally squealed with excitement, jumped from her chair, and hugged me! Everyone else in this larger office area emerged from their smaller offices and wanted to know what was going on. They all rejoiced with me, too. It was wonderful!

This secretary also told me when it was time to take college entrance exams and helped me choose between the SAT and ACT. She also asked me what I wanted to study in college (I still could not decide. It was either medicine or education or French). She told me about a scholarship opportunity for future teachers and I applied. I prayed to God and said, "Dear God, I don't know what I want to be when I grow up. I need a sign. If you want me to be a teacher and not a doctor, please give me a sign by awarding me this scholarship." And God did.

"My Head is Full of Children"

"My head is full of children" the T-shirt read in the 1990s mail order catalogue. The artwork showed a woman's countenance with diminutive figures of children placed on her head like a crown. "That is definitely me," I thought. "There's Jamal!" (Everyone said he was most-likely retarded and possibly crazy. He turned out to be one of the most brilliant and wise children who ever taught me). "And there is Yasmine!" (I dreamily recall her gleaming, caramelized cheeks framed by an explosion of beads and braids reminiscent of Independence Day sparkler shows. I smile affectionately as I remember how her fancy dresses were almost always diligently tucked into the waist of her white hosiery when she returned from using the restroom. And her proud walk that accentuated the clicking of her glossy, black Mary Janes.) "And there's Sarah. And Jason. And the other Sarah. And the other Jason." (There were so many Sarahs and Jasons in the 1980s and 90s).

During my years as a public school educator, I did not refer to myself as a "leader for social justice" or really consider myself much of a leader at all. I just knew I loved my work and felt "at home" teaching and serving children and their families. It seemed as natural as breathing for me to question leadership on why there were more "free and reduced lunch" students referred for special education and more middle-class students identified as gifted and talented. I thought it was normal to interrogate the gender divide in math and science or bring to people's attention the way gifted girls opted out of being smart as soon as they hit puberty. It never once occurred to me that I was doing something extraordinary when I worked against the grain of policy and practice to ensure equal opportunity for students. It just seemed like the right thing to do.

Depending on my principal, my questions were either met with communion or a roll of the eyes. Mr. Wise, a budding scholar, empathized with my desire to create change. Together, we began the process of working within the existing system to make needed transformations. Our first goal: changing the minds and hearts of teachers who were the gatekeepers as they were usually the preliminary "nominators" for advanced programs for students. Unfortunately, after working with Mr. Wise for only one year on our antideficit-thinking strategies, he left for an advanced career opportunity outside of the public school system.

Then came Mr. Dick, aka: The Coach. (Yes, he literally preferred that we call him, "Coach" and refer to him as, "The Coach.") All I can say is, thank God Mr. Wise was my first principal because this guy was a hot mess! Not only did he tell me to "let go" of ever trying to change things in gifted or science education because, "That's just the way things are." He also told me that I, "like most women," was too "naïve and emotional to be a principal" and advised me to drop out of the master's program! Thankfully, I saw Mr. Dick for what he really was and followed my heart, which, led me to some amazing educational positions outside of the public school system, in addition to eventually becoming a stay-at-home mom before returning to the public school system several years later.

When I returned to the public schools after working in a hospital setting for a few years and taking a sabbatical from professional life to raise my two children, I was astonished by how much things had changed! First of all, women were everywhere in leadership! I was thrilled. During the time I worked on my master's degree, very few women were principals. However, during the job search process during my reentry to the profession, almost all people with whom I interviewed were female principals. Second, the fact that the principals were doing the interviewing at the building level was a significant change. In the past, this was done at the central office level and job candidates were then placed into "holes" as openings came up. (Honestly, it was a pain having to apply separately to each opening in a single district, but it also provided an opportunity for candidates to check out the specific school site and individual principals and teachers to gauge for fit. I really appreciated this as I had become very picky in my old age and felt that I was interviewing *them* as much as they were interviewing me.) Third, my impressions of these individual schools were strikingly different from how I felt walking into my first school as a new teacher twenty years ago; from painted rock gardens to floral landscapes on the outside to beautifully decorated main offices and bathrooms on this inside, gone was the air of cold "institution" and in its place was a feeling of home. I was especially impressed that the adult bathrooms I used in each school had a pretty, little basket filled with tampons and sanitary napkins "just in case." I could not wait to get back to the classroom!

As an "older woman" reentering the field, I did not feel like an outsider at all. And the four years I spent back in the classroom before entering a PhD program did not disappoint. I was surrounded by amazing women working their butts off for kids. I left convinced that women really had changed the landscape of leadership in schools. However, it was also evident that this transformation was partial and incomplete due to what I felt was a backlash against the influx of women leaders in schools: Politicians pressed for controlling legislation from high-stakes testing and other "accountability" policies in addition to the movement to weaken teachers' unions. I was disheartened to find how nonpolitical most school folk at the local level seemed to have become. But, I remained optimistically hopeful as I entered the world of academe as a PhD student in educational policy.

"It Was the Best of Times, It Was the Worst of Times"

The five years I spent studying for the PhD were some of the most wonderful years of my life that included exponential intellectual and spiritual growth and the development of what I know will be life-long friendships and professional relationships. They were also trying times, however, as it was a very stressful trying to balance my responsibilities as a mother, wife, and daughter with those of working several part-time jobs and fulfill the various requirements of a very rigorous PhD program (please see Mansfield, 2012 for additional details).

Sometimes I felt like the educational process was more akin to fitting a "square peg in a round hole" (or, trying to stuff a woman into a manhole?). It really depended on whom you chose to hang out with. I learned very quickly that there seemed to be a rift in the academy between those who were "old school" and those who seemed more open to embracing new ways of thinking about educational leadership, research methods, and personal orientations. Dichotomous messages did not just spring forth from professors, but from students as well. Interestingly, age had nothing to do with it. Some of the ancient professors were the most enlightened and some of the youngest students were the most obnoxiously trying to preserve the status quo.

For example, one day, during my fifth year in the program, I received an email from a second-year PhD student (whom I had never met) telling me what to wear and how to act at a professional conference! Apparently, unless all of us looked like a male model in a "Lands' End" catalogue and kept our mouths shut while in the presence of eminent scholars (among several specific directives); we would be an embarrassment to him and the entire scholarly community. After thinking on it awhile, I responded to this young man. I did not reply to "all" as I did not want to humiliate him, but only wanted to let him know how his email offended me, personally.

> I do not know you, but I received an email from you today (below) telling me how to dress, what to consume and how to talk while I am at AERA. Please do not send any more patronizing emails out to the entire department... I have attended AERA 5 years and have seen all manner of dress and much of it is not "business casual." In fact, many people dress very creatively... There is no "uniform." Secondly, AERA is one of the few venues where it is entirely appropriate to have philosophical and methodological discussions (positive, negative, mixed). That is what AERA is for. It is for us to engage with ideas and fellow scholars. Encouraging your friends (one-on-one and face-to-face) to be respectful is fine, but admonishing the entire department via email to keep their ideas to themselves until they get home is an inappropriate attempt to silence voices... Thirdly, in the past 5 years at a total of 13 conferences, I have seen what you would probably label as inappropriate drinking because it led to someone saying something they might regret the next day. In the first instance, I pulled the male student aside and quietly told him to stop harassing my friend. When he refused to stop, I went and found his academic mentor and told him what was going on. He quietly pulled him aside and walked him "home." In the second instance, a female student colleague had drunk too much... One of her close friends pulled her aside and talked with her a few minutes before walking her "home." (One of these instances was a UT student; the other was a student from a different university). These scenarios are rare, but of course, do occur in any environment from time to time. And, I believe they should be handled on a case-by-case basis as needed. But to assume that we, as a department, need to be warned by you ahead of time for overindulging or there will be bad consequences is just absurd.

I did not hear back from this young man. According to others, he shared with his entire cohort my response in an attempt to make me look like a bully. However, it had the opposite effect—at least with some people. In addition to emails, women students would stop me in the halls and thank me for what I had done. The common thread among them was that they all had wanted to respond in like fashion but were too scared. They did not want to "piss this guy off" because he was a "very controlling person" and they had to "deal with him the next several years." In addition, they really weren't sure whether there was a "uniform" to wear and were so "relieved to hear from an advanced student" that they could "just be themselves." They also appreciated that any "guidance" that should be given to others would be based on a personal relationship rather than some invisible list of rules that one must follow or be denied a future job in academe.

To be fair, this young man *may* have been genuinely trying to help others. I did not know this young man, so I could not truly judge his true intentions. However, based on feedback I received from a handful of female students, it seemed my response was warranted. In addition, to be fair, I had already defended my dissertation and was now a part of the club. I was not afraid of this student and felt confident "putting him in his place." This could be interpreted as a misuse of power. I shared these misgivings with my confidants. While they understood why my heartfelt tender, they reminded me that sometimes, we must be "the bad guy" on behalf of others. I have mixed feelings. I think what I said was correct, but wonder if I should have just clicked, "respond all" and gave the entire list serve my "take" on the topics that were thrown in the public sphere.[1]

"Only the Rational Nonreligious Need Apply"

The problem with feeling like you finally "made it" is forgetting that this position is fleeting—especially for women living at the intersection of a variety of identities. This became especially clear during the job search process the spring I defended my dissertation.

On the positive side, my professors were extremely pleased that my application packages were "getting a lot of play" from some great schools. Most interviews went well and even resulted in job offers. It was just a matter of determining which offer would justify moving my entire family across the country and all that goes with that decision. Things were going rather smoothly, but a storm was on the horizon that I was not prepared for.

I was invited to Napoleon Complex University (NCU) for two days of teaching a graduate level course in law, presenting my dissertation research to faculty and doctoral students, interviewing with faculty, department heads, dean, etc. It was both exhausting and invigorating. About midway through my second day on campus, during the interview with the department faculty, a question was posed to me: "What scholars have influenced you and how?" I began telling them how my affiliation with UCEA (University Council for Educational Administration) has been especially important to my development—from working and learning with the Executive Director, Dr. Michelle Young, for three years to meeting other scholars like Dr. Linda Tillman and Dr. Catherine Lugg that have been especially helpful. I referred to these scholars as being a real "blessing" to me. "The" senior scholar in the room interrupted in a loud tone: "If you say 'blessing' one more time . . . !" I know I looked at him inquiringly. Then he added, "I am an atheist and your religiosity is very offensive to me." He then went on to ask, "I mean, how religious *are you* anyway? Because I'm *not* going to hire a *Jesus freak*!" (Does he assume I am a Christian because I'm White or what? What if I were brown? What would he say? "I hate Muslims"?) In my peripheral vision, I could see that three or four faculty were so startled by this comment that they literally jumped in their chairs! However, no one said or did anything.

I wanted to get up and run away. The hostility of this man and the lack of support from others was truly frightening. Further, I knew what was happening was against the law. I knew I could file an EEOC complaint against NCU for what was happening in this very moment. I felt so powerless and didn't feel I had any choice but to stay and make the best of it.

So, I apologized to this senior scholar for being offensive and let him know that I was only speaking so informally (saying words like "blessing") because most folks there had been so warm and inviting, that I felt very comfortable speaking in my usual vernacular. I thanked him for his criticism and went on to try to tie this criticism of "religiosity" to my academic journey and how over the past five years I had been processing my ontology, epistemology, etc. and reconciling some conflicting identities within my own persona, for example, problematizing whether it was even possible for a feminist to be comfortable within "The Church."

After several minutes of silence, a junior scholar (an openly gay man) very quietly and gently said, "I feel Katherine has some really important things to say and I feel it is important for us to be open to her. I mean, what are we going to do, say we're for diversity but then pretend we don't all have different religious or spiritual beliefs that are a part of our identities?"

I wanted to run across the room and embrace this man for coming to my defense. I quickly realized I really didn't need to. I felt his hug across the table in a deep, spiritual sense. I knew my candidacy was burning in a trash heap out back, but his words, which acted as a protective cocoon in this unsafe space, gave me the strength to go on and finish the interview. It was not until I returned home to my family that I was able to face the annihilation that had occurred and let myself mourn.

Over the next few days, I received encouragement from a handful of professors who became aware of what had happened. One professor wrote, "I hope this e-mail finds life treating you a bit more gently. A little birdie told me you had something truly shitty happen in the midst of a job interview. Here's a giant hug..." Another professor empathized and told me not to beat myself up about continuing because it was a "very tough situation to face and very unfair." Another professor wrote,

> I am sorry that happened to you. That's beyond inappropriate and just unacceptable behavior. Yes, it's illegal! It is also illegal to openly make a judgmental statement about the hiring decision to you as a candidate and tie it directly to your religion (which you should not be asked to declare in the first place!). At this point, I feel this needs to be addressed on a broader level. This is just unconscionable!

Finally, one professor offered to act as a reference in any future job applications and wrote that what I had experienced was "one of the unfortunate aspects of our profession." She added, "Don't worry. You are blessed and Highly Favored!"

REFLECTIONS AND RECOMMENDATIONS

While the experiences shared above rightly suggest that some experiences in academe directly related to resisting imposed identities, the opposite is also true. There were important moments that proved like-minded individuals were fighting the good fight to make the Ivory Tower a more inviting place for outsiders. Women, people of color, those who spoke languages other than English, gays and lesbians, Christians, Muslims, and non-believers and questioners of all walks of life. This commitment to social justice clearly led me (and others) to experience what the literature on liminality termed, c*ommunitas* means on a personal level.

Communitas began with finding fellow liminars who were also struggling. A diverse assemblage of allies that would provide a sense of belonging and hope. This rag tag collection of scholars eyeballed each other, cautiously at first. The Lesbian wondered if the Christ-lover's *Agape* would include her. The Black man wondered if the White feminist's quest for civil rights dared consider race as important as gender. The international student worried whether her accent would be misinterpreted, again, as lack of intelligence. All, hungry for *Philia*, risked further annihilation of personhood by extending the hand. Clearly, I would never have survived, even flourished, in academe if it were not for this sense of communitas that the ambiguity of liminality induced. I learned that although I am a singular soul, I really cannot claim to have done anything at all single-handedly. I have so many people to acknowledge for their support and help.

For me, the best thing about being an "outsider" is finding other "outsiders" as companions. For the most part, my companions were women who were first-generation college students still supporting their families of origin. Thankfully, professors (junior and senior ranks), who also experienced different degrees of outsiderness, came alongside us on our journeys. This entails some risk—especially for those who have been burned before. Nevertheless, finding communitas is absolutely essential to survival in academe.

The major ritual that any doctoral student goes through is, of course, the final oral defense of the dissertation. This is the final test. After that, you are called, "doctor." You have proved yourself worthy to enter the club. Unfortunately, the time it takes to get to this point is long and difficult. It is helpful if universities have a clearly drawn path with clearly marked milestones to get to this point. Qualifying exams, comprehensive exams, specialization exams, and the like do provide some direction. Another helpful practice is a formal mentoring program that might act as additional support for the liminar in her/his quest in this liminal space. Unfortunately, mentoring is often the missing piece when it comes to higher education generally and women and people of color in educational leadership preparation programs specifically (see Mansfield, Welton, Lee, and Young, 2010; Young & Brooks, 2008). This needs to change. So far, the field seems to recognize the importance of increasing the presence of women and people of color in higher educational arenas. However, to date, relatively little has been done to smooth the paths of those who attempt to do just that. Unfortunately, we still seem to insist that newcomers "fit" with the old, white, male mold. The Ivory Tower struggles to impose an outdated identity on liminars, rather than allowing itself to transform into something that is truly diverse in every way. Mentoring needs to include structure (helping students find their way through the maze that is doctoral studies requirements) and anti-structure (helping students find their own voices rather than forcing them to conform to something other than their authentic self).

CONCLUSION

As the profession witnesses the emergence of women, women—especially those who don't fit the WASP mold—still struggle to negotiate political and/or academic spaces often acknowledged as "interstitial" or "liminal." And, yet, younger (i.e., newer) female educational leadership scholars now have access to successful and, now classic works of, senior female educational leadership scholars. Thus, one can instantly recognize that we are at a threshold of expanding the purview of what it means to be identified as a woman educational leadership professor and researcher that has potential to transform the field in significant ways. We are at a historical, social, and political moment that deserves celebration as well as serious contemplation on how educational leadership preparation programs have changed due to the presence of women and people of color and those who would join them in *purposeful, perpetual liminality* to effect purposeful, perpetual and substantive change.

I look to the future with expectation because of the nomadic but substantive souls who embraced me in the borderlands. The interstices. Those who, like me, had struggled and continue to struggle with identity politics. This was only possible because of people like Papa Scribner who reaches out, takes chances, and "lets in" the riff raff that is slowly but surely, becoming a loose collective of powerful voices for change. I liken it to a choir of sorts—all of us so unique and different, with strengths and weaknesses, different gifts and contributions to make—but when conjoined by a vision for social justice, manage to blend their voices into something beautiful even if sometimes cacophonous.

The possibilities are endless. Therefore, I embrace perpetual liminality and those blessed souls in the borderlands. I invite you to take our hands and come along. The field of education needs you.

NOTE

1. Unfortunately, a couple of years later, this man misused his power against me while in a gate keeping position. I was given an opportunity to reveal his unethical behavior to those who could remedy the situation, but chose to refrain from seeking retribution. I reasoned that his ugliness would reveal itself to others, in time, without my help.

REFERENCES

Beech, N. (2011). Liminality and the practices of identity reconstruction. *Human Relations, 64*(2), 285–302.

Cook-Sather, A., & Alter, Z. (2011). What is and what can be: how a liminal position can change learning and teaching in higher education. *Anthropology & Education Quarterly, 42*(1), 37–53.

Ladson-Billings, G. (1998). Just what is critical race theory and what's it doing in a *nice* field like education? *Qualitative Studies in Education, 11*(7), 7–24.

Mansfield, K. C. (2012). "Flying by the seat of my pants." In: J. Marshall, Ed, *Juggling flaming chainsaws: Faculty in educational leadership try to balance work and life* (pp. 113–121). Charlotte, NC: Information Age Publishing, Inc.

Mansfield, K. C., Welton, A., Lee, P., & Young, M. D. (2010). The lived experiences of female educational leadership doctoral students. *Journal of Educational Administration, 48*(6), 727–740.

Mascia-Lees, F. E., Sharpe, P., & Cohen, C. B. (1987). Double liminality and the black woman writer. *American Behavioral Scientist, 31*(1), 101–114.

Sherman, W. H., Beaty, D. M. Crum K. S., & Peters, A. (2010). Unwritten: Young women faculty in educational leadership. *Journal of Educational Administration, 48*(6), 741–754.

Turner, V. (1967) *The forest of symbols: Aspects of Ndembu ritual.* Ithaca, NY: Cornell University Press.

Turner, V. (1969). The ritual process: Structure and anti-structure. The Lewis Henry Morgan Lectures 91966). Ithaca, NY: Cornell University Press.

Van Gennep, A. (1909). *Les rites de passage.* (M. B. Vizedom & G. L. Caffee, trans.). London: Routledge.

Yarnal, C. M. (2006). The Red Hat Society®: Exploring the role of play, liminality, and communitas in older women's lives. *Journal of Women and Aging, 18*(3), 51–73.

Young, M. D., & Brooks, J. S. (2008). Supporting graduate students of color in educational administration preparation programs: Faculty perspectives on best practices, possibilities, and problems. *Educational Administration Quarterly, 44*(3), 391–423.

Ziegenhals, G. E. (2011). Liminality and leadership. *Faith & Leadership: Leadership Education at Duke Divinity.* Available at: http://www.faithandleadership.com/content/liminality-and-leadership?page=full&print=true

CHAPTER 11

MY RELATIONSHIP WITH ACADEMIA AS A LATINA SCHOLAR

Melissa A. Martinez

... for better, for worse, for richer for poorer;
in sickness and in health...

THE RELATIONSHIP THAT ALMOST NEVER WAS

Crouched by the side of the bed in my hotel room, I called my mother in tears sharing my insecurities with her and my doubts of whether or not I could survive in this newfound world called academia. "I just don't think I can do it!" I said. "But you've accomplished so much already," she told me, "And you're almost done. Hang in there *mija* (little girl)." I knew she was right, but it was not completing the PhD that I was referring to really, it was what was to come after becoming Dr. Martinez that I dreaded. As she tried to console me, I knew she did not quite understand my predicament and so I turned to a dear colleague and friend, a true *hermana* (sister) I had met throughout my doctoral journey. I quickly told my mother I loved her, and then called Esperanza. Immediately, Esperanza, who was a year ahead of me in her doctoral coursework, knew what I was going through. I was at one

Continuing to Disrupt the Status Quo?, pages 145–155
Copyright © 2014 by Information Age Publishing
All rights of reproduction in any form reserved.

of the largest educational research conferences in the nation with literally thousands of other attendees but felt utterly alone and displaced.

It was my third year as a doctoral student and I had already presented at other various conferences with two of my mentors and other peers so the conference "scene" was not exactly foreign to me. However, this time it was different. I explained to Esperanza how I had become overwhelmed and disgusted by what seemed to be "normal" socialization practices at these research conferences. You would constantly see doctoral students pining over leading academics in the field and cliques of alumni from particular research one institutions gathered and traveling together in packs, often, seemingly snubbing other students like me that did not come from these particular institutions or didn't share the same mentor "bloodlines." Moreover, networking particularly disturbed me because it seemed so superficial, self-serving, and competitive; at least from my own observations and experiences up to that point. You would see people in hallways, elevators, and conference halls all doing this. You had to be able to recite your research interests, ask others' theirs, and not be ashamed to gloat a bit about yourself and any of your scholarly accomplishments thus far. I also felt like you were expected to "be on" at all times because as a doctoral student who would someday be on the job market, whether for a faculty or administrative position in higher education, you never knew who was a potential colleague or employer. This pressure to "perform" suffocated me. Seeing some of my own colleagues fall prey to these expectations and quickly become competitive, name-dropping and fame-seeking hounds was disheartening. Taking all of this in as I went from session to session that day, I began to withdraw and proceeded to have what could only be described as either a breakdown or an out of body experience. What was worse was that my close colleagues that I could truly confide in about how I was feeling were either at the conference presenting or in sessions, or not at the conference at all, like Esperanza.

As I sat there on the phone still sobbing with Esperanza, I revealed what was perhaps my biggest fear about all of this; feeling as if I had to sell my soul or compromise my authentic self in order to fit in with the right people within this small, elite world. If I did not, how would I get a faculty position? I was confronted with this realization at that exact moment. I had three mentors up to that point, and all had stressed the pressures of joining the faculty ranks; particularly the reality of "publish or perish." I expected that. However, I guess they had not quite prepared me for the reality of all of the other unwritten rules and expectations that were played out at these types of conferences. Furthermore, I had only started seriously thinking about joining the faculty ranks this year after working on a qualitative research project with a mentor and really falling in love with this whole process. Prior to that, I had pursued the PhD in Educational Administration with the hopes of being an administrator in higher education. My ultimate dream had been to be a dean of students, as I thought that complimented my experience as a teacher and school counselor and satisfied my desire to work with students. Nevertheless, I was feeling as if I simply was not good enough to join this world, did not have it in me to give of myself this way, nor did I want to.

Esperanza said something profound to me at that moment that completely changed my outlook on academia, and literally saved my relationship with it. She essentially said something to this effect, "You have to define what success means to you." She did not say I had to be a faculty member at a research one institution or morph into someone who I barely recognized. While no faculty member or colleague had explicitly said this either, the unspoken pressure to conform to this unwritten standard remained. We knew professors who at one point seemed to pursue meaningful work for their communities and in the name of social justice, but who later seemed to develop an ego and were more interested in hearing themselves speak in classrooms than actually living by what they professed. "You're right," I said. "I started this PhD because I wanted to be in a position where I could help more people, particularly more Latina/os and students of color pursue higher education." I decided immediately that my relationship with academia was going to be on my terms, at least as much on my terms as I could keep it. Success to me meant making a difference in whatever community I was in, not necessarily on a national scale or at a prestigious research one institution. Success meant doing meaningful work while maintaining balance and staying true to myself. I did not want to lose me, and so when I stood up for myself in this way I realized that I could stay with academia, or at least as long as I continued to feel confident in our relationship. At that point, I could only hope and wait to see what the future held in store for me.

Ready to Commit

I successfully graduated from The University of Texas at Austin in August of 2010, and the Division that I had worked for as a graduate research assistant while I was pursuing my doctorate offered me a postdoctoral position when I finished. I eagerly accepted and counted my blessings as I was finally earning a decent salary for the first time in four years and was able to work directly with students in a college outreach program, which I loved. At the same time, however, I was officially on the job market hustling to apply for faculty positions all over the country. I was ready to "commit" to the life of academia.

As someone who had been a bilingual teacher and school counselor in the K–12 public education system, but also had a PhD in Educational

Administration, with a concentration in Higher Education, I considered and positioned myself as a P-16 scholar able to teach in both higher education and educational leadership programs. I kept my notion of success at the forefront of my mind in the process of applying to positions, focusing more on openings at teaching institutions, but daring to apply to some research intensive schools as well. I remember seeking mentorship during this whole process from both my faculty mentors and other colleagues that had gone through the interview process. "Be prepared to answer these types of questions," they would say, and "be prepared with your own set of questions as well." They provided additional insight on what campus interviews usually entailed, explaining how they can be one to two day long processes where you get to meet faculty members, students, and often the chair of the department and dean of the college. They also educated me on the ins- and outs- of the job talk. Needless to say, I had quite a few rejections, but I did have a few phone and Skype interviews and two campus visits. The numerous rejections were a bit hard to take and I remembered the mantra that a faculty mentor shared with me, "All it takes is one yes!"

In the midst of all of this, my body began to talk to me physically to tell me that the years of stress it had undergone while I was in the PhD program had taken a toll and it was not happy. I had gained approximately 25 pounds since my first year of the program, and this definitely impacted my self-esteem. I continued to carry those extra 25 pounds while in my post-doctoral position and as I was on the job market and tried my best to accept myself for who I physically was at the time, knowing that the weight gain was part of the sacrifice for the degree. It is sad, but true. This time, however, my body was reacting differently. I began waking up nauseated every morning, with a pain in my stomach on some days, followed by irregular bowel movements. The symptoms would often subside by lunch, but it definitely affected my appetite; a clear sign that something was wrong. I thought perhaps I had the flu, a virus, or maybe even food poisoning at one point. Being a believer in alternative medicines and healers, and having been raised to believe in spiritual indigenous practices, or *curanderismo* (a mix of Catholic and indigenous spiritual practices), I asked my parents what they thought I had. "*Empacho*," they said. This stomachache occurs after eating spoiled food or food that does not agree with your system. The pain is said to be a result of the food being lodged, or stuck in your intestines. The common cure for this is for someone, usually a spiritual healer, to break an egg and hold the unbroken yolk in his/her hand then pray over you while rubbing the yolk over your belly. The yolk is supposed to break over the area where the food is stuck. Once the yolk breaks, you are wrapped in a towel and have to stay that way for a few hours while the yolk is still on your belly. I tried performing the "*empacho*" ritual on myself while praying, and even drinking a particular tea made up of a concoction of herbs that were said to help my situation but neither of these worked. After the symptoms persisted for almost two weeks, I realized I needed to consider Western medicine and sought my physician's opinion.

After speaking to my doctor, she referred me to a gastroenterologist who diagnosed me with irritable bowel syndrome (IBS). Apparently IBS is particularly common among women, often goes undiagnosed and can be brought on by high levels of stress. After discussing my plight with a female faculty mentor, she revealed that she had experienced something similar during her first year as a professor and knew of other female colleagues who had experienced the same thing. I was dumbfounded thinking of how much I did not want this to be a part of my life as a faculty member and how I needed to stay true to my understanding of academia. I would define success, and it would include balance. I share this particular aspect of my life because I think it had everything to do with the stress I had experienced in pursing my PhD and being on the job market and not knowing where or if I would be relocating for a new faculty position. The thought of not being offered a position at all frightened me the most, particularly because I had already started to repay my student loans and had never been unemployed, unable to pay my bills.

As I began taking medication to ease my IBS, exercising more often and giving myself more "me" time to ensure greater balance in my life I continued in pursuit of "the one" faculty position meant for me. It was hard not to get anxious however as the realization that I would likely have to move out-of-state to a new city where I would have to make new friends and essentially build a new community and support system became more imminent. I kept thinking that perhaps if I were in my 20s I would think this was a wonderful opportunity, an adventure. However, now in my mid 30s as a single Latina with most other faculty members my age married and/or with a partner and/or with children, I thought this would be a difficult and dreadful task. Therefore, I prayed on it, a lot. What I prayed for most often was that God send me to the university where I needed to be, where I could make a difference in whatever community I was in; again, my notion of success.

When I got the email for my first campus interview, only one of two I went on, I was thrilled. It was on the west coast at an institution that was not research one, but seemed to be striving to be. I prepared myself as much as I could, doing research on the institution, the faculty members in the department I could potentially join, preparing my questions for the search committee, and fine-tuning my job talk presentation. I arrived for the interview the night before it was scheduled, and was to leave the morning after the daylong event that was to last from 8:30 am to 8:30 pm. The itinerary included me meeting with faculty members individually and in small groups, as well as meeting students, then presenting my job talk and meeting with the dean. The night would end after dinner with a few faculty members.

Everything up through the job talk seemed to go smoothly, at least on my end. All of the faculty members I spoke with were nice, cordial, and seemingly making every effort to present the best impression of the department, college, and university.

Things began to go awry at the job talk. I noticed as I set up for my afternoon presentation that the room was getting full, with both students and faculty members. I was a bit nervous, but given that I was presenting on my dissertation research I felt quite secure. I proceeded to share my work with the audience, attempting to engage them at various points throughout my presentation using a bit of humor and what I thought were significant and common points of interest. The crowd was numb and expressionless. I sought eye contact with individuals who I thought might validate my work, my findings, my interests, but only one person seemed to nod once. As I concluded my presentation and allowed audience members to ask questions, the unwelcoming feeling that I was experiencing became overwhelming. My confidence faded, as I felt bombarded by questions primarily from faculty and the dean that seemed to be aimed at invalidating my work. I definitely felt I had to defend my research more than I ever had before, even compared to my dissertation defense. My hybrid Chicana feminist and social capital conceptual framework was questioned, and my research findings were deemed obvious. "Given the context of your study, I could have told you, you would get these results without doing the study," one audience member said. And it wasn't the mere fact that I was being questioned about my work that bothered me. It was the tone and condescending manner in which I was being questioned that was disturbing. Perhaps this is what I should have expected, a part of the job talk and interviewing process. Clearly, my mentors and colleagues had not prepped me for this. I know I looked flustered in responding to some of the last questions. One question was thrown at me that I did not understand, but tried my best to answer. I was on the verge of tears. It took everything I had in me to hold it together in front of this crowd of at least 30 to 40 people. As what seemed like a hazing ceremony concluded, I quickly excused myself and headed for the restroom so that I could gain composure and swallow the knot in my throat and silence the deafening beating heart in my ears.

Upon returning to the room where I had presented, I was informed that I was to immediately meet with the dean. My conversation with the dean was equally disconcerting. As the dean asked me questions to gain a better understanding of the type of position I was looking for, I stayed true to my understanding of academia and touched upon my notion of success. I explained that I wanted to work at an institution where I could make a difference, and that did not necessarily mean I had to be at a research one institution. "I figured you'd say that," he said. It seemed he had me all figured out only based on my job talk presentation and this brief conversation; I found this conclusion quite presumptuous and arrogant. He proceeded to explain how there were certain professors who "fit" at certain types of institutions. In not so many words, he suggested that I likely would not make the cut at a research one institution. Although his institution was not a research one, it was positioning itself to be. I made it through the meeting, and then went to dinner as scheduled. I don't remember much of the dinner except that I spoke little because I felt like I had been physically and emotionally abused and beaten after this ordeal, and the three faculty members who accompanied me to dinner did not seem very interested in me anyway. They carried on their own conversations about theory and politics; it was as if I really was not there.

As soon as I got to my hotel room, I called Esperanza and cried. I told her all of the gory details and went to sleep wishing I could magically wake up in my own bed at home. In the morning I felt numb, but began to process all that had happened on the plane. As I looked out my window and saw the beautiful sky and the Grand Canyon below me, tears quickly streamed down my face. "Even if they offer me the position, I won't take it," I told myself. I kept thinking that there had to be an institution where my work was validated, where I was validated, and where I could make a difference and find success.

Ironically, as I was wrote this portion of the chapter I sat on a plane headed to the same national conference where I first had my meltdown and almost gave up on academia. My eyes filled with tears once again as I wrote about my first interview experience because I could still recollect how it felt to be ridiculed; I had felt belittled. And I share this vulnerability now in hopes that others who have experienced this or may experience this know that feeling this way and being treated this way is not okay; it is unacceptable.

Finding "The One"

It has now been one year since I found "the one." The second campus interview I went on was at my current institution, Texas State University-San Marcos (Texas State). The interview had been for a faculty position in Educational Leadership. The faculty there knew that I was a P-16 scholar and practitioner and not necessarily just focused on work that concerned educational leadership in K–12 settings. I felt like they had seen strength in this attribute, however, and imagined how my work could compliment their own. I particularly felt this validation during my job talk, where faculty and students seemed genuinely interested in my work and saw value in it. Therefore, I left my interview at Texas State feeling completely different than I had after my first hellish interview on the west coast. I remember walking out after the full-day interview feeling exhilarated, confident, and hopeful. I had practically skipped down the stairs on my way to my parked car in what must have been 98 degree Texas heat. Looking back, I think that perhaps my first campus interview served a great purpose to prepare me for my Texas State interview. As the saying goes, I had planned for the worst and hoped for the best. In the end, being hired at my current institution left me feeling truly blessed for a number of reasons. The main one however, had to do with my not having to relocate. Since I lived only 30 miles from Texas State, I found that I did not have to move for my new position. I think this made a world of difference, particularly in my first year. The stress of adjusting to my newfound role as an assistant professor was not compounded by my having to move to a new city where I did not know anyone, as I had feared. I was now able to stay in Austin, where I had lived for almost 12 years and had made long-lasting friendships and professional networks.

Admittedly, I really enjoyed my first year as an assistant professor. I say this somewhat surprisingly, and I repeatedly told people this when they asked me how my first year was going, because I had expected my life as a tenure-track professor to be consumed by work, stress, and the pressure to publish. Not that my first year was not filled with much of this, but I think because I expected it, I was not quite so shocked or ill prepared when it happened. I had seen my mentors constantly multitasking between their research, teaching, and service, juggling to stay sane and have a personal life as assistant professors. I definitely am doing the same now, realizing that the work-life balance will always be a struggle in this profession. But with this also comes flexibility and autonomy that is definitely not found in most 8:00 a.m. to 5:00 p.m. jobs. There are days when I can simply roll out of bed and start working from the comfort of my own home, and there is not anyone looking over my shoulder to make sure I am getting my work done. Now, for people who are not self-motivated, have a hard time managing their time, or prefer to work in settings where they are always around people this flexibility and autonomy can be a detriment. After all, the life of a professor is generally one of solitude. It is you and your computer, or books, and you're writing most days as you prepare for your courses and work on your research. Nevertheless, you can choose to work in your office, where you will likely see colleagues and students, or coffee shops where you can still be around people in case this is a concern for you. In addition, you can collaborate on research projects with other faculty members as well, and even plan together for your courses. Of course, you are not alone when you are teaching, as you have a room full of students. You meet with students outside the classroom setting as well, for advice, guidance with coursework, and their dissertations.

I will say that despite the flexibility and autonomy, there are still many sacrifices that the academy asks of you, particularly as a female faculty member of Color. The reality is that the academy is still not a very welcoming place for people like me. I know this based on literature, from the personal stories that other colleagues and mentors across the country have shared with me, and now these accounts are further solidified through my own research on the experiences of tenure-track assistant professors of Color. In staying true to my commitment with academia and to myself, I crafted my research agenda my first year to reflect my lived realities: the personal/professional and activist scholar/practitioner. My interests center on postsecondary access issues for students of Color, pedagogical practices in training future educational leaders, and the experiences of faculty of Color in the academy.

Through my work on the experiences of faculty of Color in the academy, I have reflected much more on my own experiences this first year. I realize that during my first semester I was really being more observant and simply getting to know the lay of the land in my program, department, and college. It was not until the second semester that I became more vocal, exposing the real "me" at faculty meetings. While there were definitely disagreements and varying opinions shared at these meetings, I found that generally my colleagues maintained a certain level of respect for each other. I really appreciated this. However, toward the end of the spring semester, I came to the realization that my first year had really been a honeymoon period–and it had ended. Up to that point, I had not necessarily felt any microaggressions or confronted any overt instances of racism or any other forms of "isms" personally within the academy. However, ,I saw a glimpse of reality when a conversation about varying ideologies arose at one our final faculty meetings. At that moment, I knew that as a female of Color who primarily studies the experiences of communities of Color from a critical lens, my work and I would likely be considered threatening at one time or another. This is the reality for most faculty of Color in the academy. Unfortunately, conversations about this reality continue to be marginalized particularly by people that continue to believe we live in a colorblind, post-racial society.

Sacrificing for the Relationship: A Latina With a PhD

I want to devote the final portion of this chapter to discussing my personal struggles and sacrifices related to being a single Latina with a PhD, as these intersecting identities evoke uncertainties and issues related to dating, marriage, motherhood, and cultural/familial expectations. These issues might resonate with other female scholars, particularly my Black and Latina colleagues. This whole chapter in fact is purposefully written with my personal reality in mind as a Latina PhD who is in a "committed relationship," not with a man, but with academia.

I guess I should first start by saying that I am a 35-year-old single Latina interested in having a partner, getting married one day and potentially having a family. Perhaps if I did not want these things, being single would not be an issue. The reality, however, is that I do and I also have a PhD, which makes finding a man, and particularly a Latino, even more difficult. It is also a fact, however, that I have not been in a long-term relationship since 2003 (it is 2012 as I write this). I know that is a long time. I have dated since then, but no one ever lasts longer than a few dates. I have been told this is because I have expectations that are too high and that is my problem. I have also been told that my various degrees definitely limit my pool of potential suitors, not because I am not willing to date men without a college degree, but it is likely that men without a college degree, or perhaps even those with a college degree but without a PhD, will be intimidated by me.

Furthermore, between 2006 and 2010 I pursued the PhD and I did not have much time to devote to finding "the one" relationship with a man. Not necessarily having time to pursue a relationship did not make not having one any easier. Further, I would argue that as a Latina, getting married and having kids are milestones that are expected and valued; in many ways, valued more than having a PhD. At least that is how I have interpreted some of the messages family has provided over the years. For instance, while pursing the doctorate, the first question often asked of me by extended family members was about school and how it was going and the second was, "Have you met anyone?" One of my aunts who I love dearly tended to ask this of me the most. I tried to redirect her question, letting her know that I was not single because I wanted to be. I just had not yet met the right person for me. Constant inquiry about my relationship status and her feeling sorry for me only made it worse. I already had my moments where I felt it was hopeless. I felt as if my pursuing the PhD was undermined by the fact that I did not have a boyfriend, husband, and/or kids. I wanted my family to recognize the great feat that I was accomplishing, but somehow I still felt unsuccessful and lacking in their eyes. At first, I used to get this type of pressure from my parents. But, as they saw how it negatively affected me, they became much more supportive instead of interrogative. My mother, especially, had learned to stop asking about my dating life over the years because I had expressed my own frustration about this with her several times. I had even called her a couple of times when I was at my lowest; feeling lonely, depressed, and was literally sobbing. As my dad was often in the background hearing these phone conversations, they both finally got it. My aunt had not. It got to the point where I had to ask my mother to speak with my aunt so that she could stop asking me whether I was seeing anyone. This question often evoked heartache for me. I would tell my mom, "Believe me, when I start seeing someone, you all will know!"

The dating world as a Latina with a PhD has been rough. I have been told by Latina elders in particular that it will be harder than ever for me to find a Latino man because I have a PhD. While I date men from all racial/ethnic backgrounds, I do tend to date more Latino men. Some friends have even suggested that I just say I do something else instead of what I actually do. But I don't want to have to lie about who I am or what I do, and I don't think it is too much to expect to be with a partner that respects me and is not threatened by my success. I know some of my Black female colleagues have been given similar advice because we've talked about this issue before. There is research on this phenomenon. Clearly, my academic identity as a PhD, scholar, and professor are intertwined with my personal identity as a Latina woman who is a daughter, sister, niece, cousin and one day perhaps, wife and mother. There is also no doubt that my commitment to and relationship with academia will be intertwined with my commitment to and relationship with my future partner. But the reality is that I want both of these relationships, and I want them both to work. Therefore, I will close by sharing the advice that a dear friend and colleague once told me. I revert to this advice when I question my commitment to academia, or contemplate revealing my PhD status to a man, I think of her saying, "just do you!" In "doing you" you stay true to yourself. For me, this is success.

CHAPTER 12

EARNING A DOCTORATE IN EDUCATIONAL LEADERSHIP

The Perspectives and Experiences of a Deaf Female Scholar

Catherine O'Brien

Being a woman with disabilities may be described as a double-edged sword. Many researchers in women's and disability studies recommend precautions when considering education for women with disabilities, along with the development of policies to ensure equal access and equality (AAUW, 2004; Barile, 2005; Traustadottir, 1990). Both men and women with disabilities face discrimination; however, because of their gender combined with the stigma of a perceived disability, women with disabilities are often viewed in society as less significant than men with disabilities (Traustadottir, 1990). Access to education for women with disabilities has not always been readily available.

Through the years, education has been an integral part of my life. Although I have always yearned for knowledge, access to that knowledge was not always readily available. I was often told what I could not do and seldom told that I was capable of much more. Because of my stubbornness in achieving whatever goal I had set for myself, I would not allow anyone to tell me I could not accomplish something. I often had the mindset, "Watch and I will show you what I can achieve." Some describe me as a survivor, others as tenacious, and still others as obstinate. The label depends upon my decision to adapt to the prejudices or shortsightedness of members of the educational system or to fight them. Frequently, when I decided to fight for access or equality, I began that fight alone without the support of women peers or superiors.

During my school years, I was usually isolated and the only deaf person in my school. Higher education was no different. I was the first Deaf person admitted into both my undergraduate school (in 1980) and into the university's educational leadership department (in 2007). According to the 1991 Americans with Disabilities Act (ADA), I am defined as deaf and disabled; however, I perceive myself as a part of a cultural minority, the Deaf culture. Deaf people, who are members of the Deaf community, feel they are not disabled at all. We believe we can do anything anyone else can do. I communicate using American Sign Language (ASL). My mannerisms, and some of my values and beliefs, are different from my hearing peers. Because of this, I am often viewed as incapable or too much trouble. My language is often valued as less than the spoken language, English, an auditory language that is accessible to the dominant hearing society. The hearing society would prefer that I assimilate into the hearing world and act as though I am hearing, speaking like them and speech reading, denying my deafness and the existence of my identity. The following are selected accounts from my experiences in higher education/educational leadership programs. I chose these stories hoping to increase understanding and awareness. Further, I hope to assist women who face similar barriers.

Much of my story describes the audistic perceptions and actions I experienced while attempting to achieve my educational goals. An American Deaf educator, Tom Humphries, coined the term "audism" in 1975; it is defined as the discriminatory treatment of Deaf individuals (Bauman, 2004; 2008; Lane, 1999). Humphries, in an unpublished article noted that the phrase "audism" is based on the Latin term "*audire*" which means to hear (Bauman, 2008, Lane, 1999); Humphries (1975) offers this dictionary-like definition:

> Audism: (O^dizm) n. The notion that one is superior based on one's ability to hear or behave in the manner of one who hears. (Bauman, 2008, p. 240)

According to Bauman (2004), Humphries then fleshes out this definition by pointing out the common manifestations of audism:

[Audism] appears in the form of people who continually judge Deaf people's intelligence and success on the basis of their ability in the language of the hearing culture. It appears when the assumption is made that the deaf person's happiness depends on acquiring fluency in the language of the hearing culture. It appears when deaf people actively participate in the oppression of other deaf people by demanding of them the same set of standards, behavior, and values that they demand of hearing people. (p. 240)

Harlan Lane (1999) borrowed the term "audism" from Humphries and used it as a way to describe the hearing society's paternalistic and condescending treatment of the Deaf. Audistic people affirm their belief by their willingness to "help deaf" people navigate the larger hearing society. The hearing individuals Lane refers to are the professionals who "work" with deaf people, such as doctors, audiologists, school administrators, and teachers.

HIGHER EDUCATION AND EDUCATIONAL LEADERSHIP EXPERIENCES

Fighting for access to education continued throughout my academic career while earning the bachelor's, master's, education specialist, and doctoral degrees. Access is not just the right to sit in the classroom but is the opportunity to actually receive the information being taught and to be able to participate and access communication in order to interact with peers and instructors.

The Educational Leadership Cohort

After serving as a teacher for three years in a rural district, over nine years in an urban school district, and receiving a "Teacher of the Year" award, I was encouraged by my principal to apply for the educational leadership cohort that was sponsored by the district, the state's flagship university, and a private foundation for educational leadership. The district's goal for this cohort was to develop principals and other leaders for the district who were current on school leadership practices. The cohort met for an entire calendar year.

As a member of the cohort, I soon realized that becoming a school administrator, as a deaf woman, was going to be a challenge. Many of the members, both men and women, challenged my presence in the cohort. They contended that since I was deaf, I would not be able to hear student fights, emergencies, fire alarms, or be able to communicate with staff, parents, and students. The fact that I had been a successful teacher for over

12 years (even being awarded the "Teacher of the Year") did not enter into their mental models of who I was or what I could become. They had limited me simply because I could not hear. During our educational leadership classes I used ASL interpreters for communicating what was being said in class or in groups, but, in school, I relied on speech reading and body language for communication. I was successful in both modes of communication but was more comfortable using ASL interpreters. Only about 30 percent of speech is actually clearly visible on the lips. Success in communication by speech reading depends on knowing the person (having speech read the person before), the subject matter being communicated (thus reading ahead or having prior knowledge), the accent of the person speaking, the body language, the facial expressions, a clear view of the face of the person speaking, and movement of the person speaking.

Stooping Low

One day while taking a break from our educational leadership class, I noticed two men and two women in the hall, who were not members of the cohort, discussing the district's need to 'train' school principals using a cohort. I stopped and began speech reading them. As I studied them one man began to discuss the deaf woman in the cohort. He stated, "They (the district) must need people so bad in that cohort that they have stooped so low as to accept a deaf woman!" As the four began to laugh and joke about the cohort, mocking how a deaf person would speak and moving their hands about as if mocking an interpreter, I became angry inside. I decided to confront them. I walked up to them and introduced myself in a very pleasant manner. I said, "Hello, my name is Catherine and you are?" After they introduced themselves smirking at me because they knew I was a member of the cohort, I explained that I was in the cohort that the four of them were talking about. They acted surprised and apparently derisive until I added, "Oh and I am also the deaf woman you were laughing about the district stooping low enough to admit into the leadership cohort." The men immediately dispersed while the women looked at me and took their time leaving. They seemed to look at me differently, almost pleased that I had approached them or surprised that I had speech read their conversation and I had spoken to them. I thought the women might have appreciated that I stood up for myself.

Demeaning Member

It was difficult for me to work in the cohort as some members wanted to be my friends when they realized I possessed knowledge that they did not have, and I could read much faster and more than adequately discuss the subject matter. However, they still doubted that I could become a school leader because I was deaf. One day while working with my group, one man in our group began discussing his doubt of my becoming a school leader because I was a Deaf woman, and gave his rationale for believing the way he did. The man spoke as though I was not present at the table with him. I was amazed that none of the women spoke up or said anything about the inappropriate conversation. When I interrupted him and said, "Hey, I am sitting right here and I can 'hear' everything you are saying," He then replied, "See what I mean, she still does not understand." I said, "Understand what?" He replied, "She still cannot understand what I am saying, she will never make it!" He continued speaking about me as if I were not there. Then he accused me of picking a fight with him. Situations like this occurred frequently, and when I tried to address the inappropriate conversation I was often accused of picking a fight or told it would be best if I would just sit quietly and "listen."

I attempted to stop this type of discriminating behavior by asking a female professor to join our group discussion hoping the man would discontinue his inappropriate conversation about me. When the professor sat down and joined our conversation, the man's behavior continued. As he attempted to gain a reaction from me with his comments, I stayed quiet. After he made several comments, the professor asked him to explain what he was getting at and why he was inciting me. He stated that he wanted me to address the issues. She then explained that she did not see any issues. Later she told me to stay quiet and not to engage in debate with him. He was never reprimanded or spoken to about his continuing inappropriate behavior.

ISLLC

At the end of the cohort training, we were required to take the Interstate School Leaders Licensure Consortium (ISLLC) standards test. The state required a score of 168 (of a possible 200) to receive principal certification/licensure. We were required to sign up independently to take the test and to give our scores to the cohort leaders. My score of 193 was the highest in the group. When the cohort leader discussed the test results, she never mentioned my score. She did, however, mention others' scores and praised them for their hard work. I sat quietly and wondered why my score was not mentioned. Later I was told I was not being looked at seriously as a school leader. I did not have what it took to be a leader and being a deaf woman they feared for my safety and doubted my ability to lead a school.

Recognizing Power: When to Confront or Adapt

The work with the cohort resulted in my earning my Education Specialist degree. I continued to work in the urban school district for another year.

During that year the Educational Leadership and Policy Analysis department chair and a couple of the professors from the cohort program encouraged me to consider a doctoral program in Educational Leadership. As I transitioned into the Educational Leadership program in the fall of 2007 my experiences were generally good; however, there were times, because I was a Deaf woman, that I found myself in challenging situations where I had to make a decision of whether to fight against, or adapt to, the ways the people in the department saw or thought about me. To keep up with what was being taught, I purchased my books early for the next semester so that I could read them before class began. I had learned early in my educational career to write down questions or comments to ask the professor and to take notes regarding vocabulary and sign(s) that I would teach the ASL interpreters to use.

Identity

At the beginning of my PhD program in Educational Leadership, a professor told me that I was the first deaf person to be admitted into the program and that he had advocated for me. Further, he said that because I could speak and speech read, he felt that my hearing impairment would not be a problem. I explained that I was not "impaired," rather, I was Deaf. I explained that the big "D" refers to Deaf individuals who consider themselves a part of Deaf Culture and members of the Deaf community, while the little "d" refers to the physical condition or "pathology" of deafness or deafness as a "disability." In this sense it implies that something is broken and must be fixed, that the ability to hear is impaired (Moore & Levitan, 2005; Muñoz-Baell & Ruiz, 2000; Lane, 1999; Lane, Hoffmeister, Bahan, 1996; 2002; Ramsey, 1997). Further, I explained that the term "hearing impaired" was considered a cultural insult and asked that he refer to me as being Deaf.

Although I asked him to refer to me as Deaf he would always tell others that I was hearing impaired. I would cringe to see him introduce me as "hearing impaired." Often I would interject and say, "I am Deaf, not hearing impaired." However, I was most often ignored. I had to decide if this situation warranted a stronger stance and how I would go about this. I took the stance of adapting; I felt the need to teach the professor and others I met along the way. At times I felt this stance was not strong enough. At other times I would remind myself that I was just a doctoral student, and the first Deaf person to be admitted into the program. I felt I should be more patient and continue to teach them.

The Student

During my first year of PhD coursework, I experienced a number of oppressive and demeaning situations. There were times I felt that I had to confront the inequalities or perceptions of me. For example, on the first day of my first class a male peer sitting next to me said, "You know it is great that they let you into this program." I asked him, "What do you mean by 'they let me into this program'?" He replied, "You know, they let you in this program being deaf. Will you be working in a school for the deaf?" I replied, "Do you not think I passed the same entrance requirements as you?" He replied, "Well there is affirmative action, I just thought…" I interrupted him and said, "Affirmative action was not a part of my being accepted into this doctoral program. Further, for you to make an assumption about me without knowing or having a peer relationship with me is inappropriate. I worked just as hard if not harder to be here; I am just as capable as you or anyone in this classroom." I then said to him, "You know what is scary to me?" He replied "No." I explained, "The fact that you are going to become a principal and superintendent in a school district with these assumptions. How will you judge and make decisions about the students in your school when they do not fit your 'norm?' And how will you be able to understand their experiences, culture, background, or even be able to empathize with your students if you have these underlying assumptions of people like me?" At that he got up and chose another place to sit.

After this conversation I realized that was I going to have to work hard, be the best, and prove that I was worthy to be a doctoral student and earn my doctorate. I felt the need to dispel any rumors that I had special privileges because I was a Deaf woman. I also realized that I had decided to confront him and not adapt. In some ways I think I challenged his thinking because he was my peer and not my professor. It was safer. His statements and his assumptions about me, without even speaking to me or getting to know me first, felt like a stake driving through me. I felt I had to confront him and give him more information to assist him in realizing that his thoughts of me were incorrect and that his thoughts were inappropriate and demeaning.

The Male Professor

During my second year I was required to take an advanced research course. During the first class the professor announced to the class of 22 students that if we did not pass his class he would recommend to our doctoral committee that we be dropped from the program. I sat in the front row in the center, a friend sat to my right and two nursing students sat to my left. As class began, the ASL interpreter shadowed the professor.

The interpreter's placement while interpreting in a classroom situation is important. Typically, they stand to the right and slightly behind the speaker. This position gives the Deaf person the ability to see the speaker and the interpreter at the same time and allows the Deaf person to receive the whole message. As the interpreter took his place the instructor moved away from the interpreter. As the instructor continued to teach I could tell he was uncomfortable with the interpreter being next to him; it was obvious that the instructor was trying to move away from the interpreter the whole time he was teaching. After an hour into the three-hour class the instructor decided it was time for a break. During the break I approached the instructor and asked if everything was all right. He said, "Yes." I asked if he had any questions about the interpreter, placement of the interpreter, or the role of the interpreter. I attempted to converse with the instructor, provide the instructor with information, and possibly help him to become comfortable with the interpreter. He stated that he was indeed fine. I could tell he was agitated and uncomfortable with me speaking to him, so I decided to walk away after he declined my assistance. The interpreter followed the instructor until class was completed.

The next day I arrived at my office and was informed by another graduate student that the professor from the research class had arrived early that morning to speak with a professor in our department. The student said the research professor was upset and did not want the interpreter in the classroom; further, he said he was not aware that "special education" students were allowed in the doctoral program. From the student's account the professor defended me and explained that I would be one of his best students. After the graduate student spoke to me the professor invited me to his office. He explained that the research professor had visited with him earlier in the morning and had said he did not want the interpreter in the front of the room with him because the interpreter impeded his ability to teach. He asked me to work with the professor because I would learn a lot about research from him. I explained that I had tried to talk to the research professor during our class break and he refused to speak with me. The professor told me to be "flexible," that he was older and not used to people like me in his class. I was told to be quiet and put the interpreter in another place that wouldn't shadow the research professor. I tried to explain the appropriate placement of the interpreter, but the professor reiterated his position and said "You need to pass this class; let it go."

When I arrived in class the next day, the research professor grabbed a chair in the hallway, put the chair in the far right corner of the room near the door and told the interpreter to sit there. The interpreter was puzzled and looked at me for answers. At that time I had to decide who had the power in the classroom, whether it was worth fighting, and what supports I had. The interpreter signed to me, "YOU ALLOW THIS? LAW!? ADA? YOU HAVE RIGHTS!" I signed back to the interpreter, "Please, just interpret, I will handle this, I will! My way!" Next my friend to my right and the two nursing students on my left wanted to talk to me. I said, "Later, during the break."

The behavior of the professor shocked me. He was impenetrable and I was not sure what to do next. As the research professor began to teach on the opposite side of the room, I could see that I was going to be lost quickly and I needed a plan to prevent this. It was impossible for me to watch the interpreter on my far right and the research professor on my far left. It felt like my head was splitting in two. The research professor also wrote on the board and talked facing the board (a common behavior among hearing lecturers), so that I could only access about a third of what was being taught. After an hour and a half the research professor gave us a break.

I was exhausted, angry, and knew I had no power in this classroom. If I tried to confront the professor I knew I would surely lose. I did not feel I had any support in my department especially after the earlier conversation with the professor. I feared that if I said anything the research professor would give me a failing grade (my experiences in undergraduate school prove this). I needed a foolproof plan to demonstrate to the research professor that I was capable, intelligent, and could learn the material being taught.

During the break, the interpreter asked me what I was going to do. Feeling a confrontation coming on with the interpreter, I told him I would handle the situation. He then said I needed to go to student services and file a grievance and that I had rights. I thanked him for his position and told him that this was my class, my grade, and I would solve my own problem my way. I then asked the interpreter to interpret and to follow the NAD-RID Code of Professional Conduct for interpreters. Next, I asked the nursing students and my friend to talk with me in the hall. I asked them if they would share their notes with me. All three said, "Yes!" I explained my plan: I asked the nursing students to write down everything that the professor said and I asked my friend to write down everything he wrote. Next I said I would focus on the interpreter and try to pay attention to what was written on the blackboard, focusing on everything that was visual. Then, after each class I would copy all three sets of their notes and compile our notes into one complete set of notes, being sure we did not miss anything. Finally, I promised I would email the completed set of notes to everyone each night after I had finished compiling them. Further, I said I would write down any questions or missing information so we could ask the research professor questions during the next class period. Everyone was in agreement.

Beginning that night, and for every class thereafter, we photocopied the class notes. We would say our goodbyes and I would stay in the office to compile all four sets of notes into one complete set. This process often took into the early morning hours to complete. When there were questions in my mind or incomplete information on a topic, I would research the issue on the Internet and add my findings to the notes. I kept my promise and emailed a complete set of notes after each class.

During the next class period I attempted to ask questions that had emerged from compiling the class notes. The research professor overlooked my hand in the air waiting to ask him questions. So I wrote questions down and handed them to the nursing students and my friend. They asked the questions and we wrote down his responses. I could not figure out why the research professor refused to call on me or allow me to ask questions in class. After each class, I added the answers to the questions to the previous set of notes and would resend those notes along with the new set of notes for the day.

At the eighth week of class, we had our first test. The test was long (three hours), and we were allowed to use our notes. The notes were helpful and I could not have passed the test or class without them; but the process of compiling them and the information that I retained was most helpful. I received the second highest score in the class on the first test. After this test, the research professor began to answer my questions. I felt that this was because I demonstrated to him that I was capable and could do the work.

During class the professor told stories. One story he told I would never forget. He said that one way school districts could save money would be to eliminate special education. The cost of educating a student in special education was great and there were few benefits for the dollars. He felt that the state could save money if these students stayed at home. He also made comments about his wife being a professor and having a child; then he argued with my friend who was pregnant at the time. He made it clear to us that women had a place and it was not in the classroom, pregnant. My friend argued with him often. Some of the other women, including me, protested his comments and he would laugh at us. At the end of the class my friend received a grade of "B" and we both thought it was because she fought with him regarding his perceptions of women and special education. I received an "A" and knew I had earned my grade and felt my friend had also earned an "A," but did not receive one. I felt guilty about this. She shrugged it off and said she was not surprised because she argued with him and he did not like it. Still, I was not satisfied with the research professor's attitude toward women, the special education population, and the lack of access to the class and the placement of the interpreter. I had left the interpreter where the research professor had placed him on the second day of class, even though it prevented me from having direct access to class and to the material being taught.

In this research class, I decided to adapt and to problem solve my situation in a way that demonstrated to the professor that his opinion of me was wrong. I felt at the time he had the power in the classroom, and to confront him without any support would have been a losing battle. Therefore, I thought the best course of action was to show him the error of his prejudiced perception of me and hopefully make the path for others after me better.

There were many times when others told me to fight against his authority (oppressive behavior and prejudice), file a grievance, and make some noise. If I had enjoyed the support of my peers or professor(s), I might have made a different decision. I felt alone in making this decision and made the one I felt was best in the situation. Today, I am not sure I could do anything differently, without support. But, if I had support I do not believe that I would be so docile. Further, I would encourage my students and my peers to seek appropriate respect, *with* my support and encouragement. We rarely change behaviors or force respect from others by using laws that seek to force them to change.

My peers were not always supportive of allowing me access to information or participation. Some of my peers complained about the interpreter in the front of the classroom and some stated the interpreter distracted them from the lecture.

Professional Conferences: Identity and Access

When beginning my doctoral coursework, a female peer who was two years ahead of me explained to me how I might contribute in educational leadership and how I might gain standing in the professional organizations. She encouraged me to do four things: (a) to join three professional research organizations that hold annual research conferences; (b) to write research proposals/papers and submit them to the conferences; (c) to attend the conferences; and (d) to advocate for access in order to fully participate in the conferences.

First, I joined the three professional research organizations and then began the task of learning to write research proposals and concept papers. After working on a concept paper with my advisor and one other professor, and submitting it, my first presentation proposal was accepted. Elated that I had accomplished three of the four tasks, I informed my peer. She then said "Do not forget the fourth item on your list, advocate for access." I thought, "Well, we now have the ADA, and by law all professional conferences must provide access. This should not be a difficult task." I was wrong. When I sent my proposal to one of the professional research organizations, I informed them that I needed highly qualified ASL interpreters. When the proposal was accepted, I was told that someone would get back with me regarding this. I waited for two months and then asked my peer who she would recommend that I contact regarding ASL interpreters and access. She picked up the phone and called someone she knew and that person promised she would look into the situation and get back to us. Two weeks went by and we did not receive a return phone call. So my peer made another call and again was told the same information—they were "looking into it." After another three weeks went by we made another call and were told that the conference was coming up soon and asked, "Why did you wait so long to inform us?" My peer responded with whom she had spoken, when (two months earlier, and several later checks) and what she had done to obtain interpreters. Again we were informed that they would look into it. Two weeks before the conference we were assured by a man that he would "take care of hiring" two ASL interpreters. A week before the conference we called again, and again we were assured that there would be interpreters present. After the call, I felt I was set for my first professional research conference presentation.

After driving and flying all day, we arrived at the conference hotel, checked into the hotel, registered for the conference, and then spoke with the man who said he would "take care" of the ASL interpreters. I could tell that something was wrong when I saw his facial expressions. When I inquired about the interpreters, he explained that he had been too busy organizing the conference and that he had not contracted with an ASL interpreting agency for the conference. He further explained that the hotel did not know where to obtain interpreters and, thus, he did not know where to begin. I asked him why I was not informed of this prior to arriving at the conference. He explained that he was simply too busy. I was surprised at his lack of communication, problem-solving skills, and even more surprised that the professional organization did not have any knowledge regarding ASL interpreters and access for Deaf people. At that point I needed to create a plan so that I could present my paper and answer questions from the audience. I told my advisor and he said he could not offer any solutions. Then I spoke with the other professor, and he was surprised that the organization did not retain ASL interpreters for the conference. He decided to speak with the director of the organization.

The next day I did not hear from the professor or anyone prior to my presentation. I decided to go ahead with my presentation and hope for the best. The professor arrived just before our session was to begin and sat next to me. When it was my turn to present, I was nervous and was worried about the question and answer period. I voiced for myself during the presentation and the presentation was well received. During the question and answer period, the professor wrote down the questions and after reading each question I answered. I relied solely on the professor because there were many new faces and accents. It is difficult to speech read someone you have never met on a topic that you have not fully comprehended. When the session ended, I told the professor that I appreciated his assistance and I would not have been able to answer the questions or participate in the discussions without his assistance; however, I would not present again without interpreters. He said he would speak to the organization board members to ensure that next year, I would have ASL interpreters and access to the conference.

During the conference, several male professors informed me that they had never experienced a Deaf person attending "their" conference. They suggested that I needed to be patient and they would "see" what they could do to provide accommodations for "their" conference the following year. Further, I was informed that the organization had never budgeted for interpreters before. On the other hand, three female participants inquired why I did not have ASL interpreters present at the conference. After I explained, each said that interpreters should be provided because the organization needed to comply with ADA. It was important that the organization embrace differences, and that I be accepted as a member of the organization.

One year later, I wrote four presentation proposals and had one proposal accepted to each of three professional organization's conference. Two of the proposals were accepted to the previous year's professional organization conference. I informed the new professional organizations and the previous year's professional organization that I would need highly qualified ASL interpreters. Further, I explained that they should reserve and contract with the interpreters several months prior to the conference opening to secure highly qualified interpreters. I offered my assistance in locating and securing interpreters for all three professional organizations.

One of the professional organizations responded quickly and asked me to inform them of the days and session times I wished to attend. I did so and one month before I was to travel to the conference, they established a contract with ASL interpreters and informed me of the agency name, interpreter names, and location where I would meet the interpreters once the conference had begun. Further, I was informed that there would be an access booth and if I needed anything to stop at the booth and they would assist me. It was obvious to me that this professional organization had prior experience with ASL interpreter requests and knew how to go about securing highly qualified ASL interpreters. The interpreting agency contacted me prior to the conference to introduce the two interpreters who would be working with me. The interpreting agency inquired about my mode of communication; they asked for copies of my presentation and research paper, and they gave me contact information for the two interpreters assigned to me in case I needed to change my schedule. The two interpreters worked with me the entire conference and the accommodations were excellent.

These two stories reflect the extremes I experienced as I began to attend and present at professional conferences. The latter successful experience is what I sought from all professional conferences I planned to attend. I cannot stress enough the importance of having the same two interpreters for the entire conference and the ability to share my research with them prior to the conference. Interpreters exercise a lot of power over a Deaf person. They are the Deaf person's voice and represent their intellectual abilities. Interpreters have the ability to make a Deaf person appear to be stupid—by their lack of voicing skills—or intellectually competent—by their excellent voicing skills. If the interpreters are prepared and understand the Deaf person's vocabulary, research work, and communication needs, access to the conference will be successful.

Unfortunately, the unsuccessful experience from the first year was repeated in the second year with the same organization. After that conference, I met with the conference coordinator and reiterated the importance of following the necessary steps in securing the same two highly qualified ASL interpreters for the conference. I explained again that for an interpreter to be highly qualified they must satisfy four things: first, the interpreters should be certified at the highest level according to their state licensing board or the national certification board. Second, the interpreters should have experience in interpreting in higher education and professional research conferences. Third, the interpreters should communicate with me prior to the conference, with sufficient lead time, to obtain copies of my work and the presentation to assist in their preparation for interpreting to the best of their ability and communicating with me during the conference. Finally, the most satisfactory access is provided if the same two interpreters can be hired for the entire conference and they can be secured several months in advance of the opening of the conference. I was assured that the following year they would follow these guidelines.

During my fourth year of attending conferences I was no longer a student. I had completed my dissertation and had accepted a position as the first I. King Jordan Fellow at Gallaudet University. "Gallaudet University is the world's only university with programs and services specifically designed to accommodate the educational needs of deaf and hard of hearing students" (Gallaudet University, 2012). Deaf students from all over the world attend Gallaudet University to earn their undergraduate and graduate degrees. A limited number of hearing students are also admitted into the undergraduate program and a larger number of hearing students is accepted into the graduate program. While working at Gallaudet University, I enjoy 100% access to communication twenty-four hours a day, seven days a week because almost everyone communicates in ASL.

This year, I wrote two conference proposals and both were accepted. The first professional organization provided access to their conference even after it was discovered that the interpreter agency they contracted with could not meet the requirements of the contract. The organization had to scramble at the last minute to secure another interpreting agency to provide accommodations. I was amazed at how quickly the professional organization worked to ensure that all Deaf people attending the conference were provided access. This professional organization appears to be the most consistent organization in providing access to people who are Deaf. It is also true that between 4 and 10 Deaf professionals attend the conference every year, and within the organization there is a section specifically for the education of Deaf persons. When advocating for access in attending professional conferences I was successful when there were more Deaf professionals attending the conference.

The second paper was accepted by the professional organization in my field of research. It was the fourth year I would present a research paper at this conference. Again, I informed the organization of my need to have highly qualified interpreters present at the conference, and again they waited until a month before the conference was to begin to respond to me. This time they cited "lack of funds," "change in staff," "it was too late," "they were too busy preparing for the conference," and that "they were unaware that I needed highly qualified ASL interpreters to access the conference." After four years of consistently attending the conference, advocating, teaching, and being patient I was indeed frustrated.

The director of the professional organization sent me an email informing me again that there was no budget for ASL interpreters and I should consider bringing interpreters from Gallaudet University. At that point, I felt that the director did not learn much from my advocacy during the past four years, nor that the director understands that the Americans with Disability Act (ADA) mandates for accommodations. Further, I felt I was not valued as a member of the organization. The director did not know Gallaudet University's purpose and its international reputation. I decided to contact a mentor and former professor in the field to ask for her recommendations on the situation. I shared with her all of the information I had been given. This friend suggested that the situation should be brought to the board for resolution. She asked for my permission to send an email addressed to the board, the director and president of the organization. I agreed because I felt I had done all I could do and I was out of options. For the first time I felt I had a peer, a mentor, and someone who understood and was willing to assist in solving the accommodation issues with the organization before I had to resort to filing a formal ADA complaint.

This intransigence deeply saddened me. I was forced to fight for accommodations to attend a professional meeting of an organization of which I was a member. I have been told to be patient, diplomatic, and quiet, and that the members need time to be taught and educated. Further, the organization often speaks and presents about the importance of research in the areas of social justice, equality, diversity, and acceptance in education but somehow these words, speeches, and presentations did not apply to a Deaf person who wished to become a researcher in the field and a member of the professional organization.

After my mentor sent an email inquiring about ASL interpreters for the conference, I was informed that my perception of the situation was inaccurate and that interpreters would be contracted for the conference. Before arriving at the conference, I received an email from the interpreting agency informing me that they would be sending interpreters. Five interpreters were scheduled to work the three-day conference. The interpreter responsible for voice interpreting my presentation would not be able to meet me to review my presentation until an hour before the presentation. This was problematic because we would not have time to review my research or presentation and she would not be used to my style of signing. Consistency in interpreters is critical for a successful presentation. I sent my paper and presentation to the interpreter who reported that she did not have time to review the material before she arrived at the conference. By the time we met, we only had 40 minutes to review my presentation, vocabulary, and signs.

During my presentation, the voice interpreter was not able to accurately voice interpret. She, admittedly, was not prepared and did not understand the complex concepts I was attempting to convey to the audience. Several times, she also assumed the word I was finger spelling to be another word, which was inaccurate. A member of the audience alerted me to the interpreters voicing inaccuracies by pointing toward the interpreter and shaking her head, "No." For example, when I finger spelled the words "culturally relevant" she voiced the word "relevance." The PowerPoint clearly had the words "culturally relevant" in the title, but she missed it during the presentation. I signed and finger spelled the words twice and she still did not understand the terms. Further, most of the vocabulary used during the presentation was also in the PowerPoint and, had the interpreter taken the time to review the PowerPoint, she might have been better prepared. The interpreter stated she was not given enough notice or information about the job prior to the presentation. In the end, she apologized for her poor performance; however, the damage was already done. After the presentation, I wondered whether the audience thought I was incapable or intellectually incompetent, whether I was wrong and the interpreter was right, whether I should have corrected the interpreter more, etc. There is not enough time in a 15-minute presentation to correct the interpreter and present the research.

Membership of One

Advocating for interpreter accommodation during conferences was not the only barrier that I confronted while attending classes, meetings and professional conferences. During my educational leadership doctoral program, in classrooms, in social gatherings, and in professional organization meetings, I have often felt like an unwelcome outsider. It is isolating being the only Deaf educational leadership and policy researcher. I felt as though I was a visitor standing on the outside of the building peering through a window wondering how to join, how to learn, how to be accepted, and how to develop relationships with the members. Communication is key to becoming a member of any culture. When socializing with professors or peers in classes, conferences, or meetings, it is often my responsibility to understand what is said the first time. However, the more I persisted and the more I continued to socialize with peers, mentors, and colleagues the more they learned about me. Persistence and never giving up is how I am able to challenge and change their perception.

Interviews and Employment

During my dissertation writing, I began to apply for employment at colleges and universities. I was nervous and excited at the same time. As I applied for available positions, my dissertation committee members offered letters of recommendations and support. My dissertation research and writing was very difficult for me because I studied a school for the deaf and, while writing, I was hit with the horrible realization that deaf students today experience the same oppression and audistic behaviors I did when I was their age. It is hard to believe that thirty years later we have not made the necessary improvements to advance the education of deaf children. With this in mind I sought out positions where I would be supported in continuing my research in educational leadership with a focus on the education of deaf children.

I attended three conferences with the purpose of presenting my research but also to interview for positions available. Two of my dissertation committee members introduced me to colleagues who were seeking to hire assistant professors for their PK–12 educational leadership and policy programs. I appreciated their support and confidence in me during this time. They genuinely supported me and proudly discussed my accomplishments while earning my doctorate. Below are some of my experiences while searching for the best fit as an assistant professor in educational leadership.

You Want to Be a Professor? Really?

During the conferences and interviews, I was often asked about my research and what my goals were for my career. I was also asked how I would communicate and work with students and faculty members. While this is not an appropriate question to ask during an interview, and it is against the ADA, I felt I did not have a choice and did not want the committee to think I had anything to hide; therefore I reluctantly answered their questions. During an informal interview, one professor seemed shocked that I wanted to be an educational leadership professor as he replied, "You want to be a professor!" with a surprised look on his face he continued, "So you think you can do this kind of work, research and teaching? You know this is demanding work." I could tell by his word choices and facial expressions that I was wasting my time even thinking about applying for this position. I felt that I had to be on my game and interview prospective employers keeping notes of facial expressions and conversations. The last thing I wanted to do was to be hired by a university that did not have confidence in me or a vested interest in my research.

Hiring Two

During an informal interview, three professors who were looking for a PK–12 educational leadership assistant professor were questioning me about my PK–12 leadership, research, and teaching experiences. I did not have an interpreter present during the informal interview and my speech reading was on, meaning I was able to speech read the three without asking them to repeat. I know I was clearly understood because they did not ask me to clarify or repeat. When we were almost ready to go our separate ways, one of the professors asked me how I would be able to teach doctoral students using an ASL interpreter (even though I had explained that I had been a teacher and administrator, in a hearing environment, for over 14 years prior to beginning my doctoral program). I responded, "Well, let's see. I have been chatting with the three of you for over an hour and I did not see an interpreter present, did you?" The professor responded "No," but I interjected, "Well, why would you ask that question then?" She responded, "Well, if we hire you, we would have to hire an interpreter too!" At that point I realized that she had not heard anything I said during our one-hour meeting. Further, she did not focus on what I could do or how I could be an asset to their program.

SUMMARY

This chapter describes some of my experiences as a Deaf woman in educational leadership as a student and now as a faculty member. Some of my experiences relate to being a woman but most relate to being a Deaf woman. Two themes color most of my experiences in higher education. One is isolation; the other theme is related to that feeling of isolation: obtaining and advocating for access in many different situations. Access, in this context, is much more than simply being allowed to attend school and sit in the classrooms. It involves actually being able to actively participate. The incidents I have chosen to describe also demonstrate audism. I am Deaf and I am part of a minority group of people in our society who do not hear, communicate in ASL, and am a part of what is known as "Deaf Culture." Many members of society are unaware of both the existence of Deaf culture and common courtesies to observe in working with individuals who are Deaf.

In this chapter, I described in detail the attitudes and actions of educators and some of the ways in which "ordinary citizens" (in and out of schools) demean deaf individuals, either intentionally or because they do not think about the possible results of their behaviors. I have also described an apparent lack of understanding of deafness and how to provide access.

In closing, I would like to say that I wish to be treated like my peers, with respect and dignity, without having to force someone to comply with a law. When people are forced to do something, they most often impede the changes that they are forced to make. I wish to have my culture and language respected. I wish to be included and have the ability to learn from others while they at the same time are open-minded enough to learn from me. I wish for people to focus on what I CAN do! Isn't this what everyone wants and needs?

REFERENCES

AAUW, (2004). *Women and girls with disabilities.* Washington, DC: *American Association of University Women Public Policy and Government Relations.* Retrieved June 1, 2012 from http://www.aauw.org/issue_advocacy/actionpages/positionpapers/disabilities.cfm

Barile, M. (2005). Including women with disabilities in Women and Disability Studies. In Ben-Moshe, L., Cory, R., Feldbaum, M., & Sagendorf. K. (Eds.), *Building pedagogical curb cuts: Incorporating disability into the university classroom and curriculum* (pp. 21–32). Syracuse, NY: The Graduate School, Syracuse University. Retrieved June, 1, 2012 from http://gradschpdprograms.syr.edu/resources/publication_disability.pdf

Bauman, H. L. (2004). Audism: exploring the metaphysics of oppression. *Journal of Deaf Studies and Deaf Education, 9*(2): 239–246.

Bauman, H. L. (2008). (Ed.). *Open your eyes: Deaf studies talking.* Minneapolis, MN: University of Minnesota Press.

Gallaudet University. (2012). Gallaudet University Fast Facts. Retrieved June 12, 2012 from http://www.gallaudet.edu/gallaudet_university/about_gallaudet/fast_facts.html

Lane, H. (1999). *The mask of benevolence.* New York, NY: Alfred Knopf.

Lane, H., Hoffmeister, R., & Bahan, B. (1996). *A journey into the deaf- world.* San Diego: DawnSignPress.

Lane, H., Hoffmeister, R., & Bahan, B. (2002). Educational placement and the deaf child. In M. A. Byrnes (Ed.), *Taking sides: Clashing views of controversy in special education.* Boston MA: McGraw-Hill.

Moore, M., & Levitan, L. (2005). *For hearing people only.* Rochester, NY: Deaf Life Press.

Muñoz-Baell, I., & Ruiz, M. (2000). Empowering the deaf: Let the deaf be deaf. *Journal of Epidemiology and Community Health, 54*(1), 40–44.

Ramsey, C. (1997). *Deaf children in public schools.* Washington, DC: Gallaudet University Press.

Traustadottir, R. (1990). Obstacles to Equality: The double discrimination of women with disabilities. Retrieved June 2, 2012 from http://dawn.thot.net/disability.html

CHAPTER 13

SINCE SHE IS GONE, WHO WILL GET ME THROUGH?

Anjalé Welton

> *[Delores] you gave to us without ever asking for anything in return.*
> —Jabors Welton III (aka, Uncle Jimmy)

Writing this chapter offers me the opportunity to pay tribute to individuals who continue to be a source of support as I pursue tenure. The type of supports I have received along the way might be considered by dominant standards as "unconventional" or outside the norm. My aunt Delores Fagan took on a parental role, assisting my mother in the absence of my father, in raising me. After my aunt passed away, during my formal grieving process, I used this chapter to reflect upon some of the lessons my aunt taught me and the methods she used to support my educational advancement. I now realize my aunt's simple lessons could be guidelines for achieving tenure. Therefore, the subsequent sections in this chapter are presented in a nonchronological order as I flashback to critical moments when Aunt Dee served as an emotional resource. I conclude this chapter with a list of assets from my loving and community-based upbringing, what I call my *Black cultural capital* that I find to be distinctive to what *I need* to navigate the academy.

PIVOTAL MOMENTS WITH HER

As a single parent, my mother relied on the support of others to help her raise me. I commend her for that because it can be difficult to overcome pride and ask for help. My aunts, cousins, uncles, and church members surrounded me with insurmountable love and protection, and each person had a distinctive role in "project Anjalé." Aunt Jacque was my emotional support. I still pick up the phone and call her if I'm angry, sad, or just need to get a good cry out of my system. My cousin Rushcelle always made sure I looked put together, wearing one-of-a-kind dresses. My mom encouraged all of my artistic talents by signing me up for voice lessons at the local community college, and, at one point, even took on a second job as a bookkeeper for a Black professional dance company, which then enabled me to receive free dance classes. Every now and then, Uncle Jimmy, my mom's quiet brother, gave silent monetary contributions to my education. And then there was Aunt Dee, who, no matter how "funny the money," as my mom would put it, always made sure I had my basic needs met—food and a roof over my head. Aunt Dee was also my *life planner*.

My maternal grandmother passed away when my mom was a teenager, and Aunt Dee, as the oldest sibling in the family, assumed the role of matriarch. Because she was the matriarch, everyone in the family consulted with Aunt Dee in times of crisis or prior to making major life decisions. Aunt Dee was a tiny woman, 5'2 who never weighed more than 110 pounds, but she was stern and heavy handed. She never spanked me, but I always underestimated her strength given her small frame. So, when she would occasionally grab my arm with her curved fingers (due to her struggle with Rheumatoid Arthritis) to emphasize that she was serious or disappointed in my behavior, I was surprised at how powerful her grasp was (which was just strong enough to make a point and show concern.) Thus, I rarely misbehaved under Aunt Dee's watch. I lived with her every summer from birth until I graduated from college and moved to the Washington D.C. area for graduate school and my first "real" job as a teacher. She also served as my mom's primary childcare option for me and I lived with her for extended periods of time throughout my childhood when home life was tumultuous. I don't know why Aunt Dee decided to assume the role of manager of my educational goals, but we put our heads together and designed a strategy to get me to college and beyond. She was my strategist when I got my first job at 15 and decided I was going to start saving pocket change for college. She even flew out to Washington, DC when I got my first teaching job to help me negotiate the purchase of my first car. My Aunt Dee, Delores Donalene Fagan, passed away on April 14, 2012. And now my *life planner*, navigator, and confidant is gone.

Nine Days and Nine Nights

I chose to write this section in present tense to better convey to readers what I was thinking during the last moments I spent with my aunt.

I'm sitting in the desk nook of my Aunt Dee's hospital room. Since I have now made her hospital room my temporary home, the desk nook no longer resembles a desk. Instead, thanks to family and church members, the desk is now a fully stocked kitchenette. I'm frantically editing a university sponsored grant application while my Aunt Jacque and a close family friend, Brenda, sit two feet away from me chatting about my aunt's condition. Access to wi-fi in the hospital enabled me to press on with work, because even though time inside the hospital room is at a standstill, my tenure clock still clicks on. I glanced across the room at my Aunt Dee asleep in her hospital bed and then looked back at the time on my laptop. I had ten minutes left until the 3:00 p.m. deadline to upload my grant application.

The doctors weren't sure how much Aunt Dee could hear or see at this point, but she was responsive to touch. Occasionally, when we would talk to her, her eyes would open. Her eyes surprisingly opened when we turned on her favorite soap opera, the *Young and the Restless*. Every so often between editing a sentence or two of my grant application, I would look up or walk over to check on Aunt Dee to see if she presented any strain in breathing. It was 2:57 p.m. and this was my fourth attempt at uploading the grant. The online submission system was overloaded and I was having trouble processing my grant application. It was 3:02 p.m. and two minutes past the deadline... my application finally uploaded. My mini panic attacked ceased and I looked over at Aunt Dee again, who, at this point, was in a deep sleep. Relief from uploading the grant application was coupled with feelings of guilt, because even though I wasn't sure whether this was my final time with Aunt Dee, I continued to work. For nine days I had barely left the front doors of the hospital. I had developed the routine of bathing in the shower in the hospital room. Every other day my mother would bring me a clean change of clothes. I stayed in the hospital with Aunt Dee just long enough to have an "in" with the nurses and assistants. As their shifts changed, the nursing staff began to rely on me to report when my Aunt Dee's fever spiked through the night or when her bedding needed to be changed.

One ultimate lesson Aunt Dee taught me was to never press the pause button on productivity, no matter the circumstances. Even though Aunt Dee was physically unable to assist me, her mere presence meant she was performing her final call of duty as my *life planner*, making sure I was productive and maintained my momentum during my first year as an assistant professor. During those nine days and nine nights that I slept in Aunt Dee's hospital room I managed to accomplish the following:

- Completed a grant application to support funding for a graduate research assistant
- Conferenced with a few students over the phone about their papers for a class
- Conferenced via Skype with a teaching assistant to plan for subsequent class sessions
- Edited my advisee's dissertation proposal, which was due to the rest of the dissertation committee members
- Completed a conference symposium proposal for which I invited a few graduate students to contribute papers
- Directed my advisee's early research project presentation (the equivalent of a thesis defense) via Skype in a conference room on the neurological patient wing of the hospital

Despite my guilt I knew Aunt Dee would tell me if she could talk that, "No matter the level of pain or hurt, work must continue...life must continue." Aunt Dee spent most of her adult life in physical pain battling a combination of Rheumatoid Arthritis and a mild case of Parkinson's. I never witnessed Aunt Dee take a break, and there were numerous times in her life she had to take on extra physical and mental work, despite the extreme physical pain she may have been in. Extra work was necessary to get through a personal family obstacle or in support of other family members or friends. Her home consistently served as a temporary home for not just family members, but close friends, church members, or neighbors who were experiencing a period of crisis and needed shelter until they could get back up on their own two feet. So many relied on Aunt Dee for mental strength, even though she was privately battling her own physical weaknesses from multiple illnesses.

Every time we sat down together to map out some life goal I had for myself Aunt Dee would tell me her "little stories" of sacrifices she made at one time or another in order to meet a specific goal. I'm not sure why, but one story that always stuck with me was how she saved money to buy a new bedroom set for my cousin Rushcelle, her daughter, when she was a little girl. Aunt Dee decided not to use any form of motorized transportation (car or bus) to get to work and for five months she walked to work so she could use the money that would have been used on transportation to buy a new bedroom set. But, as I sit here thinking about this story, I wonder if my extra work—the work that I'm doing during the last moments of Aunt Dee's life—will enable me to reap professional rewards later?

A Temporary Home

I said my last goodbyes to my second grade class and picked up the rest of my classroom supplies. My mom and I went to the school office to begin the paperwork to withdraw me from school. Tears welled up in my eyes after I left my classmates because I would miss my peers and my teachers, but also because I was afraid they knew the real reason why I was leaving school. As my mom finished the withdrawal paperwork, the school secretary said goodbye to me, and from the look on her face, I could tell she knew why I was leaving school. My mother was laid off from her job and we were evicted from our apartment. My mom's former coworker was kind enough to let us live with her family (husband, stepson, and two daughters) temporarily until my mom found a steady job and could afford for us to move into our own apartment. Unfortunately, one of the host family's daughters had to give up her room and share a room with her sister, so my mom and I could have a bedroom. I was initially the target of name calling and resentment from the host children because of this, but at the time, I didn't realize what a sacrifice it was for a second grader to give up her room so another second grader could have shelter.

Since my mom and I were living in a house owned by a family I really didn't know, I had overwhelming anxiety every time my mom left to run errands or go to work. My mother worked as a waitress and security guard several nights a week. I often got scared and couldn't sleep when she worked nights because I was sleeping in a bedroom by myself in a house with people who were thoughtful, but strangers to me. My sleeplessness and anxiety began to impact my schooling. I generally performed well academically in my new school because it was several units behind my previous school in most subject areas; however, I was frequently falling asleep in class. I woke up at various times of the night crying and instantly picked up the phone to call Aunt Dee. It didn't matter what time of night, Aunt Dee would always pick up the phone. She would talk to me on the phone for several hours until I calmed down and fell asleep. During our late night calls, Aunt Dee would help me walk through my next school day, coming up with another game plan for me.

Aunt Dee reassured me that this new school was just temporary, this living situation was just temporary, and the life setback itself was just temporary. She encouraged me to forge ahead...to keep being...to keep doing...to keep planning. A year later, my mom and I had another shift in circumstances. My second grade insomnia continued throughout that year, but Aunt Dee still picked up the phone when I called every night until this new temporary setback came to a close and my mom saved enough money for us to get our own apartment.

Every little bit helps

I made it! I'm here! I was, generally, a conscientious student, graduating in the top ten percent of my high school class. Plus, my mother always placed emphasis on studies, using her signature phrase "Boys and books don't mix." However, for some reason I never visualized the opportunity to physically be a part of the college experience. Because I had no familial examples of the successful completion of college, graduating from college wasn't a goal of mine. I simply prayed that my hard work and diligence would at least get me through my first semester and maybe even my first year of college. Aunt Dee dropped me off at freshmen orientation—three days of activities to learn about the university, register for classes, take my picture for my student identification card, and make some initial friends.

I got everything off of the checklist my assigned orientation advisor provided, and the only item remaining was my appointment with the financial aid counselor. Aunt Dee for the year and a half prior has helped me map out all the logistics for going to college, primarily the financial piece. She decided to come with me to my appointment with the financial aid counselor to listen and take notes; then we could strategize afterward. Luckily, the financial aid counselor had mostly good news to report—that most of my tuition would be paid for through scholarships because of my academic performance in high school. I also received a few need-based grants. However, there was one line item financial aid would not cover, the one thousand dollars required for student administrative fees. After my three-day orientation, I returned to Aunt Dee's house and, for several days, we budgeted my entire first year of college—food, textbooks, and other miscellaneous necessities. I held my breath each following year when we had our college budget planning meetings, just praying that I had enough to get me through another year. These budget meetings were so important, because I often had to figure out how $8 of spending money would last me a few weeks.

The day after our college budget planning meeting, Aunt Dee had a bank envelope with $1,000 in cash that we immediately deposited in the bank. Miraculously, I was able to pay my tuition. It wasn't until several years later that I learned who the generous benefactor was. Uncle Jimmy, my mom's quiet brother who always kept to himself, served as my silent partner for my first year of college. Aunt Dee had called upon her brother to make a contribution to my education. I am not sure what she said to Uncle Jimmy. Maybe she was cashing in sacrifices she made for him at critical moments in his adult life, but, whatever her method, I was able to enroll in college and get through my first year. Every little bit helps, but I often consider what my pathway would have been if Aunt Dee had been unable to fortuitously serve as my advocate in such a critical moment.

She Is Gone

I don't remember why my sleep was unsettled and I woke up with my pillow and pajamas drenched in sweat. I looked at the hotel clock and it said 6:15 a.m. Forty-five minutes later I got up, showered and headed out the door to participate in a conference. Aunt Dee was physically transported from Baylor Hospital to a hospice care facility before I flew out to Vancouver, BC for the 2012 American Educational Research Association (AERA) Annual Meeting. Prior to attending AERA 2012, I had returned to Illinois after spending almost two weeks in the hospital with Aunt Dee. I had planned to cancel my trip to Vancouver for the conference, but I knew as a first-year tenure-track professor networking at professional conferences is critical. Plus, as the "doc" of the family, my family members were proud and didn't want anything to get in the way of my work. My family said they could take over taking care of Aunt Dee and encouraged me to continue with work and attend the conference.

I told my mother I could receive text messages while out of the country, but I had yet to hear from her on the status of Aunt Dee's condition. Instinct told me to go to the computer kiosk in my hotel and log on to check my email. There it was. The first email in my Inbox was from my mom. "Aunt Dee is struggling to breathe. She is slipping away. The doctors say she doesn't have much time." I immediately went back to my hotel room to call my mother, but, by that time, Aunt Dee already passed away. My mom updated me on everything that transpired between the few hours she emailed and up until Aunt Dee passed away. It was then that I realized the last hour Aunt Dee struggled was at the precise moment I had awakened confused and drenched in sweat earlier that morning.

From that point on I didn't attend any AERA sessions and events. I spent most of my time in my hotel room crying that day (with my roommate, writing colleague, and dearest friend Katherine Mansfield occasionally hugging me as I sobbed on her shoulder). I left the conference early and didn't present the rest of my papers. I rearranged my travel to head straight to Dallas for my aunt's memorial service. Katherine left AERA early as well to make sure I made it to the airport because of my emotional state.

It was difficult explaining to colleagues that I was cancelling all my work-related activities to assist Aunt Dee in the hospital, coupled with another set of explanations for why I was rushing to her memorial service. I found myself using more verbiage than necessary to justify my absence from work. In order to clarify I said, "my aunt raised me" or "her death is the equivalent of having a parent pass away." Since Aunt Dee replaced the role of an absent father, this latter was true. Unfortunately, I felt compelled to justify my childhood family structure because, in my professional space White, heterosexual, two-parent family units are still considered the norm. Not only does my Black single female status counter the heterosexual and married emblems that most of my colleagues wear, but also revealing my single parent upbringing placed additional identity stereotypes on me related to my social class. Disclosing my social class background was followed up with colleagues questioning whether I know how to "behave" or "act" in academia.

In my world—in my Black world—aunties, uncles, cousins, church members, and the elderly woman down the street—are all involved in the rearing of a child. The community effort of raising a child in my Black world is perceived as normal and needs no explanation, justification, or verification. I have been the vulnerable "only" in predominately White, middle class, heterosexist spaces my entire life, so one would think that even though I'm now in a vulnerable position as a pretenure professor that I would be accustomed to this level of vulnerability. So why did I feel it was still necessary to justify to others grieving for my aunt?

Since She Has Gone

When I returned to Illinois after my Aunt Dee's memorial service, I quickly threw myself back into my work routine out of sheer paranoia and fear of the internal ticking of the tenure clock. Three months after the memorial service during one of our bi-weekly phone conversations Aunt Jacque asked me, "Can I ask you a question? How are you dealing with Aunt Dee's death?" I admitted to her that I was beginning to feel physically exhausted and that work tasks that were easy and could be completed in a day or so, were now extremely challenging, taking a week or more to complete. I reassured her that other than a bit of exhaustion I was continuing to throw myself into work. Aunt Jacque admitted,

> Well, I'm grieving and have verbalized to my friends that I'm grieving. Some of them don't understand why I'm tired or sad, and I just tell them I'm still grieving, and for those who don't understand maybe we can revisit our friendship after I'm done, but right now I can't deal with people who aren't willing to understand that I'm grieving.

Hearing Aunt Jacque verbalize the word *grief* was the first time I even thought about the process of formally *grieving*. Even though my exhaustion was obviously a symptom of grief, for some reason, I considered putting a pause on work to grieve as a sign of weakness (and maybe in some ways I still do). Nonetheless, no matter what task is put on the back burner, it will still remain there waiting to be reconciled. My Aunt Dee emphasized diligence and pressing forward despite obstacles, but sometimes stepping over a pile of mess in order to get everything else done isn't always healthy. Eventually, whatever it is, in my case GRIEF that you put aside to meet work demands will eventually catch up with you. There is an extra set of exhaustion that comes with trying to act "normal." Pushing aside the grieving in order to catch up on work was a futile attempt on my part to act and appear "normal." Aunt Dee for the duration of her adult life simultaneously coped with multiple illnesses and assisted others with their personal issues. This level of selflessness often meant Aunt Dee did not take the time to attend to her personal health. Putting her own health on the back burner in order to work, work, and work ultimately led to Aunt Dee's complete immobility during the last several years of her life.

I admit when one of my mentors, Dr. Whitney Sherman Newcomb, put out the call for contributions to this book, just like my grieving, I placed finalizing this chapter on the back burner. Writing this chapter meant that I had to actually put the grieving to the page. Completing the chapter forced me to suspend other work related duties and take the time to grieve. The manuscript was over a week late to Whitney (practically a month late with the extension she gave to authors). Colleagues often say they appreciate that I am "dependable" and "reliable," but, for once, this character trait wavered because writing this chapter meant I must take the time to grieve, and I needed more time. It's easy conducting research and writing as an observer, but letting your own stuff hang out to dry is DIFFICULT and EMOTIONAL. I admit I had several reservations about completing this manuscript because of my hyper-visibility as a pretenure professor, woman of color. Revealing layers of my identity that aren't as readily visible as my skin color and gender (such as straddling between working class and poor, experiences with homelessness, being a first-generation college graduate, and coming from a single parent home) means I am further "othered" and exposed (Ford, 2011; Turner, 2002), maybe even too exposed considering I still have to achieve tenure. Many times I considered contacting Whitney to tell her I was pulling my chapter because I felt it was too much of a risk to share my personal narrative. Though what I share is deeply personal, I know it is important and worth some risk because I have several graduate students with similar intersecting identities that feel like there aren't others like them pursing a doctoral degree and a career in academia. Thus, storytelling, no matter how deeply personal, demonstrates that those with identities that are historically "othered" can infiltrate predominately White, affluent academic spaces. Still, for some reason, exposing these other identities is easier than taking the time necessary to GRIEVE.

WHO WILL GET ME THROUGH?

Aunt Dee, who, in many ways, was a coparent and codirector of "project Anjalé," is now gone. The vignettes I shared in this narrative are deeply personal and presented in a nonchronological order. I chose to present these vignettes in the order in which I reflected upon them during my formal grieving process. Despite my guilt for working during my final moments with Aunt Dee, I was awarded the grant I wrote (that barely got submitted by the deadline) while I was in the hospital with her before she passed away. This was my first grant award as an assistant professor. I realized even though Aunt Dee couldn't talk to me while she was in the hospital, her presence helped me complete the grant application. It was her final act of duty as my *life planner*. The vignettes present critical and painful moments that Aunt Dee has helped me get through, but now that I am in grieving mode I wonder who is going to help me get through the rest of life, and the biggest task of my professional career—tenure.

Throughout my life I was made to feel that my childhood family structure was a deficit and meant I was a high risk for failure. However, Aunt Dee's coparenting and other family and community members' contribution to my success, though considered nontraditional, was, for me, a valid part of my Black identity, a form of Black cultural capital (Carter, 2003) that helped me navigate often egregious predominately White spaces that I have been educated in or worked within my entire life. Education as an institution focuses on what communities of color lack, not recognizing the cultural assets, or nondominant forms of cultural capital, students of color use in their own communities, (Carter, 2003; Gonzalez & Moll, 2002; Yosso, 2005). This nondominant capital should be legitimized in institutional spaces (Yosso, 2005). However, I have noticed the skills I have used to develop familial capital, kin, ties, or social networks (Yosso, 2005; Stanton-Salazar, 2001), mirrors the way in which I navigate my professional space by building a scholarly network or community. Therefore, even though Aunt Dee, my *life planner*, is gone, there are people who will get me through to eventually earn tenure.

I was and still remain close with my PhD cohort. Most of my cohort members successfully acquired tenure-track positions and we continue to check in with each other, collaborate on research, give each other feedback on our writing, push ourselves, and hold each other accountable for getting the work done. I feel extremely fortunate to have entered my doctoral program at the right time, when I was able to be a part of a strong doctoral cohort, a family, who in some ways replaced Aunt Dee's role as *life planner* (of course there are many roles left unfilled now that she is gone). But, my time in doctoral studies had some definite imperfect moments. For instance, it took at least two and half years for me to secure a mentor in the doctoral program!

Much of the challenge in securing a faculty mentor was due to the fact that I worked full time as a teacher of students with emotional disabilities at the elementary level my first year or so in the doctoral program. Most of my students were removed from abusive home environments and lived in therapeutic group home settings. Therefore, at the time I served as both teacher and parent to my students. In fact, during that first year of both teaching and engaging in my doctoral studies fulltime, I was bestowed with the honor of Austin Independent School District's Special Education Teacher of the Year. Taking four doctoral level courses a semester as a full time graduate student plus working 60 or more hours a week hardly gave me time to network with other professors in order to get an idea of whose research I was interested in so that I could approach them as a potential faculty mentor. Engaging in both graduate school and working full time also gave me limited opportunities to seek out graduate assistantships, so I could then quit my full time teaching job and simply focus on my doctoral studies.

During this time, I received a full fellowship offer from another research-extensive university with a highly reputable educational policy doctoral program. The university paid for me to visit the campus and put together a two-day schedule of visits with faculty, students, and a campus tour. Three weeks later, the program director contacted me and said that the faculty were impressed with me and would like to offer me a full fellowship. I felt like that was the first time I was truly recognized for my scholarly potential and the work I had already put forward with the two masters degrees I had acquired in education, plus the real world experiences I gained as an urban educator. One professor at this other university told me, "You have already developed your scholarship, and you can just pick up where you left off when you enroll here and immediately move forward with conceptualizing your dissertation." However, I still chose to enroll in a university in my native state of Texas even though I was not offered any fellowship money and told there was none available when I assertively inquired. I had a number of reasons for my decision, but I had been away from Texas, my home, for quite some time, and with my Aunt Dee's health taking a turn I really wanted to be close to my family. Therefore, enrolling in a doctoral program without a fellowship meant more financial hardship due to working multiple jobs and acquiring some loan debt in order to support my studies. It was the right choice for me at the time because I needed to be closer to my family for my emotional health.

My first few years of the doctoral program were a real struggle for me because I felt like even with tactical efforts to secure a faculty mentor, the mentoring opportunities never materialized. So, in the early times of the doctoral program when mentoring was hard to obtain, my family and a few peers in my doctoral cohort (Katherine Cumings Mansfield and Pei-Ling Lee who talked me through points of personal crisis when my scholarly self-worth and self-esteem were extremely low) were the ones who recognized my scholarly potential and encouraged me to keep at it. Aunt Dee was the driving force in terms of facilitating my plan for my educational career while other family members (my mother, Aunt Jacque, Uncle Jimmy, and many others) verbalized they were proud of me. I was the first! The first to get a college degree and the first to even consider going to graduate school. My family would tell everyone they knew about my accomplishments. Upon being introduced to a family friend for the first time, they would say, "We heard about you. You are the one who is going to be the doctor, wow!" To be honest, familial capital (see Yosso, 2005) was the only fuel that got me through those first years of the doctoral program. Family members were the only ones to verbalize that I was smart! I wanted to quit so many times because I received limited encouragement during my first few years of my doctoral studies. Aside from select highly encouraging peers in my cohort, and despite insistent attempts on my part to make scholarly connections with faculty and peers, my efforts were more than often left unreciprocated. The "Why am I here?" question popped in my head every other day.

It was in my third year of my doctoral studies when opportunities and my outlook shifted in a positive direction. It took time to get others to take notice, but there were a few faculty members who began to recognize that I was a hard worker, and offered me assistantships and opportunities to collaborate on research projects. I am still publishing the data on some of these projects that faculty mentors offered opportunities for me to engage in. I was able to start a tenure-track position at least one lap ahead because I had a few publications in print or in press from these projects. A few faculty members who became formal mentors actually researched the importance and dynamics of faculty–graduate student mentoring relationships (see Reddick & Young, 2012). The fact that Dr. Young and Dr. Reddick actively researched mentoring, in turn, made them strategic in mentoring me, especially when it came to teaching me how to navigate the job search process. One mentor in particular, Dr. Holme, did not settle on only one student to work with, but offered a number of students opportunities to collaborate on research projects (see Holme, Richards, Jimerson, & Cohen, 2010; Holme, Welton, Diem, 2012; Holme, Diem, & Mansfield, 2011). Also, in my second year of doctoral studies, a professor actually verbalized to the class that I was a good student—that I was scholarly. This was the first time EVER in my educational career a teacher, let alone a professor, verbalized I was smart! This professor, Jeff Wayman, spent significant amounts of time developing his students' writing skills and securing grant funds to establish research projects that would also help support students' dissertation research. Once I secured those first few formal mentors by the third year of my doctoral studies, I had examples of what a good mentor looked like and what strategies I could use to connect to additional mentors within and external to my home institution.

In those first couple of years in my doctoral studies it was not formal mentoring, but, instead, strong familial ties and select peers who encouraged me to see my doctoral pursuits through. This Black cultural capital, the familial and cultural capital that *I feel* encapsulates *my* Black identity, has been so critical to my educational and professional success, and has seen me through thus far. Now that Aunt Dee passed away, I recognize that my Black cultural capital is *good*, it is *important*, and it is the *right* kind of capital **I NEED** to navigate academia. Since Aunt Dee passed away I continually search elsewhere for elements of capital that worked well in my dynamic with her. The following are elements I have identified in my relationships with Aunt Dee and other family and community members I consider as positive forms of *my* Black cultural capital:

- *I need people who will help me develop both a vision and strategic plan for a successful road to tenure.* My Aunt Dee strategically helped me plan each phase of my educational trajectory. In our planning meetings Aunt Dee and I planned down to the last dollar what was needed for me to continue with my studies. Similarly, every so often my former doctoral cohort members and I check in with each other or have our own informal planning meetings to make sure we are actively writing, working on finalizing a publication that has been accepted for publication, or at least have several manuscripts in progress. If any of us in the cohort is struggling, we find ways to help each other gain momentum and secure authorship on an article. We also share each other's scholarly plan and timeline for tenure to make sure we are all on the right track; learning from each other if there are areas that one peer has garnered more success in that we could then apply to our own tenure trajectory.
- *I need to* hear *people engage in counter-storytelling to demonstrate there are others "like me" in the academy.* I am taking a huge risk as a pretenure faculty of color sharing in this chapter some of my deeply personal stories from childhood to the present. When I presented my Aunt Dee with a personal dilemma she would provide personal testimonies (other family members still practice this as well) in order to demonstrate she understood my struggle, but expected me to press on in spite of the struggle. Recently a couple of scholars whose work I highly admire served as guest speakers in my signature course on education, democracy, identity politics, and social justice leadership. Both scholars engaged in counter-storytelling to demonstrate how their personal identity and struggles serve as the momentum for their educational and scholarly pursuits. One scholar expressed that her first-generation college graduate status was the impetus for pursuing a doctoral degree in education, and the other scholar shared experiences with isolation in her secondary schooling because of her sexual identity. Both of these guest speakers were nationally

renowned scholars, who served as examples for me that my complex identities can function as a positive thrust for my own work and scholarly success.

- *I need to see others "like me" successfully navigating the academy.* As I mentioned earlier in my narrative, not only did I have family members who motivated me but I also had strong examples of community members (mostly church members), Black leaders, who were educators and successful business owners. Black leaders in the community connected my mother to educational resources that would provide me greater opportunities. One church member was a school board member and helped my mother negotiate the process of transferring me to a better-resourced school. It took time to find the right academic and professional space, but currently I work in a department where more than half of the faculty members are persons of color. Even though I have a number of mentors who do not identify with my racial/ethnic background, for me it is important to have a significant number of leaders and scholars of color in my workplace to demonstrate that where I work is a place where persons of color can be successful. In previous institutions where I was employed, if there were little to no employees of color (often I was the only), it was a definite sign that limited support would be available for me to thrive in that professional space.

- *I need people to verbalize to me that I am scholarly and that my scholarship matters.* Even though most of family members do not have a college degree, they have been a positive barometer for building my scholarly self-esteem by simply telling me I am smart. I chose my current institution of employment because both faculty and students on the job search committee verbalized that they wanted someone whose scholarship was centered on social justice and pushed dialogue on issues of social justice in their coursework. So far, I have had several colleagues in my department verbalize to me that I am "collegial," and that "Other faculty want you to be successful here" and that "Faculty appreciate that you deeply care about students and teaching," and that "Faculty notice that you are a productive scholar and work hard." Words of support from my colleagues are important because they give me a since of belonging, self-efficacy, appreciation, and verbal recognition that I might be doing the right things to achieve tenure.

- *I need colleagues who will share opportunities, resources, and help me make sure I have the necessary boxes checked for obtaining tenure.* As my educational advocate, Aunt Dee, as well as numerous family and community members, made sure I had what I needed to matriculate to and complete college. Aunt Dee and I always made calculated lists of items or tasks for college. Every so often as I'm cleaning out certain boxes of bills or notes, I come across some of these list in her handwriting or documents she has sent me that were critical for college planning. Currently I have tenured colleagues in my department who voluntarily offer me opportunities and make suggestions of resources I should tap into, because they want to make sure I have the necessary boxes checked in order to make tenure. One colleague invited me to be coprincipal investigator for a grant, another colleague has offered me an opportunity to coedit a book, and a number of colleagues make suggestions for different campus-based, as well as external, grants I should apply for. These are all ways in which my colleagues make sure I know the expectations for tenure and that I am prepared to meet those expectations. Constantly sharing, providing opportunities, and making sure I understand norms and practices of the tenure-track are all ways in which my colleagues demonstrate that they want me to succeed.

- *I need emotional support.* As my narrative demonstrates, in points of considerable crisis, Aunt Dee was my greatest source of emotional support until each crisis subsided. I have a cadre of peers, especially from my doctoral cohort, who I instantly call in moments of extreme crisis. This is my first time living in the Midwest. I moved to a small college town for the job opportunity. Since I have no friends and familial connections here, it is important I reach out to my peers elsewhere for emotional support.
- *Finally, I need to be in an academic space that recognizes my Black cultural capital is vital to my survival and the way in which I navigate the academy.* Obviously I have made it this far in my career, and the Black cultural capital that I rely on is working in my favor, but why are certain academic spaces still so resistant to faculty who do not represent the academy's idea of "normal"? Why do certain academic spaces still push back with sexist, heterosexist, racist, and classist organizational and institutional standards of being and performing; despite those of us who demonstrate time and time again our way of "making it" in the academy works for us and we can be successful if we bring elements of our multilayered identities to the forefront of our professional realm? I have always relied on a complex set of resources, but most of those resources are rooted in familial and community ties, though some of the resources are from persons who are experts in navigating academia, such as faculty mentors and scholarly colleagues. However, it is interesting to note that the capital I rely on the most derives from those who know the least about the rules of the academy—my family. My family is just that, the ones who are most *famili*ar with me and know what I need. The strategies I

learned when Aunt Dee and I put our heads together and planned, planned, and planned again, even though she is gone, are skill sets (i.e., cultural capital) I learned from our relationship that I can attribute to the road to tenure.

REFERENCES

Carter, P. L. (2003). "Black" cultural capital, status positioning, and schooling conflicts for low income African American youth. *Social Problems, 50*(1), 136–155.

Ford, K. A. (2011). Race, gender, and bodily (mis)recognitions: Women of color faculty experiences with white students in the college classroom. *Journal of Higher Education, 82*(4), 444–478.

Holme, J. J., Richards, M., Jimerson, J. B., & Cohen, B. (2010). Testing the "theory of action" of high school exit exam policies: A review of research of the impact of exit testing on student achievement, attainment, post-secondary outcomes, and institutional responses. *Review of Educational Research, 80*(4), 476–526.

Holme, J. J., Welton, A., Diem, S. (2012). Pursuing "separate but equal" in suburban San Antonio: A case study of Southern Independent School District. In E. Frankenberg & G. Orfield (Eds.) *The resegregation of suburban schools: A hidden crisis in American education* (pp. 45–67). Cambridge, MA: Harvard Education Press.

Holme, J. J, Diem, S., & Mansfield, K. C. (2011). Regional coalitions and educational policy: Lessons from the Nebraska Learning Community agreement. In E. Frankenberg & E. DeBray (Eds.), *Integrating schools in a changing society: New policies and legal options for a multiracial generation* (pp. 151–164). Chapel Hill, NC: University of North Carolina Press.

Gonzalez, N. & Moll, L. C. (2002). Cruzando el puente: Building bridges to funds of knowledge, *Educational Policy, 16*(4), 623–641.

Reddick, R. J., & Young, M. D. (2012). Mentoring graduate students of color. In S. Fletcher & C. Mullen (Eds.), *The SAGE handbook of mentoring and coaching for education* (pp. 412–429). Thousand Oaks, CA: SAGE.

Stanton-Salazar, R. D. (2001). *Manufacturing hope and despair: The school and kin support networks of U.S. Mexican youth.* New York: Teachers College Press.

Turner, C. S. V. (2002). Women of color in academe: Living with multiple marginality. *The Journal of Higher Education, 73*(1), 74–94.

Yosso, T. (2005). Whose culture has capital? A critical race theory discussion of community cultural wealth. *Race, Ethnicity, and Education, 8*(1), 69–91.

CHAPTER 14

SENSE MAKING

The Fight to Claim and Continuously Reclaim a Space in Higher Education

Whitney Sherman Newcomb and Catherine Ruziak Gorman

Continuing to Disrupt the Status Quo? Young and New Women Professors of Educational Leadership was conceptualized to give young and new women professors in the field of educational leadership a space to share their voices in regard to their experiences as faculty in higher education. The authors bravely provide personal, intimate, and emotional examples of hardships and triumph that have shaped who they are as women faculty. It is painstakingly clear through narrative after narrative that although women have increased in number in departments of educational leadership, the contexts and climates in which they have entered and exist have, in many ways, remained stagnant along the lines of gender dynamics since the entry of veteran women into the field. Age and race have further complicated the experiences of women who have continued to enter the field, bringing the concepts of intersectionality and multiple subjectivities to the forefront in several instances for discussion. Women have not mastered the balance of work and home expectations more effectively as time has marched on; they continue to struggle with the demands of their identities as wives/partners, mothers, sisters, and daughters, perhaps due to societal expectations that have remained unchanged and continue to place women as primarily accountable for responsibilities at home. For these women, legislative shifts and workplace policies have, for the most part, been rendered as useless (other than Title IX which allowed them entry in the first place) due to unspoken rules and consequences made known to them from the first moments they secured their positions. The enactment of the very policies created to help them is often seen as weak and detrimental to the securing of tenure.

Returning to the question posed by Edie Rusch in Mertz (2009), we asked "How many department faculty have mastered the art of healthy gender dynamics?" (p. 184). In our search to answer this question, we read and re-read the women's narratives to search for emerging themes that capture the realities that they live as faculty so that we can better understand and make sense of the experiences of new and young women to the field of educational leadership. Their narratives, the specific stories the women chose to share, and their tone in writing, together, give readers a window into their consciousness.

Living on the Defense

We heard in many instances that women have been forced to live on the defense; albeit in different ways. For example, Melanie shared,

> However, while I am mindful of the various kinds of privilege I enjoy and constantly educate myself about and reflect on them, I also recognize that I cannot work in a state where I am constantly defending who I am or the work that I do.

For Melanie, part of the struggle she faced that required her to take a defensive stance over and over again was related to her identity as a "trailing spouse." Despite how hard she has worked to create an identity for herself as a noteworthy scholar in her own right, it has been difficult to shake the title of "the other academic in the household" or to not be seen as the "other half of a faculty package" where her husband is seen as the coveted one and she is seen as the perk, or, in some instances, the tag along. It is difficult to make advances with your work as a scholar if you are forced to live constantly defending who you are and your right to claim space in higher education.

Azadeh described the need for her defensive stance in another way:

> Many of my female colleagues and I often discuss the sad idea what we must consistently 'prove' we should be in this space; that there is a burden of proof that does not rest in our accomplishments, research, teaching, or service, but rather in the eye of the beholder. I feel the constant ebb and flow of the liminal space in which I inhabit and the constant watchful eyes waiting for me to make a mistake.

For both Azadeh and others, the obtainment of a faculty position did not bring with it a basic level of respect that is granted to most male colleagues. Instead, there is the need to constantly remind others of why they should have space in higher education and why their voices should be heard. For these women, the defensive stance has turned into a "crouch and dodge" ritual as hostile eyes lay in wait for mistakes to be made. Furthermore, for some women, defensive strategies were needed for the interview process before even attaining a faculty position. They had to not only justify their presence in academia, but their feminist research as well. Melissa described a hazing incident in the following way:

> My hybrid Chicana feminist and social capital conceptual framework was questioned, and my research findings were deemed obvious. "Given the context of your study, I could have told you, you would get these results without doing the study," one audience member said. And it wasn't the mere fact that I was being questioned about my work that bothered me. It was the tone and condescending manner in which I was being questioned that was disturbing. Perhaps this is what I should have expected, a part of the job talk and interviewing process. Clearly, my mentors and colleagues had not prepped me for this. I know I looked flustered in responding to some of the last questions. One question was thrown at me that I did not understand, but tried my best to answer. I was on the verge of tears. It took everything I had in me to hold it together in front of this crowd of at least 30 to 40 people. As what seemed like a hazing ceremony concluded, I quickly excused myself and headed for the restroom so that I could gain composure and swallow the knot in my throat and silence the deafening beating heart in my ears.

Whitney described a similar incident during an interview for an academic position when she said she was asked why her dissertation study entitled "Women's Experiences with a District-Based Aspiring Leadership Program" didn't include men to make it more equitable.

Catherine and April spoke of living on the defense related to the ways in which they experience their individual intersectionalities. For April, her defense stance was created by the complications of race, gender, and age. When she was in K–12 practice, she "noticed the need for others to 'validate' my credibility in my first administrative position in a charter school." She went on to describe this further and said,

> White masculinity is read as authority in ways that Black femininity is not. They [other administrators] had no need to prove their credibility given their subject position as White men. However, irrespective of the fact that the audience was almost always made of a majority of Black women, they implicitly understood that my authority would not be widely received without making my credibility transparent. This understanding was reified continually in my role in this school. I was often challenged by parents who would then openly accept the same communication from the White male administrator.

The need for Catherine's defensive stance was due to the intersectionality of both gender and deafness. She described multiple instances of abuses from student colleagues and professors alike in her doctoral program. She stated,

> There were many times when others told me to fight against his [a professor] authority (oppressive behavior and prejudice), file a grievance, make some noise, etc. If I had enjoyed the support of my peers or professor(s), I might have made a different decision. I felt alone in making this decision and made the one I felt was best in the situation. Today, I am not sure I could do anything differently, without support. But, if I had support I do not believe that I would be so docile. Further, I would encourage my students and my peers to seek appropriate respect, *with* my support and encouragement. We rarely change behaviors or force respect from others by using laws that seek to force them to change.

Catherine described her defensive stance as one of running for cover on several occasions, but with strategies employed for achieving success ultimately. She encountered predispositions from others uncomfortable with individuals with disabilities and torture due to ignorance and advice to ignore the insults: "Later she [a professor she had gone to for counsel] told me to stay quiet and not to engage in debate with him. He was never reprimanded or spoken to about his continuing inappropriate behavior."

Catherine sums up this overbearing need to defend with the following, "We rarely change behaviors or force respect from others by using laws that seek to force them to change." In good faith we create laws and policies meant to protect those that have less of a voice within the systems in place; however, historically we have seen that no matter how many policies we create the mindset doesn't change. The underlying factors for this seem to be twofold: policies cannot change overnight the preconceived prejudices that exist or the climates in which they thrive. The change must come at a deeper level, an earlier recognition of an individual's value from childhood and less of a predisposed purpose based on gender alone. While these changes in attitude have evolved over the years, they remain slow to evolve; thus, making it difficult to level the playing field later in life. So the sense of gender and being solely defined by gender can still remain a point of contention and an obstacle to achieving individual goals.

Failure to Walk the Line: Unmentorable and Intolerable

Almost every author described instances of expressed discontent from colleagues due to discomfort with the women's difference and behaviors that were seen as straying from "the norm." Katherine described her narrative as, "...a story of being 'betwixt and between' and my failure to fall in line with prescribed forms of conduct and my resistance to those who would hold me back from living my authentic self." For Katherine, the intolerances described to her by her colleagues were the very behaviors that kept her authentic to herself (i.e., speaking out against injustice, voicing her opinion). Azadeh described specific instances of the negative connotations the word "strong" brings when applied to women:

> It has interested me to know when the word "strong" became a pejorative in relation to women faculty members in education—whether the term is used in relation to dispositions, personality, or tone. I wonder, was there ever an option for a space invader, like me, to not be strong? Would I be sitting at the same table as you, watching you as you curiously watch me, if I were not strong? Pervasive sexist and racist systems perpetuated by the hegemonic exclusionary elite require strong action. It is this type of action that will help me push past the liminal space, into a more solid realm. I do not have the luxury to be passive.

She went on to describe a verbal exchange with a White male colleague: "I want to talk to you about your tone," he said. "My tone?" I said. "Yes, *YOUR* tone," he said and further described her consciousness of this "dialogue:"

> I learned that day that my tone is perceived as tough, aggressive, and strong. This is what the older White man told me in his fancy office. And he told me I needed to "watch it" because two White faculty members did not like "it." What he did not know was that my mother, whose will and strength mirrors that of the Gods of the Pantheon, taught all three of her daughters to be strong, to be intelligent, to be independent, and to be assertive. Intellectual prowess combined with verbal dexterity—that was her Persian recipe for raising her daughters... I looked at him. He looked at me. I apprised him of my skillful mother's child-raising philosophies and reminded him that the cultural codes inherent in my family structure would not mirror those of the White faculty members to whom he was referring. I advised him that I would not succumb to or believe in hegemony of language, which allows a certain way of speaking (a white way) to be privileged over my way. As a woman of color, I was raised to speak carefully and with intelligence, knowledge, and assertiveness.

For Azadeh, the intersectionality of gender, race, and age interacted to create such discomfort for a colleague that he had no idea what to do with her other than try to assert his authority and privilege as a White male to reprimand her. Her failure to walk the line rendered her intolerable by this colleague.

Karen shared an instance where failure to walk the line could have had high-stakes consequences and cost her to be denied tenure:

> It was an uncomfortable situation that felt negatively patriarchal and it was clear my gender and age was a strong influencing factor in their level of discomfort with me going up for tenure. Their concerns had nothing to do with me meeting the tenure criteria. Both acknowledged I was fine in those areas. However, they did have a problem with my personality and communication style. While not overly vocal, I have no problem speaking my mind and making clear my thoughts on situations of importance. This was something they did not like. I have always made it a point to speak my mind. I could tell this made both of them uncomfortable—a young woman with a mind of her own—and they imposed on me they wanted me to "be seen and not heard" on future faculty issues.

For Karen, the enactment of the right to speak her mind as a young woman resulted in an unethical discussion by male colleagues with power as influencers of tenure decisions at her university and threats to deny tenure for not walking the line.

For many of the women, the act of walking the line was akin to keeping their mouths shut, not sharing opinions, and cowering in the corner as weak-minded individuals. Anything else rendered them as intolerable colleagues incapable of having the rules "beat into them," whether through mentoring or scolding. Whitney described instances of being told her personality is "too strong" and to "take a chill pill and tone it down a notch" and was even told administrators were probably "sick of seeing her face" for expressing her opinion and defending herself when necessary. And, she described an instance where a student expected her to know her place as a female in society when she was told by him that she couldn't take his brand of intellect due to being a women.

And, for a few women, the battle between walking the line and not walking the line ran deeper and caused conflicts with their families due to their intersecting ethnic identities and gender expectations. Both Gaëtane and Melissa described the struggle with sexist traditions in their backgrounds. Gaëtane explained, "Culturally, a female leaving her parents' home to live independently is frowned upon. Nevertheless, I was in search of a new path, one that would lead to a fulfilling career."

Space Invaders and "Otherness"

All of the women spoke of instances of being "othered" and, therefore, were classified as space invaders in a sense. For Cosette, being a space invader was due to her ethnicity and gender:

> I am the only African-American female faculty in my program. I am one of two tenure track faculty producing scholarship in my program and with graduate faculty status, which has allowed me a direct line of access to leadership equal to the program coordinator and support unavailable to other peers and the program coordinator. This has caused some backlash from White peers as a result.

Melanie described her "otherness" in a different way:

> I started my career in higher education as a trailing spouse—a following, dragging, straggling, lagging, shadowing, stalking, pulling, and bringing-up-the-rear wife. As many dual career couples know, finding a workplace that accommodates and supports the careers of both spouses is akin to finding the proverbial needle in a haystack. It took my husband Jeff and I four years and three universities before we were offered tenure-track and tenured positions at the same institution. The toll was high. Moving was difficult on our finances, marriage, and children. More challenging, though, were the many unwelcomed opportunities to learn about the dark side of academe: the politics; dishonesty; backbiting; misconduct; carelessness; sexism; and mismanagement that were common in each workplace.

And Katherine described the otherness she experienced as a female child of poverty who held high expectations for herself while surrounded by others who did not:

> After introducing myself to the counselor, I asked, "What do I need to do to go to college?" Laughter immediately ruptured the silence. I waited for her words, but none were forthcoming. I repeated my question, to which she shook her head and chuckled again. I asked, "Did I say something funny?" She answered, "Well, you aren't exactly college material." I felt ashamed of my ragged hand-me-downs and her gape that named me *white trash*. My cheeks were aflame as I realized she must know about the verbal taunts. The punching. The kicking.

As she recounted the shame she experienced as a child, Katherine went on to try to make sense of some of her experiences as a female adult in higher education and said,

> I was struck by how on the one hand; change *has* taken place in academe. There are more women studying and earning advanced degrees than ever before. On the other hand, however, the huge growth of female graduate students and the modest visibility of women professors has not, in and of itself, allowed an immediate and thorough overhaul in the reign of the status quo in the Ivory Tower. I was reminded of some of the literature I read while completing a doctoral portfolio in Women's and Gender Studies concerning the concept of liminality—or what I call, "outsiderness"—and how women may

be *allowed* in the so-called club, but still struggle for full membership with the rights and responsibilities that come with it.

Even as an adult, Katherine continues to struggle for full membership to "the club."

Several of the women wrote about health consequences of their space invader status. Azadeh talked about academic schizophrenia and the feeling of not belonging:

> By academic schizophrenia, I offer that although I am a relatively young academician (37 years old) with some accomplishments under my belt, the ever-pulsating knowledge of not fitting in and not belonging *here* wears on my conscience. I never thought of myself as a weak or naive person, however in the six, going on seven, years I have been *here*, my thin, worn skin and navigational naïveté have not only become situated in my own weary head, but have been repeatedly confirmed by those around me. My identity and the identity that others put upon have comingled to create this ugly third space that houses feelings of inadequacy, incompetency, and self-defeat. No matter where I go I know that I do not belong... *here*.

For Azadeh, the intersectionality between gender, race, and age has created a sense of not belonging and a wariness that has come much too early in her career. She went on to describe her disappointment once achieving a position in higher education as her hopes of being a champion for those who have been "othered" have been stifled by her classification by others as an "other" or space invader and the difficulty in being heard when you are rendered invisible yourself.

> I naively thought that if I worked at an institution that championed minority causes and was designated as an HSI that I would feel a sense of belonging—a transnational version of feminist collusion and cohabitation that was global in scope, and encouraged women to unite, not further divide. However, I was totally wrong. I came here so innocent, thinking we were all fighting for the same causes, the disenfranchised student, the forgotten youth of tomorrow, and the returning adult learner looking to make sense of the world through a newly earned degree. However, I was totally wrong. I have come here to know and understand the othering of the other. I am a theorist; you think my thoughts and ideas are worthless. I am a Persian; I do not fit into any of your confines, and thus you dislike and distrust me even more. I am Middle-Eastern; and in the post 9/11 world your fear and disgust with regards to me are tangible; and most of all I am an invader of your space; I am sitting right next to you. Right *here*.

For Catherine, being a deaf woman rendered her as an "other" who was not only incapable of being a student, but incapable of ever being a school leader. She said,

> As a member of the cohort, I soon realized that becoming a school administrator, as a deaf woman, was going to be a challenge. Many of the members, both men and women, challenged my presence in the cohort. They contended that since I was deaf, I would not be able to hear student fights, emergencies, fire alarms, or be able to communicate with staff, parents, and students. The fact that I had been a successful teacher for over 12 years (even being awarded the "Teacher of the Year") did not enter into their mental models of who I was or what I could become. They had limited me simply because I could not hear.

And, in yet another instance, Melissa talked about "otherness" in terms of isolation and not fitting in with the socialization practices of networking to become a professor:

> I explained to Esperanza how I had become overwhelmed and disgusted by what seemed to be "normal" socialization practices at these research conferences. You would constantly see doctoral students pining over leading academics in the field and cliques of alumni from particular research one institutions gathered and traveling together in packs, often, seemingly snubbing other students like me that did not come from these particular institutions or didn't share the same mentor "bloodlines." Moreover, networking particularly disturbed me because it seemed so superficial, self-serving, and competitive; at least from my own observations and experiences up to that point. You would see people in hallways, elevators, and conference halls all doing this. You had to be able to recite your research interests, ask others' theirs, and not be ashamed to gloat a bit about yourself and any of your scholarly accomplishments thus far. I also felt like you were expected to "be on" at all times because as a doctoral student who would someday be on the job market, whether for a faculty or administrative position in higher education, you never knew who was a potential colleague or employer. This pressure to "perform" suffocated me. Seeing some of my own colleagues fall prey to these expectations and quickly become competitive, name-dropping and fame-seeking hounds was disheartening. Taking all of this in as I went from session to session that day, I began to withdraw and proceeded to have what could only be described as either a breakdown or an out of body experience.

Overall, Katherine's statement of feeling "...like the educational process was more akin to fitting a 'square peg in a round hole' (or, trying to stuff a woman into a manhole?)" seems to capture the experiences of many of the women well. Others who have been "othered?" Yes, indeed. Space invaders? Absolutely. Phenomenal women faculty who have managed to thrive despite their imposed status? Hell, yes.

Firestarters

As we read each story, it became apparent how many of the women held "firestarter" status in the eyes of some colleagues. Failure to walk the line and conform to the norm, an ever present theme throughout the narratives, resulted in being considered not only intolerable and unmentorable, but active trouble makers as well. Gaëtane described her struggle as a young Black woman from the Caribbean to raise issues of social justice in her classroom:

> No matter how I structured my course syllabus in an honest effort to disclose through course objectives and student learning outcomes, the evaluations usually criticized the amount of time spent discussing race or more precisely "bashing whites". At times, I developed a hypersensitivity to these tensions and consistently had to adjust my "mask" to fit the classroom environment, as Paul Dunbar avers in *We Wear the Mask* (1993): "We wear the mask that grins and lies. It hides our cheeks and shades our eyes…" However, there were momentary lapses in the adjustment process of my mask where a rage flooded my being.

For Gaetane, pushing boundaries required the wearing of a mask at times to hide disappointment and disgust. Katherine described being a firestarter in a different way as a result of actions from a male student colleague:

> For example, one day, during my fifth year in the program, I received an email from a second-year PhD student (whom I had never met) telling me what to wear and how to act at a professional conference! Apparently, unless all of us looked like a male model in a "Lands' End" catalogue and kept our mouths shut while in the presence of eminent scholars (among several specific directives); we would be an embarrassment to him and the entire scholarly community. After thinking on it awhile, I responded to this young man. I did not reply to "all" as I did not want to humiliate him, but only wanted to let him know how his email offended me, personally… I did not hear back from this young man. According to others, he shared with his entire cohort my response in an attempt to make me look like a bully.

The pushing back from Katherine caused defensiveness in this student for his actions as he labeled her a bully for being vocal about her disapproval of his e-mail. Whitney also described multiple instances of being considered a firestarter; more as a response from unsubstantiated allegations to her character, rather than trying to instigate discord within her academic environment:

> I went into this meeting with my gloves off and back open to attack (I had no other reason to act otherwise) because I assumed that whatever the purpose

of the meeting, it was for the good of the faculty as a whole and would result in a positive outcome. Instead, I spent an hour and a half being verbally and emotionally assaulted by two of the faculty [...]

Furthermore, she went on to say that the simple act of asking a clarifying question defined her as "combative."

Throughout all of the narratives we see a common theme of women being told that they are difficult, pushy, obstinate, and combative—simply because these women wish to have a voice and an active role in their own futures. These women were told that taking charge of their own lives, taking responsibility for life's outcomes, and defending themselves when necessary made them somehow less desirable in their inability to stay silent and tow the line. Sadly, many of these negative events were perpetuated not only by men, but by fellow women. It would seem that women would find a sense of community to nurture one another, especially in environments that have proven predominantly male. And, sometimes they do. However, as many of these narratives have indicated, this, unfortunately, is not always the case.

Sexism and Racist Microaggression

Many of the women talked about sexism and racist microaggression. For some, while sexist behaviors are still present, they have become more subtle rather than overt, causing women to second-guess what they have experienced. Jennifer put it this way:

> Now, we see examples of smaller decisions, side comments, joke telling, and what seem to be harmless commentary that actually cause women to second-guess their own worth, qualifications, and sense of belonging.

Others described annoying instances of being overlooked due to their gender. Karen described an instance of sexist bewilderment on the part of a male interviewer:

> About fifteen minutes into the interview conversation, my co-PI walked in (who is a male) and the gentleman interviewing me looked right at me and asked "So he is your boss?," to which my colleague and I looked at each other and started to laugh, which clearly confused the person interviewing me. My colleague then said "no"—that I was the grant Director and Principal Investigator, not him. The man looked even more confused because it did not make sense to him that I was the one running the grant.

For others, their experiences with sexism were further complicated by ethnicity and age. Cosette discussed this subtle process of the undermining of her value as a Black woman and said,

> Scholar Solorzano (1998) recognizes micro-aggression as subtle insults (verbal, nonverbal, and/or visual) directed toward people of color, often automatically or unconsciously as "put downs" of Blacks by "offenders" (Pierce, Carew, Pierce-Gonzalez, & Wills, 1978, p. 66). They further maintain that these "offensive mechanisms used against Blacks often are innocuous" and that the "cumulative weight of their never-ending burden is the major ingredient in Black-White interactions" (p. 66). Additionally, Davis (1989) defined racial micro-aggressions as "stunning, automatic acts of disregard that stem from unconscious attitudes of white superiority and constitute a verification of black inferiority." (p. 1576)

April described her experience this way,

> In particular, I noticed certain faculty making note and commenting on certain things about me such as the style of my hair, the style of my dress, where I parked in the lot, how long I stayed at work, and how early I arrived to work. Patricia Hill Collins (1998) terms this kind of observation "surveillance," and defines it as being intensely observed by others within the organization. Needless to say this was very uncomfortable for me. I often felt alone and isolated in an environment where I was being watched.

For both April and Cosette, gender and age were further complicated by their experiences as Black individuals who were under constant surveillance and undermined subtly, but consciously by others. Azadeh described a more direct encounter with a White male colleague,

> **Me:** I don't think you are taking into account the tenet of White privilege. It is not a racist way of thinking about privilege and space.
> **Him:** (yelling) You're a racist.
> **Me:** I am not a racist. In fact, given structural and institutional oppression, I cannot be a racist. I am happy to discuss this further with you when you are not yelling at me.
> **Him:** (hand waving in my face) You're just a naughty little girl. Does daddy needs to tame this naughty little girl? Daddy does need to tame the naughty girl.

Azadeh not only encountered sexism and racism in the same instance, but also ageism as she was referred to as a "naughty little girl."

Creating Community for Survival

All of the Black women authors described the reliance on networks of support to persevere through and past hard times. April mentioned that, "Research suggests that often Black women have to cultivate networks outside of the academy in order to sustain themselves inside the academy." And, Gaëtane stated that, "Women faculty of color benefit more in seeking out multiple mentors…" Anjalé extended this notion outside of the work setting to family and discussed how the support she received as a child and now receives as an adult are seen as nontraditional:

> The type of supports I have received along the way might be considered by dominant standards as "unconventional" or "outside the norm"… Throughout my life I was made to feel that my childhood family structure was a deficit and meant I was a high risk for failure. However, Aunt Dee's coparenting and other family and community members' contribution to my success, though considered nontraditional, was, for me, a valid part of my Black identity, a form of Black cultural capital (Carter, 2003) that helped me navigate often egregious predominately white spaces that I have been educated in or worked within my entire life. Education as an institution focuses on what communities of color lack, not recognizing the cultural assets, or nondominant forms of cultural capital, students of color use in their own communities, (Carter, 2003; Gonzalez & Moll, 2002; Yosso, 2005). This nondominant capital should be legitimized in institutional spaces (Yosso, 2005). However, I have noticed the skills I have used to develop familial capital, kin, ties, or social networks (Yosso, 2005; Stanton-Salazar, 2001), mirrors the way in which I navigate my professional space by building a scholarly network or community.

While some of the women described communities and networks of support, others discussed the struggle to identify mentors. Cosette described the search for mentors who could share "insider knowledge" and "teach her the ropes:"

> While I received great content knowledge on courses taken throughout my doctoral preparation experience and was supported by my doctoral program to participate in an educational leadership mentoring program for students interested in the professoriate, no faculty member within my doctoral program offered crucial insider knowledge essential to the process for preparation and successful transitioning and first time entry into the professoriate. Sherman et al., (2010, p. 10) indicate this as "hunting and gathering" in leadership education, hence looking outside of the "clan" so as not to starve as seminal to their preparation process. As such, similar to the some of the study participants in the Sherman et al., (2010) study, I had to go outside of the academy to receive specific guidance and preparation support.

And, others talked about finding community by identifying those in similar situations so as to build a forcefield of support; a type of "rag tag collection of scholars" as described by Katherine. She went on to say that her,

> ...commitment to social justice clearly led me (and others) to experience what the literature on liminality termed, *communitas* means on a personal level... Communitas began with finding fellow liminars who were also struggling. A diverse assemblage of allies that would provide a sense of belonging and hope.

The women authors themselves had networked among themselves to establish mentoring support systems, or, communitas. For instance, Jennifer and Karen commented that several other women authors of these chapters had been essential to their success. Jennifer indicated, "This also may serve as an example of where the road was paved more readily for me than for some of my peers. It is interesting to me even now that along with these opportunities came a sense of guilt about my own privilege."

For Jennifer, the recognition of the privilege mentoring afforded her brought guilt in knowing that these opportunities and relationships are not always available to other women. The mere fact that Jennifer associates a level of guilt with her own positive experiences of being mentored proves that mentoring does not exist as it should within the current climate of higher education. Mentoring should be a valuable tool to prepare new faculty to the specific expectations of a university. However, it simply isn't. Does this exist because males more naturally bond in the university environment; thus, bolstering one another's ego and skill sets? Or is this an issue that prevails across the board regardless of gender, because we, as a society, have forgotten the benefits of creating a community based on shared efforts and successes? Perhaps we are so enamored of ourselves and our own achievements that we cannot share the spotlight with others and lend necessary support to those that are new, fearing that if we do they may supersede us.

Invisibility

All of the women talked about instances of being invisible whether due to gender, race, age, or a combination of the three. April, Azadeh, and Whitney spoke about the invisibility that race and/or gender afforded them:

> To embrace the perspective of colorblindness and to engage with me through this lens is to render me invisible. That is, my experiences as a Black woman become negated through the lens of colorblindness. (April)
>
> It is easy to imagine my younger self, looking up at the fence, wondering—to the point of intellectual schizophrenia—how I was going to surpass all these

> intangible chain-links...to help identify myself in a work in which I am no underrepresented, but unrepresented. (Azadeh)

> Making countless suggestions in department faculty meetings only to be ignored and then have the male colleague sitting next to me repeat my suggestion and be told it is an amazing idea. (Whitney)

> I looked at him. He looked away. Invisible again. Thank you for letting me invade your office, nay, *YOUR* space. (Azadeh)

Karen talked about the intersectionality of gender and age:

> When I was hired, there was no hint my age and youthful appearance would have any bearing on how I would be treated and how colleagues would interact with me. There was no cautionary probation term set in my contract because of my age, no stipulations, and no other requirements because of my age (which of course would have been both ridiculous and illegal), yet some faculty colleagues felt they could still talk about it to me and to others as if it were an oddity and I was not as qualified as other people.

> I often wondered what would happen if I brought up the age of those people who were being so cruel to me and making comments about my age in a negative light; if they would laugh at any jokes I could potentially make. Of course I never did and never would; that's not in my nature, but, all the same, I did think about it on occasion. I wondered if they would be as pleasant as I was when I "laughed off" yet another hurtful comment about my youth. These jokes were hurtful and embarrassing and often made in a large group setting, but I found no other way to handle these than to just listen, smile politely, and leave the situation if possible. I found it disturbing it was generally accepted as funny and normal to make derisive asides about my age and others would laugh along with the person who was making the negative comment "just in good fun." This contributed to my feelings of isolation previously mentioned.

And, Jennifer talked about being rendered invisible for being a stay-at-home mother while working on her doctorate:

> I was not employed outside of the home during my doctoral studies; a badge I quickly learned was not valued by many peers. I endured many comments about the large amount of time I must have had to dedicate to doctoral work and how much easier it would be for them if they were not working. There will likely be a persistent debate for generations to come about the value of work done by men and women in the home in the care of children. Through my experience, I can only say that my choices were viewed as second class by many of my peers.

Clearly, whether due to race, gender, age, or a combination of these identifying factors, these women authors often found themselves as invisible "players" in their academic environments.

The Continued Struggle to Balance Home and Work

Several of the women talked about the continuous struggle to find a balance between home and work and the guilt of never feeling fully present in either realm. Jennifer first spoke of her struggle in terms of geographics:

> One challenge I face is geographic isolation. As our main campus is in Washington, DC and my office is based three hours away, I feel a constant tension between my personal and professional obligations in my area and the opportunities, committees, special events, and daily interactions that occur in DC. Before I began my work at GW and during the interview process, I was reminded that I would need to make a conscientious effort to "see and be seen" in DC. This pressure is ever-present in my mind as I also work to balance the needs of the students served by the satellite campus and my own personal life. The corridor of Interstate 95 provides a gateway to many opportunities on the main campus, but also provides a minimum of six hours of idle time in the driver's seat. For an early career professor working toward tenure, this valuable time is difficult to spend in the car.

And, she continued to describe her struggle with multiple subject positions:

> The greatest challenge I have faced in my life as a student and professor has been the ever evasive trial of balancing professional obligations and aspirations with the joys and challenges of being a mother and wife. The societal debate which surfaces around the possibility of this balance existing seems to be ever present, with the most recently publicized visitation happening just this past summer with an article by Anne-Marie Slaughter (2012). On the one hand, my work as a professor has provided me with a quality of life balance unparalleled by my colleagues who work in other fields. For example, if one of my children has a performance at school, Kindergarten graduation, or athletic event, I usually can tweak my schedule to be there. Management of one's own time is a gift. It is true, however, that at the end of the day, those trying to strike this balance sometimes feel as though they have pleased no one and that both home and work have concurrently been underserved.

And, Jennifer went even further to outline the pressures to multitask due to having a flexible schedule as a professor in the first place:

> I have networked with other mothers of young children who are also professors and it seems there are several themes which we experience. Two such themes include a unique schedule and the extraordinary support of spouse/partner/family members. I do not pretend to speak for all mothers of young children in the professoriate, but rather can only speak to my own experience. The first theme of a unique schedule includes some specific nuances about work hours, conference attendance, and professional development opportunities. I have discovered that I work very different hours than my col-

leagues, often reporting to work hours ahead of the general crowd, leaving hours before, and working late into the evening after my children have gone to sleep. This leaves me often feeling that others might not be aware of the work I do as it is not measured always by an open office door. The time stamp on emails to and from my students demonstrates the late nights that often occur in my home. While I wait at a doctor's appointment with a child, I am constantly checking email and responding to student inquiries. Conference attendance, similarly, usually entails me flying in just as the conference begins and leaving on the earliest possible flight at its completion. Often, I have to look at the presentation schedule and miss a day of a conference. This results in fewer networking opportunities and more leisurely travel schedules than some of my colleagues enjoy. Finally, many of the professional development opportunities occur at times or on days that conflict with my availability. If I were to ask my family, they might say I miss a large number of events and am "always teaching or with students," whereas my work colleagues might report my lack of presence in evening hours at my office. This is a further example of trying to please all, while pleasing none.

Karen described this pressure in her narrative as well:

I do not have a 9:00 a.m. to 5:00 p.m. job spanning Monday through Friday. Sometimes I will work on email at three in the morning, other times I will be at a coffee shop at 6:30 a.m. working on an article, I will teach until 10:00 at night, and facilitate weekend professional development sessions related to a grant. It is difficult to find time for myself between making sure I am the best mother I can be to my wonderful boys and ensuring I am meeting not only the standards and expectations set forth by my institution, but the standards and expectations I continually set (and increase all of the time) for myself.

Even women who were single without children at the time they wrote their narratives described their struggle with personal and professional imbalance. For instance, Melissa felt no room in her life for the presence of a partner because of the fact that her position as a new faculty member required total, nonstop devotion to the exclusion of watching her personal life suffer:

I want to devote the final portion of this chapter to discussing my personal struggles and sacrifices related to being a single Latina with a PhD, as these intersecting identities evoke uncertainties and issues related to dating, marriage, motherhood, and cultural/familial expectations. These issues might resonate with other female scholars, particularly my Black and Latina colleagues. This whole chapter in fact is purposefully written with my personal reality in mind as a Latina PhD who is in a "committed relationship," not with a man, but with academia.

And, Whitney described the struggle to be both a successful academic scholar and caregiver:

> There is an assumption made...that women without children have no responsibilities. There is a belief by some that women faculty with no children should have to shoulder the burden of travel to conferences or more service work and that they don't need salary raises because they have no families to support. The work that I do as the caregiver of a person with a disability is often greater than that of the care of the average child or children. But, it is discounted nonetheless.

DISCUSSION

Thousands of years of social conditioning have certainly created a climate where our society still, sometimes boldly and sometimes with subtlety, views women and minorities as *others*. Without doubt, there are biological differences between genders that create different purposes within our roles regarding reproduction and sustaining life. However, when and why did these differences spill over into our contributions regarding our skills, insights, and intellect? Why do these differences then have bearing on our abilities to contribute within our chosen professions? And when certainly did race and age become acceptable as new layers of obstacles within the framework of our culture? Instead of viewing all of these factors as obstacles, why are they not instead viewed as another element to enrich the overall experience and value of the individual? Instead of helping each individual use his or her talents to fit into the whole and improve upon the entire community, we subjugate that individual and fear what we perceive are insurmountable differences.

Regardless of the underlying motivations for why mentoring does not come naturally, each of these narratives recognized the need for this mentality to change. All of these authors actively sought guidance, support, and wisdom from those that forged ahead. All of them cast aside their own egos in order to seek the help of others, and for many of them this call went unheeded. They were forced to establish community and support beyond academia and sought mentors instead from their families and other professional contacts.

What saddened us the most in reading these narratives was not only our inability seemingly as fellow humans to uplift one another to create a whole stronger and more brilliant than its components, but the fact that many times these authors' tormentors were fellow women. The need for new/young scholars to find mentors amongst fellow women in the field and not being able to satisfy that need, because above all other barriers, many times, other women were the worst offenders and biggest obstacles to finding acceptance. The nastiness of women against one another reared its head repeatedly in these narratives and seems to stem from the need to compete to a fault; the need to ostracize; the need to single out women and make further distinctions and barriers based on race. Interestingly, other women colleagues served as both vital rescuers and conduits for success throughout the narratives *and* bullies and tormentors right alongside with many men.

Women should not feel the need to find fault with themselves or others in creating a sense of community with one another to forge mentorships and liaisons to further the successes and agendas of all women in the field. It is only when this sense of *other* is stricken from our mindsets that our voices as women will truly be heard among the collective efforts of humanity. This must first start with both men and women bolstering women and not making distinctions based on age, race, or "newness" to the field. If we insist on drawing lines between ourselves regarding our intrinsic value based on these parameters, how can we then expect the respect we deserve when we, as women, refuse to treat each other as equals? And, how can we expect others to do so as well?

This books begs the question, "If the women from *Breaking Into the All-Male Club* are "firsts," "pioneers," and "groundbreakers," then who are we, the young and new women of the field? We know the entrance of women into the field of educational leadership was threatening enough for the veteran women (and still is for many of the young and new women). If not for these women, the narratives in the present book would not exist because the women authors would likely have never found positions in the academy. And, we now know, through the women's narratives here, that the addition of age and ethnicity as confounding factors has, without a doubt, created continued dissonance forty years later! Young women are still breaking ground. Minority women are still breaking ground. So, continuing pioneers? Yes. Continuing ground breakers? Yes. Continuing to be firsts? Yes. Young and new women to the field continue to carry these titles; albeit it in different ways.

CHAPTER 15

THEN... AND NOW

Reflections on Women Faculty in Educational Administration

Norma T. Mertz

Breaking into the all-male club: Female professors of educational administration (2009) was written to remember how recently women had moved into the ranks of faculty preparing school administrators, and to preserve the stories of women who broke into what was once a long-standing male (predominantly White male) sanctuary; sanctuary in the sense of a protected space where their norms could remain unchallenged and their sense of superiority for the task undisputed. The first women to challenge the sanctity of this place and these spaces formerly uninhabited by women faced a variety of challenges to their legitimacy, appropriateness, and right to be there. It seemed important to capture the stories of these "firsts" for the women that had and would come after them, for the instructive lessons they could offer to other women seeking to join them, and for the males who did or did not welcome them into their ranks. These women faced normative, and in a number of cases, overt challenges to their entry into and advancement in the departments they entered; and they had to deal with their status as "onlys" since the unusual step of hiring a female faculty member tended to come with the unwritten proviso that only one be hired into a department.

The stories of how these pioneers managed to get hired and what they faced once hired framed the stories they told in the book. For some, the entry was relatively smooth, and because they entered an environment in which they found colleagues who were open to their entry and because they had largely been brokered into the position by professors in their doctoral programs with ties to those in the institutions they joined, they faced few significant challenges to their acceptance and advancement. Many more, however, entered a workplace that was unwelcoming, even hostile, and where they had to work hard, if not fight, for acceptance and advancement. But fight they did, and they successfully broke the barriers to females in departments of educational administration, with due acknowledgement to the role that anti-discrimination legislation played, principally Title IX and Title VII.

The stories in this book are testimony to the fact that these pioneer women helped to remove barriers to the hiring of women, and that their successful efforts to establish the legitimacy of women in the position paved the way for other women. Today, women faculty in departments of educational leadership are neither uncommon nor unusual. Indeed, one can hardly find a department that is all-male. Whether solely attributable to these firsts is not certain, however, it is a legacy they can rightly claim to have helped to establish.

Continuing to disrupt the status quo? Young and new women professors in educational leadership was written to capture the stories of females who have joined the ranks of faculty in departments of educational leadership more recently than those chronicled in *Breaking into the all-male club*. The stories not only make fascinating and instructive reading for us pioneers, but for the field of educational administration. We read about the struggles these women are facing, some not unlike those faced by firsts, but also some very different, and the stories reveal how far we still have to go to ensure that equity is achieved.

Reflecting on the stories in this book and what they have to tell us now, versus then, I was struck by the fact that few of the women who shared their stories spoke about obstacles they faced to being hired, except perhaps for the trailing spouse. It is not entirely clear whether or not there were no barriers to their being hired, or they did not perceive ones they faced to be significant, or they chose not to mention any. I would like to think they did not face barriers to being hired because they were women, and that they were hired because their competence for the position was recognized and they met the open-to-interpretation criteria that characterize faculty position announcements. However, I am anything but naïve, and I am not unmindful of the change in student demographics of preparation programs, or the significant changes in the number of women in administrative positions in school districts since the 70s. That there might have been a growing awareness that formerly all-male departments needed to change their profiles in response to these changes and to institutional pressures to meet diversity mandates is not an unreasoned assumption. It leaves the question of how open existing faculty have been to the hiring of women unresolved, particularly where women may still be one of few.

It was exciting to see how many of the stories in this book were written by women of color, and to appreciate the number of women of color who are joining departments of educational leadership. When *Breaking into the all-male club* was written, only two women of color were identified, although curiously, they had been among the first women hired into departments of educational administration. And, sadly enough, the story of only one ended up in the book. As I noted in the preface, the majority of females who were firsts in departments of educational administration were Caucasian, and I repeated the off- the-cuff remark of one of these women: "Women were threatening enough. To introduce gender and race at the same time may have been too big a leap for all-White, all-males departments" (Mertz, 2009, p. ix). The relative absence of women of color as firsts, and the paucity of stories about their multiple marginality until quite recently, rendered their experience "invisible, hidden within studies that look at the experiences of women faculty, and within studies that examine the lives of faculty of color" (Turner, 2002, pp. 75–76). In a growing number of journal articles and books, including this one, we are reading that invisibility is being reduced, and we are learning of the experiences of women of color and what it means to struggle with barriers across gender and race/ethnicity.

The stories in this book raise profound and disturbing questions about the situation of women in their departments, in particular, women of color. To a woman, the women of color sharing their stories in this book spoke of the isolation, lack of support or help, and unwelcoming culture women of color experience in the academy; the sense that they must continually prove they should be there and of having to deal with the "subtle practices to undermine my credibility" (Jean-Marie, 2014, p. 35). Other women spoke of being challenged because of their feminist research agenda (Sherman Newcomb, 2014, p. 15), of being excluded from networks and opportunities (See chapters in this volume by O'Brien and Peters), of being "invisible others" (Osanloo, 2014, p. 55) and of living in a "state of in-between-ness and ambiguity" (Mansfield, 2014, p. 130). And many spoke of the difficulties faced in managing an academic career and negotiating a personal life (See chapters in this volume by Brooks, Clayton, Martinez, Sanzo, Sherman Newcomb, and Welton).

The plaint of these women new to the field, particularly women of color, was painful to read about. I had always hoped that breaking the barriers to the inclusion of women would lead to the inclusion of all women, and that women who followed the firsts would slowly (as our numbers increased) find a more welcoming environment. Further, I had hoped that women already in such positions would embrace their sisters. It is difficult to know what the situation is over the many departments of educational leadership, but I was sad to read of the real or perceived exclusion expressed in a number of the stories, and to *not* read of women already in departments embracing and supporting their new colleagues. And to add insult to injury, a woman of color who chose to work at a minority serving institution found herself in exactly the same situation as her compatriots who were working at predominantly White institutions. As one woman remarked, "Women may be allowed into the so-called club, but still struggle for full membership" (Mansfield, 2014, p. 129).

As I read the stories in the book, I was struck by what seemed to me to be differences between then and now. In the stories in *Breaking into the all-make club*, the notion of fitting in dominated. The women sought to fit into the existing culture, to be accepted into it, to gain the respect and recognition of their colleagues and administrative superiors (overwhelmingly White males) as scholars, and to lose their status as *women* scholars. If any theme characterizes the stories in this new book, it seems to be the desire to be recognized as women of color or women who are scholars; not to fit in, but to disrupt the culture that is a barrier to their being allowed to be who and what they are, and to find ways commensurate with their identities to be members of the academy. It is intriguing that the title of the book is *Continuing to disrupt the status quo?* both because of its recognition that women's entry into educational leadership was a disruption of the status quo, and the intimation that newer entries are charged with disrupting it further, or at the very least might, by their presence, disrupt it. No less noteworthy is the use of the question mark in the title; questioning whether newer women, with their diversity, can and will accomplish the task of changing the culture. There is a persistence to cultures that defies logic, and, in spite of the significant movement of women into departments of educational leadership, and indeed into fields and departments across fields in academe, the norms of the academy remain long-standing, owing much to the White males that set them ever so long ago.

In *Breaking into the all-male club*, many of the stories spoke of the day-to day sexism the women firsts faced; to the crude jokes, to sexual harassment, to being unheard and ignored, and to being treated unfairly in tenure and promotion. At first I found it curious (and hopeful) that only some of the women spoke openly about the sexism they faced. Was it possible that women no longer faced bias and discrimination on a daily basis? Was it becoming less common or even fading? Surely not my experience told me. While hardly a daily occurrence, I still see and hear sexist comments and perceive that women are treated as "less than" in the academy, even where more of them are moving up into positions of authority, and tenure and promotion decisions more often than not, allow for a notable inclusiveness. So, was it possible that these newer women did not experience sexism and racism in their positions to the same extent as the veteran women? Some of the women did write about facing one or both of them, but I continued to be perplexed by the fact that few women wrote of overt sexism. And, while others spoke about racism in the academy or hinted at overt racism, for the most part, they did not speak about it explicitly. The more I thought about these hints and the more I pondered why so many of the women of color, in particular, spoke about the obstacles they noted in the academy in general terms (i.e., not that they personally faced them but that women of color faced them), the more I sought some reason for this. Then I remembered that the women who wrote their stories for *Breaking into the all-male club* wrote them after, even long after, the events described, after they had successfully achieved tenure and found a place for themselves in the departments they joined. I also recalled things I knew from these same women about why they had not felt comfortable sharing everything they had faced then, particularly where the people involved were still alive. These musings led me to consider that the women writing stories for this book might well be in academically vulnerable situations, untenured or not yet promoted, and certainly not integrated into their departments, and that it would not be unreasonable to hypothesize that a reticence to include specific examples derived from a need to be cautious and self-protective out of fear. It is far safer to speak about the plight of women or the plight of women of color as has already been described in the literature than to be seen to complain about their particular situation.

It is difficult to generalize from the two books how and if the experience of women faculty has changed since women first moved into departments of educational leadership. The stories in both books come from women who chose to tell their stories. However, it is clear that the number of women faculty in such departments has increased, that they are, today, rarely, the only women in the department, whether or not that has any meaning in the sense of camaraderie, and that women faculty, at least those who shared their stories, still perceive themselves to be seen as "not quite," as a kind of second class citizen who is tolerated, perhaps even well treated, but not truly an equal member. As one of those firsts who is still standing, someone who is a full professor and has outlived and out-served all of the men who were in the department when I first came, it is something I still see and feel. For women of color, the experience appears to be even more problematic. Their multiple marginality makes their vulnerability and fight for acceptance on equal terms a "two front war," even at a time when the academy is becoming more diverse.

Reflecting on then and now leads me to think about later. What does the future hold for women, both White and of color? Will the academy change as even more women enter? Will the norms that have defined it for centuries begin to yield to ones that are more embracing with the passing of more time? Will the women themselves join together, not merely to support one another, but to challenge and ridicule those norms? Clearly, I do not know, and the skeptic in me wars with my essential optimism. I can see and savor the beauty of a diverse, perhaps woman dominated academy, an academy devoted to education where the prevailing norms focus on the pursuit of scholarship and the education of diverse students to achieve their full potential in a humane and democratic environment. A pipedream? Maybe... but maybe not.

REFERENCES

Jean-Marie, G. (2014). Navigating uncharted territories in the academy through mentoring networks. In W. S. Newcomb (Ed.), *Continuing to disrupt the status quo? Young and new women professors of educational leadership* (pp. 25–39). Charlotte, NC: Information Age.

Mansfield, K. C. (2014). Reflections on perpetual liminality. In W. S. Newcomb (Ed.), *Continuing to disrupt the status quo? Young and new women professors of educational leadership* (pp. 129–144). Charlotte, NC: Information Age.

Mertz, N. T. (2009). *Breaking into the all-male club. Female professors of educational administration.* Albany, NY: State University of New York Press.

Newcomb, W. S. (2014). Cage fighting in higher education: Same old fight in a 21st century ring. In W. S. Newcomb (Ed.), *Continuing to disrupt the status quo? Young and new women professors of educational leadership* (pp. 7–24). Charlotte, NC: Information Age.

Osanloo, A. F. (2014). The invisible other: Ruminations on transcending "La Cerca" in academia. In W. S. Newcomb (Ed.), *Continuing to disrupt the status quo? Young and new women professors of educational leadership* (pp. 55–64). Charlotte, NC: Information Age.

Turner, C. S. V. (2002, January/February). Women of color in academe. *Journal of Higher Education, 73*(1), 74–93.

CHRONOLOGY OF YOUNG AND NEW WOMEN PROFESSORS' ENTRY INTO DEPARTMENTS OF EDUCATIONAL LEADERSHIP AND THEIR AGES UPON ENTRANCE

2002	Whitney Sherman Newcomb, age 27, Georgia State University
2002	Gaëtane Jean-Marie, age 29, University of Oklahoma
2006	April L. Peters, age 35, University of Georgia
2006	Azadeh F. Osanloo, age 31, New Mexico State University
2006	Karen Sanzo, age 29, Old Dominion University
2010	Jennifer K. Clayton, age 36, George Washington University
2010	Cosette M. Grant, under 40
2011	Melanie C. Brooks, age 38, Iowa State University
2011	Katherine Cumings Mansfield, age 49, Virginia Commonwealth University
2011	Melissa A. Martinez, age 34, Texas State University-San Marcos
2011	Catherine O'Brien, Gallaudet University
2011	Anjalé Welton, age 32, University of Illinois, Urbana-Champaign

ABOUT THE CONTRIBUTORS

Melanie C. Brooks is an Assistant Professor in the School of Education at Iowa State University. She was a Peace Corps volunteer in Thailand and holds a PhD in Sociocultural International Development Education Studies from Florida State University. Dr. Brooks began her career as a high school teacher and a librarian. She also has experience coordinating international education programs for students and teachers. She has conducted research in Egypt, Thailand, the Philippines and the United States using sociological theories as a way to understand issues related to religion and conflict in education. Her work has been published in *Educational Policy, Etc: A Review of General Semantics, Encyclopedia of the Social and Cultural Foundations of Education,* and *International Journal of Urban Educational Leadership.*

Jennifer K. Clayton is an Assistant Professor in Educational Leadership with The George Washington University. Prior to joining The George Washington University, she served as a Visiting Assistant Professor at Old Dominion University. Dr. Clayton is a career educator and has taught at the middle and high school levels. She also served as a curriculum developer and evaluator, testing coordinator, and new teacher mentor. Dr. Clayton earned her PhD in Educational Leadership at Old Dominion University, Master's of Education in Educational Administration at Rutgers University, and Bachelor of Arts at James Madison University. Her research interests include leadership development and preparation, experiential learning for leaders, effective leadership for social justice in K–12 schools, and university-community-district education partnerships.

Catherine Ruziak Gorman is a professor at ECPI University where she teaches various English courses, serves as the Head Tutor for the Writing Assistance Center, and develops curriculum for the Arts & Sciences Department. She has also applied her skills to the administrative side of education as Director of the Bachelor Programs for both Richmond campuses before moving to the online campus of the university. Prior to teaching she was a technical writer and editor at various corporations. She received her Masters of Fine Arts in Creative Writing from Virginia Commonwealth University, and in her spare time works on having her own writing in the genres of poetry and creative nonfiction published.

Cosette M. Grant is an Assistant Professor in the Educational Leadership Department at University of Cincinnati and a member of the graduate faculty. She is the director of the Center for the Study of Leadership in Urban Schools and editor of the *International Journal of Educational Leadership (IJUEL)*. Her research focuses on culturally-relevant mentoring strategies that might improve the academic and career success for students. Her work also includes emergent work on effective leadership for educational equity in P–12 schools and the inclusion of social justice in leadership development and preparation of educational leaders. Dr. Grant is a former UCEA Jackson Scholar and David L. Clark National Scholar. She currently serves on the advisory board of the UCEA Jackson Scholars Advisory Council.

Gaëtane Jean-Marie is a professor of educational leadership and chair of the Department of Educational Leadership, Foundations & Human Resource Education at the University of Louisville. Prior to that, she was faculty at the University of Oklahoma and Florida International University. Her research focuses on leadership development and preparation, educational equity, women and leadership in K–12 and higher education contexts, and urban school reform. To date, she has over 60 publications which include books, book chapters, and academic articles in numerous peer-reviewed journals. Her achievements as an educator, leader, and researcher have been acknowledged by receipt of several awards to include but not limited to College's *Research/Scholarship Award* (2012), ELPS Department's *Researcher of the Year Award* (2011), *Faculty of the Year Award* for teaching, research and service (2009), *Interdisciplinary Initiatives Award (2004), and Most Promising Faculty (2003)*. Also, she is the incoming editor of the *Journal of School Leadership*, book review editor of the *Journal of Educational Administration*, past chair/president of the Leadership for Social Justice AERA/SIG, and co-founder of Advancing Women of Color in the Academy (AWOCA).

Katherine Mansfield is an Assistant Professor at Virginia Commonwealth University. She graduated in 2011 from The University of Texas in Austin with a PhD in Educational Policy and Planning and a Doctoral Portfolio in Women's and Gender Studies. Mansfield's interdisciplinary scholarship focuses on the history and politics of education and the relationship of class, gender, race/ethnicity, and religion on educational and vocational access and achievement. Mansfield is published in a variety of venues including: *Educational Policy Analysis Archives; International Journal of Urban Educational Leadership; Intersections: Women's Studies in Review Across Disciplines; Journal of Educational Administration; Journal of Research on Leadership Education*, and; *Journal of School Leadership*. In 2012, Mansfield was awarded the "Leadership for Social Justice Dissertation Award," sponsored by the American Educational Research Association's (AERA) Leadership for Social Justice Special Interest Group (SIG) and the "Selma Greenberg Outstanding Dissertation Award," sponsored by AERA's Research on Women and Education SIG. Mansfield is a first-generation college graduate with 20 years teaching and leadership experience throughout the Preschool to PhD pipeline.

Melissa A. Martinez is an Assistant Professor in the Education and Community Leadership Master's Program, and PhD in Education-School Improvement at Texas State University-San Marcos. She is a native of the Rio Grande Valley in South Texas, and a former bilingual elementary school teacher and school counselor. She earned her PhD in Educational Administration, with a concentration in Higher Education, from The University of Texas at Austin in 2010 and earned her BA (1998) and MEd (2002) at The University of Texas at Brownsville. Her research focuses on three areas: (a) equity and access issues along the P-16 educational pipeline for students of color, primarily college access and readiness issues for Latina/os and Latina/o parent engagement, (b) the preparation of equity-oriented educational leaders, and (c) the experiences of faculty of color in academia. Through her research and teaching, Dr. Martinez is committed to preparing future educational leaders who are thoughtful, critical, and reflective in their practice and adhere to the tenets of social justice.

Norma T. Mertz is a professor of Educational Leadership and Policy Studies where she coordinates the Higher Education Administration and College Student Personnel Programs. A graduate of Teachers College, Columbia University, Dr. Mertz teaches courses in higher education administration including values and ethics in educational leadership and research design, and directs doctoral dissertations and masters' theses. Dr. Mertz is the editor and a contributor to the 2009 book, *Breaking into the All-Male Club: Female Professors of Educational Administration*, from SUNY Press, and coeditor, with Vincent Anfara Jr., of *Theoretical Frameworks in Qualitative Research*, from Sage. Recent publications include a chapter on Woman of color faculty: Recruiting, hiring, and retention in *Women of Color in Higher Education:*

Contemporary Perspectives and New Directions, vol. 9, edited by J.M. Gaetane and B. Lloyd-Jones, and one with S. L. Pfleeger in *The Diversity Mentoring Casebook,* edited by D. Clutterbuck and K.M. Poulsen, entitled, "If everyone who makes it has a mentor, does everyone who has a mentor make it?" Case study of a corporate mentoring project.

Dr. Mertz's research interests center on gender and leadership, faculty hiring practices, mentoring, and role socialization.

Whitney Sherman Newcomb is an associate professor in the Department of Educational Leadership at Virginia Commonwealth University. Her research interests include: leadership preparation and mentoring; women's issues in leadership; and social justice in leadership. Dr. Newcomb's work has been featured in journals including: Educational Administration Quarterly, the Journal of School Leadership, the Journal of Educational Administration, Educational Policy, and the Journal for Research on Leadership Education. She received the 2011 Distinguished Scholarship Award for VCU's School of Education for her contribution to research and the 2012 Distinguished Teaching Award for excellence in teaching. She serves on the editorial boards of Educational Administration Quarterly, the Journal of School Leadership, and the Journal for Research on Leadership Education. Dr. Newcomb was presented with the Emerald Literati Award for Excellence for the Outstanding Special Issue of 2011 for her work as guest editor of "Globalization: Expanding Horizons in Women's Leadership," a special issue of the Journal of Educational Administration. She also received the 2011 Social Justice Teaching Award from the Leadership for Social Justice SIG of the American Educational Research Association "for work that represents exemplary commitment to teaching that promotes social justice, equity, diversity, and inclusion in the field of educational administration."

Catherine O'Brien was born in St. Louis, Missouri. She became a deaf child at a young age and attended an urban city school. Until fifth grade she had little encouragement in the area academics. Then, a fifth grade teacher showed her the world of books and demonstrated a great enthusiasm for teaching and learning. In 1986, she completed her Bachelor of Science in Education degree at Truman State University as the first deaf graduate. Then she became a teacher and administrator and earned numerous awards including a teacher of the year award. In 2004, while teaching, she continued her education at University of Missouri-St. Louis and earned a Master of Arts in Special Education. Then she attended the University of Missouri and earned an Education Specialist Degree in 2006 and her PhD in 2011. In 2011 she became the first I. King Jordan Fellow at Gallaudet University where she continued her research into understanding how Deaf culture influenced school culture and leadership in schools for the deaf.

In 2012 she was hired at Gallaudet as a visiting professor in educational leadership and research. During this time she has prepared and presented numerous papers from her research.

Azadeh F. Osanloo is an Associate Professor in the Department of Educational Management and Development at New Mexico State University. Dr. Osanloo received her doctorate in the Educational Leadership and Policy Studies Program, specializing in the Social and Philosophical Foundations of Education, at Arizona State University. Her research addressed civic and social justice education in a post 9/11 climate focusing on the concepts of democracy, cosmopolitanism, xenophobia, and citizenship from theory to praxis in the K–12 educational system. She has merged her work in civics and social justice with her newer research agenda, which is aimed at establishing and integrating collaborative systemic diversity-based interventions for bullying in middle schools. Prior to being in Arizona she taught in the New York City public school system working with junior high school students in the South Bronx and jointly worked as a program director at the Harlem Educational Activities Fund–a not-for-profit that specialized in closing the gap between educational attainment and disenfranchised students from Harlem, Washington Heights, and the Bronx. While in New York City, she obtained her Master's in Public Administration from New York University's Robert F. Wagner School. In general, her research agenda focuses on issues of educational equity; social justice leadership and policy; the philosophical foundations of education; diversity, multiculturalism, and social egalitarianism; and bullying interventions.

April L. Peters is an Assistant Professor of Educational Administration in the Department of Lifelong Education, Administration and Policy at the University of Georgia. She earned an MA and PhD Educational Policy and Leadership from The Ohio State University in Educational Policy and Leadership, an MSW from Columbia University in New York and a BS Ed. from Northwestern University, Evanston, IL. She has worked in the K–12 context as a middle school teacher, a school social worker, Dean of students and a high school principal. Dr. Peters served four years as a consultant for the Institute for Student Achievement (ISA) in the Atlanta Public Schools. Her work there specifically focused on assisting school leaders and teachers in implementing small school reform model in select high schools within the district. Dr. Peters' research interests include: (a) women in school leadership; (b) examining the ways that districts provide mentoring and support for early career administrators; and (c) leadership and small school reform. Dr. Peters can be reached at alpeters@uga.edu.

Karen Sanzo is the Program Coordinator and an Associate Professor for the PK–12 Educational Leadership Program in the Department of Educational Foundations and Leadership at Old Dominion University. Dr. Sanzo is a veteran of the PK–12 public schools, having served as a middle school mathematics teacher and an elementary school administrator. Dr. Sanzo has been Principal Investigator for several national and state-level grants, totaling over $1.4 million dollars. Her grant work has revolved around leadership preparation and development, and science and math instructional leadership and formative assessment with public school teachers and leaders. Dr. Sanzo's areas of research interests are leadership preparation and development, university-school district partnerships, and data-based decision making.

Anjalé Welton primarily examines the educational opportunity structures of students of color from low socioeconomic backgrounds. Welton examines how institutional and social structures (race, social class, faculty support, tracking, etc.) shape the connections students of color make to educational resources, navigate school and ultimately matriculate to postsecondary education. Other research interests include issues of equity and social justice in school reform and improvement, underrepresented groups (persons of color and women) navigating the pipeline to academia, and youth of color voice and leadership. She has representative publications in *Teachers College Record, Journal of Educational Administration*, and the *Journal of School Leadership*. Her professional experiences include coordinator of a leadership and empowerment program for urban youth, a facilitator of an urban education teacher preparation program, and a special education teacher in large urban districts. Welton's greatest accolade is that she is the proud first in the family to graduate college and can now be called "doctor."

CPSIA information can be obtained at www.ICGtesting.com
Printed in the USA
BVOW08s2111250215

389271BV00004B/142/P